R 808.81
world's

The World's Best Poetry

Supplement III

Critical Companion

Poetry Anthology Press

The World's Best Poetry

Survey of American Poetry

The World's Best Poetry

Supplement III

Critical Companion

Explication and interpretation
of poems selected from the
Foundation Volumes (I-X) with
biographical data on poets
included in the Foundation Volumes
and in Supplements I and II

Prepared by
The Editorial Board, Roth Publishing, Inc.
(formerly Granger Book Co., Inc.)
In consultation with Benjamin Sloan

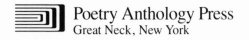 Poetry Anthology Press
Great Neck, New York

Contents

Critical Essays On:

Introduction

A poem, like the language from which it is constructed, is a living presence. Poetry has a vitality of its own and is perceived through the essential act of reading. To appreciate a poem the reader must strive towards personal participation. To do so, it is always necessary to be aware of the creative energy inherent in the poet's thought. Poetry invites the reader "in". — Poetry is an art form. Indeed, this is its basic challenge.

How, then, does one go about reading a poem? To start, it is vital to understand that a poem is not a telegram. In other words, poetry, like music and the visual arts, is not required to have a specific, paraphrasable "meaning" or "message". Approaching a poem with this expectation may create problems; it may actually prevent appreciation or understanding of a particular work. In reading poetry, as in viewing art, one must accept the work on its own, self-defined terms and suspend certain prejudices, thereby allowing the poem to speak freely. In the final analysis, the encounter with poetry must occur in a highly intimate, personal way. Although some poems may be analyzed in terms of reference to realms of experience lying outside the work itself, it is important to understand that the tradition of poetry as a whole is diametrically opposed to the prevailing contemporary emphasis on rational analysis of information-value.

Poetry involves the reader in many different ways. At the same time, it requires that certain important realizations be consciously cultivated. Fundamental to the experience is the recognition that each poem creates its own "world" which must be understood on its own idiosyncratic terms. A knowledge of poetic technique is important; structure and the use of poetic form must especially be carefully investigated. However, even more crucial is a flexibility of mind. —A ready imagination and sympathy allow the reader to enter into the poem on terms defined by the work itself and not by any preconception of what the poem ought to be. In view of this, the special skill of slow, deliberate reading generally proves to be most beneficial. Similarly, the art of oral declamation offers invaluable insight.

In addition, for all that a reader may understand about the traditional techniques of poetry—rhythm, rhyme, allusion, metaphor, imagery, etc.—it is useful to keep in mind that in every poem the implementation of recognizable procedures must be understood within the context of a poet's underlying concerns. Every poem is in some way a unique creation and the reflection of personal experience. Accordingly, the reader's task is to remember that poetry does not rely only on the actual meaning of words, but also on a variety of other dimensions. Some of these are: the musical quality of language, the degree to which color and visual images are implicit, the way in which setting and tone give a poem overall impact, how diction—the choice of words—serves to alter a poem's message, the emotional, literary, historical, and psychological associations which a poem may conjure; and, finally, any combination of these or other elements.

As a final suggestion, a good dictionary, frequently consulted, is indispensable. Shakespeare is a good example of a poet who knew the most obscure meanings of common words; he could, and often did, construct entire poems out of esoteric puns which today's reader, without a dictionary, is sure to overlook. The good poet always keeps the language alive. His work is constantly challenging and puts trust in the reader's intelligence, ability, and, above all, desire to pursue even the narrowest of etymological passageways.

This volume presents examples of ways in which particular, well-known poems may be read. A reader might ascribe to different or conflicting interpretations than those suggested here. This, however, does not detract from the essential usefulness of the volume. In dealing with poetry, as with any art form, it is hardly appropriate to attempt imposing a uniformity of critical judgement. Moreover, it seems that debate and controversy are in all likelihood a desirable outcome compatible with the passionate nature of art in general. It is hoped that the reader will, through step-by-step examples, learn to approach poetry without fear or apprehension and will eventually read with ease and confidence previously daunting or seemingly inaccessible works. This volume will have accomplished its purpose if it succeeds in showing that poetry is not inherently difficult, that it is there to be enjoyed and can offer the willing reader a good deal of what is pleasurable and unexpected.

Preface

The publications of **Poetry Anthology Press** constitute a comprehensive conspectus of international verse in English designed to form the core of a library's poetry collection. Covering the entire range of poetic literature, these anthologies encompass all topics and national literatures.

Each collection, published in a multivolume continuing series format, is devoted to a major area of the whole undertaking and contains complete author, title, and first line indexes. Biographical data is also provided.

The World's Best Poetry, with coverage through the 19th century, is topically classified and arranged by subject matter. Supplements keep the 10 volume foundation collection current and complete.

Survey of American Poetry is an anthology of American verse arranged chronologically in 10 volumes. Each volume presents a significant period of American poetic history, from 1607 to date.

I
Home and Friendship

Preface

The themes of "home" and "friendship" have been of continuous interest to poets of all ages. They are innate to world literature. In addressing positive manifestations of "man as a social creature", they convey concepts of comfort and assurance essential for human survival in the midst of a cold and hostile universe.

Nevertheless, such topics do not always communicate unconditional optimism: individuals are destined to eke out existence in different ways. Poetry on "home" and "friendship", therefore, may tell us different things depending on the particular circumstances described. Moreover, we will find that the range of metaphors it uses is broad. Home, for example, can be discussed in terms of a sturdy house or domicile; at other times, it may become an image of transitory motion. We might recall the character in Mark Twain's world-famous classic *The Adventures of Huckleberry Finn* who believed "there warn't no home like a raft after all (Other places do seem so cramped up and smothery, but a raft don't)."*

---

*Mark Twain, *The Adventures of Huckleberry Finn*
(Hartford: The American Publishing Company, 1901), p. 160.

Algernon Charles Swinburne
(1837–1909)

Étude Réaliste

There are several helpful approaches to Algernon Charles
Swinburne's deceptively simple poem. In the first place,
the poem's title leads us in two directions. Since "etude"
(study, in French) is drawn from the lexicon of music, we
inevitably anticipate a degree of importance attached to the
use of audible patterns and textured sound. Secondly,
"realiste" or "realistic" suggests that an emphasis will be
placed on concrete actuality as opposed to idealized or sentimental abstraction.

   Without reading a word of the poem itself, we may get
a further idea of what to expect merely by glancing at the
visual arrangement on the page. We observe the following:
the poem is divided into three sections clearly designated
with roman numerals. Each section, in turn, contains three
stanzas; in each case, the middle stanza consists of exactly
three lines; and, finally, each individual section is introduced by a three-word phrase and the last line of both
the first and third stanzas always consists of the same three
words. This interesting repetition of three-fold units is significant. It is a reflection of an eminent sacred symbol; it
echoes a central doctrine of Christianity which states that
God is the Trinity—Father, Son, and Holy Spirit. After exhibiting an emotionally strong religious devotion early in

his life, Swinburne became an atheist and eventually a militant anti-Christian. These facts, along with the symbolic depiction of the poem on the page, lead to the expectation that religious ideas are fundamental in this work.

In a very basic way, however, Swinburne's poem offers something of a surprise, and, instead of focusing on the traditional notion of deity, it creates a sacred image of the human person and stresses the intrinsic beauty and power of man. Thus, along with the use of essentially religious images such as "heaven", "angel", "bless", and "paradise", the subject of the poem is the new-born baby.

Etude Realiste represents a reaction to Swinburne's famous predecessor, John Milton (1608-1674). Milton, in his monumental **Paradise Lost**, defends the doctrine of original sin and asserts the innate spiritual corruption of the individual. For centuries it was assumed that, since the individual is born in a state of sin, the only way to heaven and redemption is to live in accord with Christian teaching. Swinburne, on the other hand, implies that this view does not conform to reality and that it underestimates the enormous potential and latent possibilities of the infant.

If we look further and keep in mind that Christianity emphasizes the soul rather than the body (the triumph of moral truth over physical reality), the dimension of sensuality becomes overwhelmingly important. Early Christian philosophy taught that the opportunity to reunite with God comes only with the sacrifice of earthly pleasure. Swinburne, however, concentrates on the physical or animal side of man's nature. This is evident in the inventory of the child's physical attributes as well as in the use of images as "An angel's lips to kiss", "toward the heat / They (the baby's toes) stretch and spread and wink", and "warriors grip their brands". In each case, the emphasis is purely tactile or sensory. In the concluding stanzas, moreover, it is suggested that the baby is not born into sin, as Milton propounded, but into beauty, wisdom, and love, and that the pristine quality of nature offers room for hope and pleasure in earthly existence.

Evidently, there is an undercurrent of tension which places Swinburne at a specific intellectual crossroad in the historical evolution of inherited religious attitudes. Of course, **Etude Realiste** can be enjoyed purely on the level of textured sound and image; careful craftsman that he was, Swinburne certainly intended this. But a somewhat more extensive exploration of underlying ideas makes the work all the more resonant. Poetry, we should remember, is "expressive" in the same terms as song, gesture, and dance; it articulates the rhythm of a unique but representative individual's breath-soul. At the same time, poetry is argument and it is precisely its argumentative nature that lends perspective on its message of value.

Alexander Pope
(1688–1744)

Ode to Solitude

The seventeenth century was a turbulent period in English history. The religious, social, and political upheavals of this time were the growing pains of a nation shedding its medieval values; at the time, England was in the midst of acquiring the more modern, rational flair of the epoch known as "the Age of Enlightenment". After peace was established, England entered a period of relatively calm, tolerant debate. The philosopher John Locke (1632-1704), a notable figure in the political arena of the time, emphasized reason rather than religious faith, an approach which deeply influenced the subsequent development of English thought. The "Augustan Age", as this period is also known, took its name from the reign of Caesar Augustus (27 B.C.-A.D. 14) when Virgil, Horace, and Ovid flourished. The term is used in connection with a period exhibiting the classical aesthetic values of order, clarity, and symmetry.

Alexander Pope wrote **Ode to Solitude** at the age of 12. The structure of the work typifies early eighteenth-century English poetry. The rhythm in the first four lines is identical and regular; the lines are also related through rhyme. The lines are iambic and octosyllabic (except for the last) and can be scanned as follows:

Happy the man, whose with and care
A few paternal acres bound,
Content to breathe his native air
    In his own ground.
                                    thus:
(/)∪ ∪/∪/∪/
∪/∪/∪/∪/
∪/∪/∪/∪/
    ∪/∪/

To "scan" a line involves describing it in terms of accented (/) and unaccented (∪) syllables. One unaccented and one accented syllable (in this order) define what is known as the iamb, a verse foot favored by poets on account of its closeness to the rhythm of normal English speech. Thus, iambic pentameter consists of five iambs (pente, in Greek means five) and is a standard line in iambic verse. In his poem, Pope shortens the line to four iambs, but rigidly maintains the unstressed/stressed arrangement. His fourth line is truncated, or shortened, to two iambs, but completes the rhyme scheme (*abab*). The shortening of the last line can be taken as an instance of counterpoint, or irregular beat, intended to break the monotony of the verse rhythm. The music effect of such variation allows the poet to enliven what is otherwise a predictable and straightforward metrical scheme.

In rejecting the hierarchic values of the Middle Ages, the Enlightenment gave equal emphasis to man's physical and intellectual needs; thus, the concern for a "civilized" life resulting from "health of body" and "peace of mind" (third stanza) is the focus of Pope's poem. Religious concerns linger in words such as "blest" and "meditation". But the overall understanding is that the physical activities of daily existence involving both the body and intellect are aspects of life's central undertaking. There is nothing mystical, hidden, or metaphysical about the poem; it reflects an approach stressing direct and rational response to the surrounding world. For example, in contrast to **Paradise Lost**, the tense, complicated, and multi-level spiritual work by John Milton (1608-1674), **Ode to Solitude**, written at the beginning of the eighteenth century, addresses the individual's ability to survive on his own terms. The end of the poem especially emphasizes the secular and personal over the spiritual and universal; it does not speculate on the nature of life after death but simply requests the death be "unlamented, and not a stone / Tell where I lie".

Pope's poem expresses a secular notion of hope, a hallmark of the Enlightenment. It invokes faith in the achievement of individual initiative. Pope and other poets of the Augustan Age were convinced that, because of the new awareness of the mind's potential, mankind stood at the dawn of a bright, promising future.

Lewis Carroll
(1832–1898)

The Walrus and The Carpenter

Among friends, Charles Lutwidge Dodgson, the brilliant English author and mathematician, was known for a love of children. It was even said that his painful stammer, the sign of a shy personality, would vanish in the comfortable surroundings of youth. Today, Dodgson is best remembered as the author of *Adventures of Alice in Wonderland*. Published under a pseudonym (Lewis Carroll) and dedicated to a child (Alice Liddell), this glib and whimsical book has served to entertain millions of readers. Among its highlights is the poem **The Walrus and the Carpenter**.

Involvement in literature for youngsters, a cherished pastime, led Lewis Carroll to adopt a particular approach. The author well understood the extraordinary value of good children's fiction. Such literature, he realized, inevitably has a significant place in the individual's up-bringing: it offers important relief from daily routine. The success of children's authors, therefore, would seem to depend on an unaffected, genuine ability to push back the boundaries of reason and to embrace a world which most adults tend to dismiss—the world of make-believe and absurdity. Carroll's unusual penchant for child-like vision nurtured characteristic leaps into fantasy; taking the real as a point of departure, his transition to the inexplicable, magical, and wondrous is always rapid and often quite sudden. **Alice in Wonderland**, now irrefutably a children's classic, exemplifies this approach.

Although the value of Lewis Carroll's intellectual contribution is often underrated, his books have become some of the best-known throughout the world—and with good reason. Their astounding rise to popularity and their impact on an ever-growing audience can be readily comprehended. In addressing children, the writing, it turns out, speaks also to adults who find themselves constrained by routine existence in today's society. Children's books, we should remember, are often read aloud. To a great extent, therefore, the success of such books is determined by their appeal to a wide audience. Analysis of **The Walrus and the Carpenter** can help to uncover a dimension of possible interest to a mature mind.

No one would deny that the poem is absurd in the most obvious way. Indeed, it is humorous. But its humor dwells on the ridiculous and senseless. The mere title raises an immediate question: what do the two figures or personages—the walrus and the carpenter—have in common? In everyday terms, we quickly realize, there is simply no possible link.

Thereafter, the reader's expectations are easily fulfilled. The very first stanza makes clear that the poem is a silly one. Its overt simple-mindedness, moreover, is seemingly underscored by a naive-sounding metrical lilt.

> The sun was shining on the sea,
>   Shining with all his might:
> He did his very best to make
>   The billows smooth and bright—

And this was odd, because it was
The middle of the night.

One can hardly imagine a more bizarre-sounding opening!
The subsequent stanzas continue in more or less the same
manner. Startling contradictions and *non sequiturs* are a
norm; they are encountered one after another, stanza after
stanza. Ideas and images are left dangling without explanation. The general tone of speech remains frivolous and superficial.

Nevertheless, the poem is not without an element of
delight. At the very least, it manages to hold our attention;
it succeeds in keeping us wondering about what is next. Finally, it leaves us with a modest laugh or chuckle. But is
this all? For what possible reason do we find something
sympathetic in the work? In other words, does the poem
have a level of "hidden" significance?

Broadly speaking, in spite of its burlesque, nonsensical
quality, the poem is focused on an identifiable subject. (Interestingly enough, the child may pick this up sooner than
the adult; it will be obvious from the start. What the child
will not see, however, is Carroll's "adult" point of view
on the matter.) **The Walrus and the Carpenter** is a poem
about friends; by extension, it is also a poem about behavior. No matter how ridiculous they may appear, the two
main characters are portrayed as companions; in the course
of the poem, moreover, they are joined by other
acquaintances—the ill-fated oysters.

But, in the midst of this, it takes some sophistication
to spot the poem's element of benign mockery, and this
dimension only really concerns the adult. Well-versed in
the ways of society, the grown-up can perceive that, in
fact, Carroll pokes fun at the nature of so-called civilized
etiquette. This would have been an especially sensitive fea-

ture of the poem during the author's lifetime. Towards the
end of the nineteenth century, the "Victorian Age", known
for its deceptively mannered refinement, middle-class
stuffiness, and superficiality, was at a peak of development.

Carroll makes his point through a use of curious imagery. In the beginning of the poem, for example, the sun
is anthropomorphized as hard-working, "shining with all
his might." This positive social quality, however, is immediately shown to be dependent on circumstances; when
conditions change, it assumes an odd, negative aspect: "it
was / the middle of the night." The moon, in turn, is
shown to be hypersensitive to the sun's blunder: "It's very
rude of him," she says. Here, the poet is bringing to our
attention the ridiculous side of people's assumptions about
proper behavior. In stanzas four and five, Carroll expresses
man's arrogant notion of progress involving improvement
upon nature. Hence, regarding the sand on the beach, the
walrus and carpenter make a silly claim: "If this were only
cleared away . . . it would be grand!" Excessive concern
with external, well-groomed appearances is further made
fun of when the poet describes the "clean and neat" shoes
of the oysters who "hadn't any feet". Stanza eleven makes
a burlesque sketch of a luncheon social. The small talk associated with that type of gathering is shown to be trite and
full of pretense: "And why the sea is boiling hot— / And
whether pigs have wings." In the final stanzas the mockery
touches on a more serious subject. The poet shows how
politeness and good manners can be used to disguise what
is really "a dismal thing to do"—to feed on one's friends,
in this case, the oysters.

> "The night is fine," the Walrus said,
>   "Do you admire the view?

"It was so kind of you to come!
And you are very nice!"

This is what the walrus says in order to avoid responding to the oysters' cry: "But not on us!" False sentimentality escalates in the subsequent exchange:

"I weep for you," the Walrus said;
"I deeply sympathize."
With sobs and tears he sorted out
Those of the largest size,

Finally, the carpenter carries out his hidden intentions. As a true hypocrite, however, in the last stanza he feigns innocence and addresses the oysters...as if nothing had ever happened. "But answer came there none— / And this was scarcely odd, because / They'd eaten every one."

In retaining at all times a delightful sense of play and humor, therefore, Carroll is able to touch on a broad range of serious concerns. Ultimately, he draws a caricature of human behavior which speaks directly to mature sensitivities and cautions against hyper-sophistication, lies, deceit, and pompous views of adulthood. And since the poem indeed seems to offer such a message, it also immediately provides a much-needed remedy or antidote. For what better way can there be to journey "home" and to "touch base" with simple, naive emotions, than to read and thoroughly enjoy a poem overtly written for the child.

Ralph Waldo Emerson
(1803–1882)

Friendship

The first four lines of the poem **Friendship** by Ralph
Waldo Emerson set up a contrast which the rest of the
poem will interpret: the microcosm of "A ruddy drop of
blood" is said to "outweigh" the macrocosmic "surging
sea"; likewise, the larger "world uncertain comes and
goes" while the smaller world of "The lover rooted
stays". As a transcendentalist writing in the 1830's and
40's, Emerson is responding to the world and man's place
in it as understood by the Puritans who settled America
over two hundred years earlier; in this poem the reader
senses the change in religious and philosophical ideals
which took place in the time elapsing between the Massachusetts Bay Colony settled in 1603 and pre-Civil War
America.

In the differences between a drop of blood and the
world uncertain [which] comes and goes, Emerson points
to a fundamental distinction between the Puritan world
view and his own. The Puritans saw themselves as corrupted by Adam and Eve's original sin and subject to the
kind of hierarchical Christian universe described in John
Milton's **Paradise Lost.** (Milton himself was a Puritan.)
Their sense of piety is portrayed by the scholar Perry
Miller in his book *The New England Mind:*

Puritanism allowed men no help from tradition or legend; it took away the props of convention and the pillows of custom; it demanded that the individual confront existence directly on all sides at once, that he test all things by the touchstone of absolute truth, that no allowance be made for circumstances or for human frailty. It showed no mercy to the spiritually lame and the intellectually halt; everybody had to advance at the double-quick under full pack. It demanded unblinking perception of the facts, though they should slay us. It was without any feeling for the twilight zones of the mind, it could do nothing with nuances or with half-grasped, fragmentary insights and oracular intuitions.*

As the imagery in Emerson's poem suggests ("surging sea"), the spiritual world of the Puritans was unified, large, and subject to God's unpredictable will. Transcendentalism, however, took the centrality given to mankind's spiritual relationship with God and diffused it into each individual's relationship with that which has spiritually heightened potential within the self. As Emerson describes in his essay *Nature*:

The high and divine beauty which can be loved without effeminacy, is that which is found in combination with the human will. Beauty is the mark God sets upon virtue. Every natural action is graceful. Every heroic act is also decent, and causes the place and the bystanders to shine. We are taught by great actions that the universe is the property of every individual in it. It is his, if he will. He may divest himself of it; he may creep into a corner, and abdicate his kingdom, as most men

---

*Perry Miller, *The New England Mind: The Seventeenth Century* (Cambridge, MA: Harvard University Press, 1982), I, p. 45.

do, but he is entitled to the world by his constitution.
In proportion to the energy of his thought and will, he
takes up the world into himself.**

To summarize the difference between Puritanism and
Emersonian transcendentalism we may list two main points:
(1) Emerson's world was fragmented since the potential for
spiritual growth existed privately within each individual,
while the Puritans' spiritual confrontation involved an arbitrary God who permeated all things; and (2) transcendentalism optimistically emphasized each individual's uninhibited capacity for spiritual growth while Puritanism
pessimistically stressed man's original sin and the need for
redemption.

Friendship is essentially a transcendentalist poem for
several reasons. In the first place, it rejects the tension
produced by an unpredictable and spiritually threatening
Puritan God who watches over us like a hawk. The image
of the "surging sea" in the second line—like the related
word "despair" in the poem's antepenultimate line—is
drawn from the Puritan's view of things as uncertain and
dark. In terms of diction, some of the words corresponding
to the transcendental world view are "lover", "glowed",
"unexhausted", "kindness", "sunrise", "rose", "fountains", etc. Coming from a Puritan, the line "All things
through thee take nobler form" would have to refer to
god; but here, Emerson is suggesting that a fellow human
being's existence ennobles the world around him. When in-
spected more closely, the process Emerson describes is an
unusual one; it is as if all existence—"all things"—
experienced in terms of the friend's world become trans-

**Ralph Waldo Emerson, *Selections from Ralph Waldo
Emerson: An Organic Anthology,* ed. Stephen E. Whicher
(Boston: Houghton Mifflin Company, 1960), pp. 28-29.

formed into a "nobler form". Transcendentalism, then, is a radical reversal of the Puritan point of view; it is not the individual who is subject to God's "uncertain" will, but, given the proper circumstances, "all things" are transformed into a nobler form by the mere existence of a "friend".

Through transcendentalism, Emerson has found a way out of the spiritual pessimism he inherited from the Puritans and, as he says, "...master my despair;/The fountains of my hidden life/Are through thy friendship fair." **Friendship,** when put into such a philosophical and historical context, reveals the radical about-face in America over the two centuries between the landing of the first settlers and the period following Emerson's resignation as Unitarian Minister in 1832 when he took up a brilliant career as lecturer and essayist for a new philosophical cause.

William Wordsworth
(1770–1850)

To Hartley Coleridge

Wordsworth's so-called "Great Decade"—the years 1797-1807—came while the poet lived in England's beautiful lake district, at Grasmere, very near to his friend and colleague, Samuel Taylor Coleridge. This and other fortunate circumstances contributed to the poet's productivity during the period. The friendship with Coleridge, however, had special significance. Like that between T.S. Eliot (1888-1965) and Ezra Pound (1885-1972), it served as a source of stimulation for both men and even resulted in a joint publication entitled *Lyrical Ballads, With a Few Other Poems* (1798). This volume, expanded and reprinted in 1800, was considered "experimental"; nevertheless, it quickly achieved renown as a revolutionary manifesto for poets of the era. **To Hartley Coleridge** was written in 1802 and dedicated to Coleridge's first child at the age of six.

Burgeoning "Romanticism" and democratic ideals of the French Revolution played an important role in Wordsworth's output. On one occasion, the poet himself put this issue into perspective: "The principal object, then, which I proposed to myself in these poems was to choose incidents and situations from common life, and to relate or describe them, throughout, as far as possible, in a selection of language really used by men."* This statement reveals a purposeful outlook antithetical to the strictures of "Classical" form and content. It goes along with Wordsworth's distaste for hyperbolic language and the use of pompous, inflated subjects from mythology or legend. In the poet's own words, extreme rhetoric is inappropriate for "that sort of pleasure...which a poet may rationally endeavor to impart." "Low and rustic life was generally chosen," the poet says, "because in that condition...the passions of men are incorporated with the beautiful and permanent forms of nature.... [And] being less under the influence of social vanity they convey their feelings and notions in simple and unelaborated expressions." In this way, utterance "may be more accurately contemplated, and more forcibly communicated."*

Recognizing the best in what is simple and natural, Wordsworth and other Romantic poets looked to childhood as an ideal state certainly preferable to maturity. In **To Hartley Coleridge**, for example, the line "O blessed vision! happy child!" is contrasted to a morose and sickly view of adulthood: "O too industrious folly!/O vain and causeless melancholy!"

This viewpoint, however, must be carefully considered, for it has to do not only with basic qualitative comparison, but also with a deeper, poetic notion about the nature of creative endeavor and its source in human thought. In another masterpiece entitled *The Prelude,* Wordsworth comes close to revealing a truly astounding, personal evaluation:

> This efficacious spirit chiefly lurks
> Among those passages of life that give
> Profoundest knowledge to what point, and how

---

*M.H. Abrams, Gen, Ed., *The Norton Anthology of English Literature,* 4th Ed. (New York, W.W. Norton & Company, 1979), II, pp 160 ff.

> The mind is lord and mast—outward sense
> The obedient servant of her will. Such moments
> Are scattered everywhere, taking their date
> From our first childhood.

In short, "life" and temporal existence are taken as a composite of isolated, fleeting moments, "those passages of life...scattered everywhere", whose single point of reference is true consciousness. Since this consciousness first emerges during the individual's early years as a child, childhood itself becomes a focus of natural preoccupation, concern, interest, and, ultimately, boundless inspiration.

In **To Hartley Coleridge** we see that the poet's idealization of childhood originates in a longing for unencumbered imagination. The first line singles out the attribute: "O thou whose fancies from afar are brought." Based on this, the poet leads onward and in the following lines tells us that the child has unique means of communication; moreover, he is capable of expressing purer ideas than the adult. The child demonstrates "unutterable thought" through (a) nonsensical babble ("thy words dost make a mock apparel"), (b) spontaneity ("the breeze-like motion"), and (c) naive song ("the self-born carol"). Where a thought is so profound as to be ineffable, the child's vocabulary remains appropriate, direct and does not get involved in the contorted metaphysical convolutions of the adult mind. In Wordsworth's estimation, then, the child is "suspended in a stream as clear as sky, / Where earth and heaven do make one imagery"; "fancies from afar" are assimilated with such ease ("blessed vision") that their expression emerges with unusual lucidity and directness. The adult must only learn to comprehend the fact.

Thus, in Wordsworth's understanding, longevity is a dismal prospect. He specifically discusses his view of "future years" in another passage from **The Prelude**:

> The days gone by
> Return upon me almost from the dawn
> Of life: the hiding place of man's power
> Open, I would approach them, but they close.
> I see by glimpses now; when age comes on,
> May scarcely see at all.

All too evidently, the poet sees the power of imagination as diminishing over time; according to him, the mere recall of bygone days decreases with age. —And then, eventually comes the tragedy: the adult life becomes littered with "pain", "grief", "injuries", and "sorrow", so that existence no longer is "as clear as sky", but muddied and filthy, as if "trailed along the soiled earth". He laments the frail human psyche "ill-fitted to sustain unkindly shocks"; it is "A gem that glitters while it lives", but its existence is constantly under threat ("the touch of wrongs") and finally "slips in a moment out of life".

Nevertheless, Wordsworth realizes that creativity as such must endure against all odds. In other words, the present cannot dwindle but must keep its catalytic energy and remain a focus of attention at all times. Against the background of the past, it serves the artist in a unique way: it fulfills an essential requirement. —It constitutes the mind's solid point of departure in all forms of creative activity. For a poet who wrote of "emotion recollected in tranquility", the subject of "childhood" offers a valuable occasion to make the point. The idea, however, is a pervasive one and is found echoed throughout his entire *oeuvre:*

> . . .I had known,
> Too forcibly, too early in my life
> Visitings of imaginative power
> . . .and again
> In Nature's presence stood, as I now stand
> A sensitive being, a *creative* soul.

II
Love

Preface

The subject of love lends itself to highly subjective understanding involving the innermost emotions of the poet. Throughout the history of poetry, poets have dwelt on its various forms: romantic love (Lord Byron, Rainer Maria Rilke); religious love (George Herbert); familial love (Robert Frost); and, love between friends (Alfred Lord Tennyson). Perhaps the best known author of love poetry, however, is Shakespeare. The unharnessed power of love is beautifully expressed in many of his works, particularly the sonnets. On one occasion, he wrote the famous line: "Love's fire heats water, water cools not love."* Shakespeare's use of basic, accessible imagery lends universal appeal to his poetry. Moreover, it shows how the master is able to comply with one of the main criteria of good art—a disciplined approach to creativity. Even when he writes on an intense and passionate subject, Shakespeare's prime objective is to communicate and to remain understood by others. Thus, his poetry typically offsets elements of personal interpretation and introduces subjectivity only in connection with a firm grip on an identifiable or real world.

---

*William Shakespeare, *William Shakespeare: The Complete Works,* ed. Alfred Harbage, et al. (Baltimore: Penguin Books, 1972), p. 1479.

Ben Jonson
(1572–1637)

Drink To Me Only With Thine Eyes

"In 1600, the educated Englishman's mind and world were more than half medieval; by 1660, they were more than half modern."* This observation by Douglas Bush in *English Literature in the Early Seventeenth Century* concerns a period of great philosophical and political upheaval—a time when exciting ideas and discoveries became instrumental in the formation of a new social consciousness among English people.

The changes which took place during that time reflect developments in the broad arena of European culture. In particular, certain advancements in the realm of science had an especially powerful impact on a range of spiritual, intellectual, and artistic concerns. The result was a final collapse of the stable philosophical framework inherited from the Middle Ages. We need only to remember that this was the time when European society at large took hold of two fundamental realities: (a) that the planet Earth was not the center of the universe; and (b) that the so-called "New

---

*Douglas Bush, *English Literature in the Early Seventeenth Century* (Oxford: The Clarendon Press, 1962), p. 1.

World'', laying far beyond the oceans of the continent, promised the seemingly limitless possibilities of a vast uncharted territory.

The overriding concern of this period was the emergence of empirical thought. Prior to the seventeenth century, the world view of most Europeans was based on Christian belief, which interpreted the universe in terms of an unchanging, hierarchical order established by Divine Providence. But, as the century came of age, many prominent intellectuals were led to question this belief and suggested that science had the authority to contribute new evidence towards religious understanding. Needless to say, on some occasions, this involved innovations unknown in sacred tradition. The resulting conflict was especially evident in the famous trial of Galileo in 1633. At the trial, the church authorities accused the renowned astronomer of blasphemy for suggesting a radical revision of cosmology based on scientific observation.

In the course of such events, the unsettling impact of intellectual trends also became evident in the realm of the arts. Although the period is characterized by the work of many creative thinkers, there is much evidence that new developments were the cause of considerable inner turmoil and conflict. As a result, the seventeenth century is also dominated by a basic quest for stability and permanence. Shakespeare was among the first to express concern with this important and thoroughly modern psychological problem. For example, the magnificent dramas *King Lear* and *Hamlet* are exemplary and show the tragic struggle of individuals torn between two worlds; on the one hand, there is the world of religious conviction which places faith in the existence of eternal harmony and God's law and, on the other hand, there is the surrounding secular society which is fleeting and constantly in a state of transition.

Ben Jonson, a life-long friend of Shakespeare, was another prominent literary figure who met the challenge of the times. His role in the history of English literature is connected with the rise of *neo-classicism*—the aesthetic code based on a revival of ancient art and literature. Having been well trained especially in the great Latin poets such as Catullus, Seneca, Horace, and Virgil, Jonson was able to develop a special style of poetry which was particularly suited for current needs.* To his contemporaries, this poetry had a particular element of dignity and credence; it was based on the conviction that the aesthetic principles behind pagan Greek and Roman art offer a "classical" standard. This idea had far-reaching consequences and helped to lead numerous thinkers out of a state of unproductive, intellectual disorder. Jonson, therefore, exerted powerful influence on subsequent English literature. He is best known as a poet of stature and a man of important, forward-looking ideas. It is of some significance that his closest circle of associates numbered many young students who later became the focus of an outstanding generation of English scholars, poets, and writers. Among these figures were leading names such as John Donne, George Chapman, Robert Herrick, and Sir John Suckling.

Drink to Me Only with Thine Eyes introduces some of the ways in which Jonson was able to exert his influence. Although the famous poem is ostensibly about "love", the poet's treatment of the subject is somewhat surprising and shows a special approach from the very onset. In writing a poem on a highly personal theme, Jonson instructs his lover to drink to him "only with...eyes" and

---

*Michael Stapleton, *The Cambridge Guide to English Literature* (Cambridge: Cambridge University Press and Newnes Books, 1983), p. 464.

to "leave a kiss but in the cup". Following this, the poem expresses a number of internal contradictions in the course of which Jonson seems to both extol and belittle the special qualities. Thus, in lines 4 through 8, he gives praise and promises eternal allegiance: "But might I of Jove's nectar sup,/I would not change for thine." In the second stanza, however, he seems "not so much to honor" as to express astonishment at the lover's supposed supernatural and life-giving power capable of preserving the "rosy wreath".

The substantive message of the poem, therefore, is strongly affected by the rational, calculated approach with which the author treats personal experience. In a sense, he has deified his beloved but seems to expect or need no more than mere ability to worship her from afar. Traditionally, love poetry strives to express overwhelming, powerful human feeling and stresses a determination for total complete union between lovers—both spiritual and physical. In Jonson's poem, however, we see a radically different approach. The poet adopts a cool, candid tone and simply tells his beloved to remain at a "safe" distance. In other words, Jonson's masterpiece is indeed about love, but its underlying message seems to offer something of an unexpected twist; it tells us that actual contact between lovers is not a necessary component of passionate involvement.

What was the origin of Jonson's strange conception? In part, the situation probably has to do with private experience; the poem could have been directed at an actual person. But the real answer almost surely also lies in another realm and has to do with the particular milieu in which Jonson was writing. In fact, to a great extent, an understanding of what the poem really has to say apparently depends on the interpretation of "hidden" meaning. It's ultimate aim is to address the issue of subjective truth and to caution against thoughtless adherence to traditional feelings of belief. The burning question of Jonson's day had to do with the relationship between religious dogma and empirical fact. Therefore, it is reasonable to suspect that, in the final analysis, the poem has a very specific target. Its objective is to affirm that a rational or "scientific" mind must co-exist with the experience of profound sentiment and should be adapted for the purpose of finding new ways to probe the unknown. In developing an allegory on this matter, Jonson reveals his deep respect for the ancient authors, many of whom relied on myth, legend, and symbolism as useful means to shed light on basic human concerns.

Robert Herrick
(1591–1674)

Whenas in Silks My Julia Goes

As one of the famed Cavalier poets, Robert Herrick is associated with the seventeenth-century English court. His poetry, therefore, reflects the mood of a very special literary milieu. It is light, playful, and written for an audience largely concerned with ceremony and the pursuit of pleasure.

Although many of his works appear trite and deal with overt superficiality, there are sufficient traces of brilliance and ingenuity to suggest that Herrick was indeed extraordinarily gifted, perceptive, and a craftsman of superior talent. In particular, his work shows a keen sense of structure and an unusual skill at utilizing the elements of a classical poetic technique. Moreover, his poetry is written in a lucid manner which exhibits careful attention to form. No doubt, to a great extent, this is due to the influence of his mentor, Ben Jonson; we should note that during his student years, he was involved in the well-known Tribe of Ben, a group of ardent, young scholars who advocated the imitation of ancient Greek and Latin authors.

As an exponent of "neo-classical" ideals, however, Herrick developed a special approach. In respect to Jonson, he conveys an easy-going, witty, charming, and cheerful disposition capable of overriding all manifestations of obstinate dogma. His characters, as a result, are sometimes irreverent and often idealized to an extreme. They are portrayed in "ultra lyrical" or mythological terms and are frequently presented in the guise of deities adorned with exquisite flowers and other regalia. Interestingly enough, later in life Herrick became a clergyman and shifted his focus to a more inspirational kind of poetry dealing primarily with nature. The critic Douglas Bush describes his work as "the sober interweaving of rustic, pagan, and Christian elements...of nature, myth, and ritual: which incorporates both an earthly and sensuous concreteness".* **Whenas in Silks My Julia Goes** is something of a miniature which exemplifies Herrick's masterful control and discipline as a poet.

There is a basic realization that, in all forms of art, literature, and music, brevity and economy of means require a special approach. To achieve a desired effect, therefore, the short poem must utilize every ingredient of a condensed aesthetic and must find a clear, appealing way to express a thoroughly distilled idea. From this standpoint, Herrick's piece exhibits nothing other than sheer brilliance. The poet molds a complete, intelligible work within a span of thirty-seven words and six lines. His method is to proceed carefully, word by word, and to construct a tight arrangement of lines in a recognizable pattern that elicits a specific emotional response. The poem is bound by linear development "in time" with a beginning, climax, and conclusion. In the first line, rising action comes with the ap-

---

*Douglas Bush, *English Literature in the Early Seventeenth Century* (Oxford: The Clarendon Press, 1962), pp. 115-119.

pearance of Julia in the silk dress. This establishes an image of the subject in terms of a royal being endowed with astonishing beauty. The climax is expressed by the use of "liquefaction"; this somewhat exotic-sounding word perfectly describes the movement of Julia's dress and also suggests the intensity of the poet's feelings—a state of virtual intoxication with the rich, sensuous image of the woman in flowing fabric. A resolution or decline in action occurs as the speaker tacitly accepts the powerful impression made by Julia; with the use of the word "vibration", he echoes what has already transpired and reinforces the rapidly vanishing image of the rippling gown in liquid glory. The calculated movement of the poem is articulated in a clear-cut way. Herrick uses words such as "whenas", "then", and "next" to establish anticipatory tension at critical points in the drama. The double use of "then" at the beginning of the second line especially underscores the sense of latent expectation and the possibility of savoring the fruits of ecstasy.

In fact, in the course of the short poem, the feelings of expectation become so intense that the conclusion remains open and leaves the reader in a state of wonder and suspense. Evidently, this is exactly what the poet wishes to achieve, for he only alludes to a possible final outcome. Having taken us to the heights of passion and soaring tribute to Julia's garments, he withdraws, drops his eyes, and resigns himself to inner contemplation. In other words, he finds himself at a loss to appropriately deal with private exhilaration. This, in particular, typifies the dilemma of the Cavalier poets and helps to explain their unique response to the subject of love. Julia, in her flowing apparel, is deified, and the poet's adoration becomes so complete that it need not go any further. Moreover, the need for physical involvement is, apparently, obviated. In short, Herrick's personal experience as a poet is consummate, for the vision of beauty lives on in his imagination and transports him to unearthly realms—even when his eyes are cast down.

Finally, an analysis of the poem would not be complete without addressing the issue of diction. Robert Herrick had an extraordinary ear for the sound of words, and his poetry can be appreciated for its mellifluous quality, quite apart from the actual meaning of the words and phrases. As such, it is designed to operate on a level of "musical" or sound perception. Herrick's natural ability to highlight the unique attributes of the English language is central to his poetry and exhibits an unusually precise choice of word images. In **Whenas in Silks My Julia Goes,** the soft, subdued consonants of "sweetly", "clothes", and "mine eyes" create a rustling sensation of beatific contentment. But then, suddenly, Herrick interjects with a concluding cacaphony of harsh sounds. It is almost as if he wishes to end on a tumultuous note of anguish. As a result, the last line, "O how that glittering taketh me!" stands in diametric opposition to the smooth and gentle opening; its emphatic "O" and discordant "glittering" are like the unexpected intrusion of loud clamor onto an otherwise tranquil, relaxed setting.

This, perhaps, is one of the reasons why Charles Swinburne later described Herrick as "the greatest song writer ever born of English race."*

---

*Algernon Charles Swinburne, *The Complete Works of Algernon Charles Swinburne* (New York: Russell & Russell, 1968), V, p. 260.

William Shakespeare
(1564–1616)

Sonnet CXVI

"Let Me Not to the Marriage of True Minds"

In order to appreciate the genius of Shakespeare, it may be
helpful to keep three important points in mind: first, that
the author is deeply philosophical and deals with serious
questions of universal concern; second, that he does not
presume to furnish ready answers but merely offers
processes by which an individual may come to experience
"truth"; and third, that the particular style of language in
his work is eminently expressive of an underlying message.
In taking account of these basic realizations, the reader can
come to a reasoned understanding of Shakespeare's art—an
art which makes rigorous use of poetic expression in order
to explore a broad and lofty dominion of human thought.

A glance at **Sonnet CXVI** immediately shows the
breadth of ideas which Shakespeare embraces. In particular, "marriage" at the onset and "doom" towards the end
mark opposite points on the continuum of life's experience;
"marriage" implies intimate union while "doom" suggests
ultimate disintegration. The two words also have to do with
inherently contradictory issues of eternity because "marriage" promises the possibility of a final bond which then
nevertheless dissolves in the transient manner of all earthly

things. Similarly, we find that the poem's diction falls into two categories; on the one hand, there is a sense of fleeting impermanence (e.g. "alters", "remove", "tempests", "wandering", "bending", "brief") and, on the other hand, there is the affirmation of a terminal goal and stability ("true", "ever-fixed mark", "star", and "doom").

Upon closer inspection, however, it becomes evident that the enormous sweep of the poet's imagination ultimately has to do with a rather focused concern and that the preoccupation with opposing issues such as time, eternity, decay, and stability, in fact originates in a discourse on "love".

The poem begins with a positive affirmation of "love" which shows that an ultimate human concern is to safeguard the prosperity of precious reality. The opening request—"Let me not to the marriage of true minds / Admit impediments"—tells us that, in spite of what we are about to hear, the speaker does not wish to intrude on "the marriage of true minds", presently joining faithful individuals to each other. This, we soon realize, is a note of warning because the fundamental idea behind his poem is to bring into focus the threatening temporal context of man's daily life. Thus, he cautions that "...love is not love / Which alters when it alteration finds, / Or bends with the remover to remove". These lines clearly show that the reality of worldly circumstances requires a careful examination of personal motives. In short, Shakespeare introduces an element of doubt and tells us that love is not always what it appears to be.

In the next lines, the poet develops thought through the use of metaphor:

O, no! it is an ever-fixed mark,
That looks on tempests, and is never shaken;

It is the star to every wandering bark,
Whose worth's unknown, although his height be taken.

Here the image of the "wandering bark" or ship tossed in
the "tempests" is contrasted with the "ever-fixed mark"
or star which, though occasionally hidden by clouds during
a storm, is nonetheless a reliable point of reference for
navigation. The line "Whose worth's unknown...", however, indicates that the navigator does not "possess" the
star, nor can he ever come to know its full value or significance. His approach is simply to make use of one of
the star's apparent qualities—permanence—in order to ar-
rive safely into port.

The extraordinary sophistication of Shakespeare's poetry is therefore visible in the poet's thorough grasp and
articulation of basic thought processes. We should especially note the manner in which the abstract idea is given
shape through the use of language. Although the poem is
anchored to a form of direct statement, its thrust lies in a
different sort of approach. The poem begins and ends with
the voice in the first person singular. But, as the poet
moves to the essence of his thought, he resorts to the use
of metaphor (i.e. "love...is an ever-fixed mark...It is a
star"). In general, we might say, metaphor is an "interpre-
tive" or "indirect" form of speech. Accordingly, its contrasting function in the context of this sonnet is linked to
the poet's belief that, while moving through an unreliable,
transient world, one should come to emulate the ultimate
reliability of the timeless entity—the "ever-fixed mark"
called "love".

The final two lines bring the poem around full circle:
having begun with a candid request, Shakespeare now concludes on a somewhat apologetic note. He assumes the
blame, as it were, for having risked the possibility of con-

troversy on a sensitive subject of personal nature. Moreover, his statement in the form of an afterthought is perfectly frank about the limitations he sees in his own thought. "Nothing is certain!", he seems to say. The point is that, in the end, he is left with a basic predicament because his vantage point is that of an artist who operates in terms of a specific set of ideals. At the same time, he realizes that the "real" world—the world he has been speaking about in the preceding lines—is fraught with difficulties and offers many obstacles which put into jeopardy the outcome of positive action. To live with "ideals", therefore, becomes an act of enormous heroism; it embodies a struggle with the basic philosophical problem once formulated by the ancient Greek thinker, Plato, who stated a conviction that the "earthly" or "terrestrial" world is a flawed copy of an unattainable "ideal". "Flawed love" among people on earth, Shakespeare argues, must incorporate elements of understanding which continually transport the individual's realm of thought and experience to a state of transcendent stability and permanence. It is perhaps in this context that we can begin to contemplate the final two lines of the poem in which Shakespeare ultimately leaves open the possibility of error in his own dogged convictions.

John Keats
(1795–1821)

The Last Sonnet

Verse written in sonnet form normally takes a particular
approach: a thought or problem initially presented in the
space of eight lines (octet), is immediately offset by a sestet (six lines), offering a response or resolution. **The Last
Sonnet** by Keats furnishes a good example of this procedure and shows the way in which a poet's idea assumes the
shape of a standard fourteen-line structure. It also illustrates two other common features of the sonnet, namely,
rhyme in the so-called "English" or "Shakespearean" pattern (ababcdcdefefgg), and meter in iambic pentameter.

Keat's poem focuses on the subject of "love" and examines its conditional nature from the standpoint of personal
experience. The theme is delineated in the very first line
and is expressed in terms of the poet's longing for the
quality of a star's silent gaze.

> Bright star! would I were steadfast as thou art

This striking gesture of a vocative preface serves to trigger
the subsequent discussion. The first eight lines of the sonnet describe the star's quintessential "steadfastness". At
the same time, there emerges a central predicament: although the poet desires the ideal, the star remains out of

reach. The impossibility of attaining its lofty height begins to unfold almost immediately; as early as the second line, the poet hints at an innate reaction to the qualities he describes. He wishes to experience the calm stability of the star, but realizes that his existence is a passionate one and, therefore, is antithetical to that of an inanimate object. To develop and explain his point, Keats resorts to a common poetic device; in the course of the final six lines, he attempts to translate a heavenly ideal into human terms. This process is initiated in the first line of the sestet:

No—yet still steadfast, still unchangeable.

Here we see an interface between the poem's two sections marked by a brief recapitulation of the original themes of longing and denial. At this point, the basic argument begins: the poet shifts attention away from the star and addresses his own existence.

The approach centers on a special manipulation of imagery. The two worlds Keats describes are compared and contrasted only to reveal a danger inherent in the undertaking. "For humans," the poet seems to say, "the ideal is unattainable." Thus, for example, the wish to be "pillowed" on a "fair love's ripening breast" and "To feel for ever its soft fall and swell" becomes the antipode of "lone splendor hung aloft the night". It also disagrees with the idea of untroubled chastity in the earlier allusions to "Nature's patient sleepless Eremite" and "The moving waters at their priestlike task / Of pure ablution round earth's human shores". Of similar significance is the phrase "Awake for ever in a sweet unrest" which blatantly contradicts the patient "watching with eternal lids apart". Finally, we might note that the spring-like youth and fertility implicit in the "love's ripening breast" constitutes a reversal of the cold, wintery vision of "snow upon the mountains and the moors".

Nevertheless, in renouncing the chaste and frozen qualities of the star's "steadfastness", Keats never completely severs ties with the object of his contemplation; on the contrary, he sustains an element of kinship by means of subtle links between the two sections of the poem. This is evident in several strains of imagery which appear to run a consistent course throughout the poem: thus, (a) the rhythmic motion of "the moving waters" is echoed in the undulating, wave-like "fall and swell"; (b) the color and shape of the snowy mountains is recalled in the attributes of a "fair" female breast; (c) the religious experience of the "Eremite" and "priest" offers a possible parallel to the feelings which bind two lovers; (d) finally, in the context of a short, tightly constructed poem, the use of "soft fallen" in the octet and "soft fall" in the sestet can hardly be accidental; the purpose is to establish an underlying link through an abstract association of repeated words.

In his last sonnet, therefore, Keats sets up a kind of equation; he attempts to strike a balance between the nature of a star and human intimacy only to find that "steadfastness" in the inanimate and animate realms is achieved under radically different conditions. "The star", a symbol, is devoid of the kind of feelings experienced by the poet. As the "embodiment" of a concept, however, it remains important; thus, in the end, we find that, in spite of everything, the poet's longing for the ideal is destined to linger. The tension which this creates becomes explosive in the final line. The poet reaches for the impossible; the ultimatum, as a result, becomes:

And so live ever—or else swoon to death.

What does this mean? The line comes in two parts separated by a dash. This accentuates a predicament: in striving for ideals, humans are left to choose between two alternatives—life or death. The reason is the following: in the case of "steadfastness", the ideal which is impossible in life, seems possible in death. Just as life can be understood only in terms of time and change, death leads "out of time" and permanently suspends the individual in changeless eternity.

This sonnet is one of Keat's last works. Written during a trip to Italy in September 1820, it is known to have been composed on the fly leaf of a book of poems by Shakespeare. Keats died four months later, on February 23, 1821.

III

Sorrow and Consolation

Preface

"Sorrow is better than laughter: for by the sadness of the countenance the heart is made better," says the Bible (Ecclesiastes VII:3). This suggests that outward displays of sorrow are sometimes inwardly redeeming. A good example is Walt Whitman's great poem on the death of Lincoln, expressing the sorrow felt by an entire nation. By articulating pain, the poet sometimes becomes the agent through which suffering is shared and purged. This has been a recognized function of the poet since antiquity.

Alfred Lord Tennyson
(1809–1902)

In Memoriam

In 1833, Alfred Lord Tennyson began to compose a series of meditations on the death of a friend, Arthur Henry Hallam. These pieces, written at various times and places over a period of years, were not intended as a single collection until after 1849 when work on the individual poems had already been completed. The title **In Memoriam** was suggested by Tennyson's fiancée, Emily Sellwood, whom he married just before publishing the set in June 1850. Immensely popular with critics and public alike, over 60,000 copies of **In Memoriam** were sold before the end of the year.*

After the death of Hallam, Tennyson entered a period of religious questioning, and although he remained a devout Christian, his writing betrays evidence of a deep inner quest. In particular, his preoccupation with the existence of absolute Good (i.e. God) became the focus of his writing and the source of his work's universal appeal. Originally, it was not his intention to write a formal poem on the subject and his idea was rather along the lines of a series of

---

*Michael Stapleton, *The Cambridge Guide to English Literature* (Cambridge: Cambridge University Press and Newnes Books, 1983), p. 868.

private musings in which he could freely engage in introspection without confronting issues of established religion. His primary concern was to discover the fundamental sources of spiritual hope during times of despair. **In Memoriam** exhibits a wide range of approaches to a very serious philosophical problem and reflects the development of a man's thought between the ages of twenty-four and forty-one.

When D.H. Lawrence, the modern poet and novelist, said that "a demon wrote what is most valuable in Tennyson's early poems; he is an aesthetic split personality," he was probably alluding to **In Memoriam.** The work opens with a prayer:

> Strong Son of God, immortal Love,
> Whom we, that have not seen thy face,
> By faith, and faith alone, embrace,
> Believing where we cannot prove.

Man's fall from God's grace and the subsequent need for spiritual devotion are universal subjects. But Tennyson's poetry can be analyzed as a kind of synthetic investigation into these questions. The selections from **In Memoriam** quoted in *The World's Best Poetry* (vol. III, pp. 349-55) are abstract and ethereal enough to be addressed to the Son of God—indeed, as is the stanza quoted above. Yet, they are intended for Tennyson's deceased friend. Strangely enough, throughout the poem there is an absence of nostalgia as well as a lack of specific dwelling on the subject's physical or psychological characteristics. But, in view of Tennyson's aim, this is understandable. His main objective seems to be to commemorate Hallam by elevating personal reflection to the level of religious discourse.

Thus, **In Memoriam** operates on two levels (1) the metaphysical and (2) the personal; and, it's overwhelming success at the time of publication can be attributed to the poet's special ability to express highly emotional ideas without creating controversy over everyday religious precepts. Towards this end, Tennyson has developed a unique usage of vocabulary and poetic form. The fragmented nature of the work allowed him to keep a safe distance from the issue which could have overwhelmed a less astute artist. His poem, as a result, remains sober, carefully balanced and is not unduly sentimental. **In Memoriam** is one of the most important religious creations in English literature. T.S. Eliot, a modern poet whose concerns were very similar, once said that "it is a diary of which we have to read every word."*

---

*T.S. Eliot, *Selected Prose of T.S. Eliot,* ed. Frank Kermode (New York: Harcourt Brace Jovanovich / Farrar Straus Giroux, 1975), p. 243.

John Keats
(1795–1821)

Ode to a Nightingale

The poetry of John Keats is best known for (1) the broad range of styles it represents and (2) the imaginative sympathy it expresses towards the subject. Keats is noted for a special "impersonality"—an ability to transcend the self or leave it behind. Without analyzing or prejudging, he manages to explore an unusually wide range of characters and dramatic settings. This ability, exhibited especially by Shakespeare, is to some extent present in all the masters.

Ode to A Nightingale, for example, is not an abstract poem, but is told from the point of view of someone situated near a forest or perhaps a rural village; moreover, the speaker is aware of the "Dance, and Provencal song, and sunburnt mirth!" of the day's local festival. A specific season and a particular time of day are indicated: the poem begins at dusk after a summer day and continues into the night. The careful use of concrete images to indicate time and locale is further observed in the descriptive drama of the second stanza: a drinker holds a wine glass "With beaded bubbles winking at the brim / And purple-stained mouth".

At the same time, however, Keats takes an interesting approach to launch a meditation on aging. To do so, he invokes a series of concrete details pertaining to the evening setting. These, in turn, become metaphors for uninhibited joy and childlike pleasure. The central image, however, is the nightingale which almost magically appears to set the poem into motion. It endows the speaker with a vision of transient joy and a desire to relive the happiness of youth. But all of this happens against the background of a conscious malaise and dissatisfaction with the general condition of men living in society:

> The weariness, the fever, and the fret
> There, where men sit and hear each other groan

To underscore this feeling of frustration, the nightingale finally disappears into the forest. Its sudden departure leaves the poet speechless with no time to make a conclusion or final evaluation of what is all too clearly a fundamentally elusive subject.

The poem moves from pleasure and mirth in the first and second stanzas to the "weariness" and "fret" of old age in the third. It returns (this time with the help of the word "poesy") to a pleasurable setting of flowers and natural imagery in the fourth through seventh stanzas. The culmination, however, is in the eighth stanza: a changed but now ambiguous "self" no longer knows whether it resides with the nightingale's pleasure or with human anxiety. Significantly enough, Keats ends with the final question: "do I wake or sleep?"

Consequently, within the framework of a specific time and place, the reader experiences a number of polarities: intoxicating revelry and sober reality, the invocation of village life as well as the forest and wilderness of nature, life and death, youth and old age, and, finally, the realm of subjective feelings and objective reality. To be human is to embrace all these things and to experience the pendulum swinging from ecstasy to gloominess. In the confusing shift between different worlds—the exterior and the interior— Keats does not mislead the reader and stays close to the particulars of experience. Thus, for example, the mind alights upon "beaded bubbles winking at the brim" then quickly withdraws to make parallel associations within its own realm of sensual response.

Rather than provide straightforward descriptions of interrelated forces, most writers attempt to instill in the reader the idea of a closed, formulaic, or systematic world view—"a last word". According to Keats, however, theories and ideas often become obsolete; hence, only an impartial or objective description of the way our mind operates is of lasting interest and only the poet who can patiently observe and candidly recreate the process has accomplished something unique. As the distinguished scholar and author, Harold Bloom, wrote in *The Visionary Company:* "That Keats had the healthiest of imaginations, balanced at least in a harmony to its own impulses, is now generally and rightly believed. The world of Keats is our world as Shakespeare's is, at once actual and visionary, sensuous, probable, yet open to possibility".*

*Harold Bloom, *The Visionary Company: A Reading of English Romantic Poetry* (London: Faber & Faber Ltd., 1961), p. XV.

Walt Whitman
(1819–1892)

When Lilacs Last In The Dooryard Bloomed

If we associate England with poetry based (1) on iambic pentameter, that is, on ten alternating stressed and un-stressed syllables and (2) on a traditional use of consistent rhyme patterns, then, Walt Whitman's publication of *Leaves of Grass* in 1851 represents a decisive step in America's historical rejection of the British poetic style. In this collection, Whitman ignored strict form altogether; he favored long, usually unrhymed lines lending the feeling of breadth and liberation readily associated with America's vast size and political ideals of democracy.

Among the major art forms, poetry has often been considered one of the oldest and most exalted modes of ex-pression. However, poets of all ages, no matter how radi-cal their themes or concerns, have always adhered to in-herited prosodic laws. In the on-going debate concerning exactly how strict these laws should be, John Milton (1608-1674) argued in his preface to **Paradise Lost** that "rhyme [is] no necessary adjunct or true ornament of poem or good verse...but the invention of a barbarous age, to set off wretched matter and lame meter..."* Mil-

---

*John Milton, *Paradise Lost,* ed. Scott Elledge (New York: W.W. Norton & Company, 1975), p. 4.

ton was a Puritan, and his dislike of poetic ornament went hand in hand with the Protestant rejection of Catholic ritual and ceremony. (Interestingly enough, some three centuries later, the use of traditional rhyme schemes was brought back by W.H. Auden, a twentieth-century poet and devout Catholic.) Milton's case, however, is also an example of a broader historical conflict: poetry has long been a battleground for those who, on the one hand, wish to protect its status as "high" art and those others, who believe in the complete freedom of the artist and in the unconstrained use of poetic license.

Whitman, living as he did in a predominantly Protestant country, inherited Milton's rebellious attitude; he wrote not only poetry that did not rhyme but also poetry that was no longer restricted to higher themes. His subject was America, and he emulated in poetic terms that which he considered truly "American". Upon comparison to Milton's verse, **When Lilacs Last In The Dooryard Bloomed** reminds us more of prose than poetry. This, together with the fact that the poet's choice of themes was considered inappropriate, has led many critics to judge Whitman's work as vulgar. His concerns were democratic in the fullest sense. —He was open to the whole of life. There was nothing which Whitman was not able to incorporate into his world view; at the end, even death is welcomed with open arms:

> Dark mother, always gliding near with soft feet,
> Have none chanted for thee a chant of fullest welcome?
> Then I chant it for thee, I glorify thee above all,
> I bring thee a song that when thou must indeed come,
>   come unfalteringly

A merging and happy co-existence of all beings distinguishes Whitman's world. That his ideas survived the Civil

War (1861-65), the bloodiest ever fought on American territory, speaks for his openness to all humanity—in a
democratic language of the soil.

The most revolutionary quality of Whitman's work was
the vastness of its panorama. Generally speaking, poetic
forms focus on a particular emotion, concept, or, in the
case of narrative poetry, on a series of events leading up to
a specific incident. Whitman sought to expand the scope of
such an approach. Thus it is now commonly understood
that he must be regarded as America's national poet. Whitman truly stands for the spirit of burgeoning America; his
account of the events of the day has no parallel. This was
possible only in the context of his wholly new approach to
poetry. As Whitman described it: "We need a language
fanned by the breath of Nature, which leaps overhead,
cares mostly for impetus and effects, and for what it plants
and invigorates to grow."* In an unpublished essay written
in 1909, Ezra Pound stated the following about Whitman:
"I see him as America's poet. He is America. Entirely
free from the renaissance humanist ideal of the complete
man or from the Greek idealism, he is content to be what
he is, and he is his time and his people... Like Dante he
wrote in the "vulgar tongue" in a new metric. The first
great man to write in the language of his people."**

In **When Lilacs Last In The Dooryard Bloomed**,
form and content work hand in hand towards a poetic syn-

---

*Walt Whitman, *Complete Poetry and Selected Prose*
(Boston: Houghton Mifflin Company, 1959), p. 500. The
quote is from "Democratic Vistas."

**Ezra Pound, "What I Feel About Walt Whitman,"
American Literature, Concord NH, XXVII (March 1955),
56-61.

thesis of stylistic and thematic elements. As can be seen in
the diction and images of Sections 1 and 2 (*World's Best
Poetry,* vol. III, p. 362), the poem opens with an emphasis
on religious ideas—"the great star", "trinity", "perennial", and "soul"; it gives the feeling of someone overwhelmed by his surroundings. The opening line—"lilacs in
the dooryard bloomed"—also suggests a world which operates according to predetermined, unchanging laws in the
same way that Section 2 focuses on "O cruel hands that
hold me powerless...O helpless soul of me".

Section 3 similarly implies universal issues with the
"lilac-bush tall-growing with heart-shaped leaves of rich
green,/...with every leaf a miracle". Section 4 presents
"A shy and hidden bird" (suggesting the human soul)
whose song is "Death's outlet song of life...". Finally, in
Section 5 we have Lincoln's coffin "passing" through a
spring-time countryside filled with images of rebirth, including "old woods, where lately the violets peeped from
the ground, spotting the gray debris...". Such emphasis in
the opening sections on the uniqueness of constructive images is achieved not only by the normal visual break between stanzas (which roughly connotes the break between
paragraphs in prose) but also by the added mechanism of a
section number (which corresponds to the numbering of
chapters in a novel).

At the same time, however, this "distancing" contrasts
with a central thematic concern of the poem—the search
for a metaphysical common denominator and an unspecified, spiritual unification of fragmentary elements in nature. Thus, the use of consecutive section numbers may
also be seen as a kind of visual or intellectual hinge between the disjunct sections. The word "comrades" used

near the end of the poem is, in social terms, an operative word for the harmonious unity Whitman ultimately perceives. This vision is further articulated in the use of the word "and" in the final lines of the poem; the conjunction is used in a special function to serve as a grammatical link between what were, in the beginning, disparate elements— "lilac", "star", and "bird". As Whitman explicitly states, these are "twined with the chant of my soul".

IV
Higher Life

Preface

Poetry about "higher life" deals with the realm of the divine—the sacred, or what is generally recognized as being different from the secular or mundane. We might even say that this is "the invisible life" lying beyond the boundaries of time and space. Although the existence of a spiritual dimension has always been known, concepts of the "higher life" have changed drastically. During the Middle Ages, the spiritual world was commonly perceived in terms of an ordered hierarchy such as the one described in Dante's *Divine Comedy*. By the eighteenth century, however, this sacred view was brought into serious question; during the Age of Enlightenment, reason and "the Western scientific mind" touched off a speculative discourse. This shook traditional religion to the core. The authority of church dogma was denied; floodgates of the imagination were thrown open; brand new visions of the non-material world began to take shape. Works such as **Brahma** and *Paradise Lost* can be discussed in terms of the remarkably different religious views expressed by poets over the ages.

Ralph Waldo Emerson
(1803–1882)

Brahma

According to *The Hindu Religious Tradition* by Thomas J.
Hopkins, "Brahman is viewed as the One, the totality of
the existent and the non-existent. It is the underlying truth
of all that exists, the reality on which all name and form
depend. Brahman itself is beyond specification, beyond
name and form, identifiable with only one other reality: the
atman or self of man."*

Through his poetry and essays, Ralph Waldo Emerson
introduced Oriental philosophy to America. By the 1830's,
America, formerly unified around a religious, political, and
philosophical struggle for independence, was divided by
factionalism which eventually erupted into the Civil War.
Emerson sought to heal this disintegration through the idea
of "self-reliance", i.e. the concept that genuine spiritual
growth can take place only by awareness of "the truth
within the self". This coincides with the special emphasis
on Hinduism, a major religion of the East, which has always advocated a knowledge of the self and an inner
awareness surpassing religious ritual. In accordance with
his beliefs, Emerson thus turned away from organized re-

---

*Thomas J. Hopkins, *The Hindu Religious Tradition* (Encino CA: Dickenson Publishing Co., Inc., 1971), pp. 38-39.

ligion and adopted an individual quest for spiritual fulfill-
ment. In his book *The American Procession,* Alfred Kazin
has given a perceptive assessment of Emerson's essay
"The Poet" (1844). As Professor Kazin states, "All true
writers were types of "the poet", not sub-divided and classified but integral of mind and spirit, able to see life whole
and to express the 'All'."**

Emerson is closely associated with the philosophical
and literary school in America called transcendentalism.
There are good reasons for his participation in this intellectual movement. Following the Salem witch trials of 1692,
America experienced profound dismay at the obvious
ramifications of religious fanaticism. Consequently, be-
lievers abandoned the extremist views of Puritanism; they
continued to attend their churches regularly, but not with
the former conviction. In fact, much of the religious fervor
was re-directed to material concerns such as conquering the
wilderness, building factories, machines, and cities. It is
essential to emphasize that the pathologically self-conscious
nature of Puritan life, culturally short-lived as it was, could
not help but leave a certain psychological mold which was
passed on to subsequent generations. In other words, while
the Puritan world view could not endure because of its ri-
gidity, underlying precepts continued into the future. Emerson picked up the thread and gave Americans a way to
bring into practice their largely dormant religious feelings;
he saw transcendentalism as the way to channel energies
back into true spirituality.

Some people believe that Emersonian ideas lead only
to an isolation of the individual. This idea, however, is
based on a misunderstanding of the times and the facts. In

**Alfred Kazin, *An American Procession* (New York:
Alfred A. Knopf, 1984), p. 30.

the first place, it was Martin Luther—the father of Protestantism—who originally stressed the importance of personal salvation; it was he that discarded the role of "good work" and initiated a previously unknown emphasis on an individual's private life. Emerson, of course, remained in the mainstream of the Protestant tradition. Nevertheless, he gave it a new dimension. He adopted Luther's ideas and minimized the role of original sin, thus eliminating the fear and guilt associated with spiritual activity; he also discarded the dualistic, divided, Western "self", encouraging the kind of spiritual "oneness" described in his poem.

In **Brahma,** the reader should immediately observe the use of strategically-placed sense-pauses. In particular, the poem exhibits the kind of pause which is independent of metrical division and allows a medial break based on the natural rhythm of language. This type of division called caesura almost always falls in the middle of a line. Although the effect of such medial "breath" points can be manipulated by a shift in position towards the beginning or the end of verse lines, Emerson keeps the caesurae (pl.) as close to the middle as possible. He does this to underscore the duality found in the main words of the stanza, i.e. slayer / slain, shadow / sunlight etc. In short, the recurring dual theme is present not only in thematic opposites but also in the way each line naturally breaks at the middle.

In his book *Beyond Good and Evil,* the nineteenth-century German philosopher Friederich Nietzsche, a staunch atheist and one of Emerson's greatest admirers, argues that an important flaw in Western thought is the Judeo-Christian emphasis on opposites. This is evident, he says, in popular symbolic notions such as "good and evil", "right and wrong", "light and darkness", etc. Eastern religions, however, do not share this preoccupation with a dualistic spiritual life. Thus, Hinduism sees the breaking-off of one thing and beginning of another (be it the dying of a person whose atman, or soul, is reborn into a new body, or simply the place where any object ends and another begins) as that which can be defined by the word "death". Death, according to this understanding, surrounds us and is an essential part of the world. Hence, the goal of man is to gain knowledge of the self and to end the cycle of earthly rebirth; the atman must reunite with the brahman, the spiritual oneness of all things. As T.J. Hopkins put it: "One who sees diversity in the self attains death after death, but one who knows it as the one great Brahman is free of endless death and rebirth."*

The distinction between Eastern and Western notions of the nature of death lies in the emphasis on "two" in the West and "one" in the East. The poetic structure of Emerson's **Brahma** (including the strict caesurae which split each line at a medial point) can be interpreted as an articulation of the intellectual polarities defining Western culture. Thus, the end rhyme in the first stanza is about death and finality ("slays" and "slain"), and also about life and possibility ("ways" and "again"). But the seemingly perverse last line which instructs the reader to "turn thy back to heaven" is Emerson's ultimate rejection of dualistic categories such as heaven and hell and an invitation to explore the spiritual element contained in and running through all things—the spiritual dimension of the Hindu brahma. Emerson argued that the development of human potential must rely on intuitive awareness more than reasoned understanding. The basic tension of precisely this important Emersonian theme is brought to the fore in the contrast between the poem's radically liberated "inner" content and the rigorous framework of its formal "external" structure.

---

*Thomas J. Hopkins, *The Hindu Religious Tradition* (Encino CA: Dickenson Publishing Co., Inc., 1971), p. 42.

George Santayana
(1863–1952)

Faith

George Santayana, best remembered for his work in philosophy, was a versatile thinker and talented writer. His poems, essays, and novel (*The Last Pilgrim*) are all distinguished for their exceptional logic and clarity.

The poem **Faith** is modeled on what is known as a Petrarchan (or Italian) sonnet. This means that its rhyme scheme consists of an octet (a set of eight lines), rhyming ABBA ABBA and a sestet (six lines), with an option of two or three rhymes. In this case, the sestet adopts the form cdd cdc. We might note that the use of this particular poetic mold distinguishes the poem from other common forms of the sonnet. For example, the English sonnet consists of three Sicilian quatrains (groups of four lines) and a Heroic couplet (two lines) usually in the form ABAB CDCD EFEF GG, while the Spenserian sonnet is similar to the English, but has a rhyme scheme of ABAB BCBC CDCD EE.

The first and last phrases of the poem—"O World" and "The thought divine"—represent opposite realities: one is tangible, concrete, and profane, while the second is hidden, mysterious, and sacred. In the poet's understanding, the two realities have a symmetrical relationship and represent end points along a single continuum. As one of the important themes of the work, this idea is critical for an appreciation of the philosophical underpinning of the poem and, consequently, of the particular techniques the poet chooses to implement.

One of Santayana's main objectives is to integrate the use of standard form into a conceptual treatment of seemingly amorphous, symbolic ideas such as "faith" and "divine thought". To achieve this, the poet first develops a clear idea or "vision" pertaining to the spiritual realm— i.e. the concept that realms of the sacred and profane are symmetrical opposites—and then delicately infuses his poem with an appropriate diction and imagery. Thus, the first line opening in the form of direct address—"O World"—is immediately followed by an allusion to the Bible. The unspecified reference is to a well-known episode of the New Testament (Luke X: 38) in which Martha, the daughter of Lazarus and sister of Mary, does not feel appreciated for acting as a servant while her sister is occupied elsewhere. She complains to Jesus who replies: "Martha, Martha you are anxious about many things; one thing is needful. Mary has chosen the better part which shall not be taken away from her." Accordingly, from the onset, the poet makes a kind of "private" justification for tackling lofty discourse in the context of a secular or "worldly" poetic form.

The message returns in the fourth line. This again involves the transforming power of "inner vision"; the heart, a physical organ of the human body, is discovered to be the source of "wisdom". The next four lines extend "vision" into the notion of "discovery"; hence, the reference to Columbus, who "found the world, and had no chart". The "world", as a result, is now endowed with positive qualities which the poet tells us are apparently worth finding. And here, again, we are led upwards to a higher plane of understanding: the word "faith" in the

sixth line becomes associated with "vision" and "found";
it is described as the instrument which "deciphered a chart
in the skies". Thus also, in line eight, the word "trust"
takes over the former function of "to believe" (line four)
and allows the poet to gradually disclose a highly personal
realm of understanding.

By establishing unusual relationships and bringing together ordinarily disjunct words and concepts, Santayana
molds a peculiar aesthetic model. Words take on uncom-
mon meanings which exist and evolve within a new context
having little to do with normal usage. Poetry relies on an
essential freedom lacking in prose, and it is up to the creative imagination of the poet to devise an appropriate
semantic basis. In view of this, Santayana's approach
seems to be characterized by a thorough distillation of
thought. —Everything is sophisticated. Yet, nothing
emerges as being complex or convoluted; ideas are
straightforward and pure. The main thrust of **Faith** hinges
on a sequence of seemingly self-evident associations. For
example, when the poet speaks of "knowledge" (line 9),
the word becomes associated with the prior invocation of
"wisdom", "heart", and "inward vision". "Knowledge"
is further put into context through the understanding that,
ultimately, the source of what we know—the source "that
lights"—is shrouded by uncertainty and is "a torch of
smokey pine". Naturally, this strikes at the very core of a
fundamental dilemma the solution to which is found in the
final four lines: "a void of mystery and dread", reminiscent of the "world" in line one, is linked to the necessity
of experiencing a more reliable kind of knowledge—
"faith"— by which, the poet says, anyone is able to see
"thought divine".

The ancient thinkers such as Socrates and Aristotle emphasized a secular "knowledge" based on reason alone.

With the arrival of early Christianity, however, faith, independent of reason and the five senses, was established as
the source of real knowledge. Consequently, to describe
the basic intellectual process of the Middle Ages and
Renaissance, historians have arrived at the term humanism,
which suggests an aesthetic struggle to combine elements
of Christian faith with ancient principles of pagan reason.
Milton's *Paradise Lost,* considered to be a crowning
achievement of European literature, offers an exemplary
treatment of the humanistic conflict between "wisdom"
and "knowledge". The poem by Santayana, on the other
hand, appears to carry the age-old problem a step
further—into the modern context. In our age, science and
technology have replaced religion and faith as guiding cultural forces. In view of this, Santayana pleas for a special
"searching" brand of faith grounded in personal intuition
(as opposed to rigid Calvinistic doctrine). According to
him, this kind of faith is accessible to contemporary man
and should intercede between religious fundamentalism and
scientific materialism.

One should note the skill with which Santayana conveys his thought. Within the span of a short poem, he has
given full development to a complex philosophical idea.
His poem evolves slowly and with calculated effect—as if
turning on an axis of gradually unfolding word images and
patterns. The master approaches the craft through careful
handling of numerous intricacies. To see a poem's intricacies in a creative melding of verbal form and content is essential and should be the main objective of any analysis of
poetry.

Samuel Butler
(1612–1680)

Hudibras

For most of his life, Samuel Butler worked as a secretary
in service to wealthy country gentlemen. Charles II of England, however, was so impressed with his long poem
Hudibras (part one was published in 1663, part two in
1664, and part three in 1678) that he honored him with
grants, special stipends, and eventually an overseas government post.* **Hudibras** is generally considered Butler's
most notable work.

In this poem, Butler draws a satire of society and
launches an attack by using an outdated formal structure.
To convey his ideas, he uses an octosyllabic line (eight
syllables per line) in mock heroic couplets (adjacent rhyming lines). Since the time of Chaucer, the heroic couplet
had been a popular mode of poetic expression, especially
with neo-classical poets such as Ben Jonson (who died
when Butler was twenty-five).

To understand the motive behind Butler's poem we
must first briefly consider the theoretical role of form and
structure. Any technical feature of poetic form affects the

---

*Michael Stapleton, *The Cambridge Guide to English
Literature* (Cambridge: Cambridge University Press and
Newnes Books, 1983), p. 121.

poem's sound (or sonic) quality and creates an impression of either agreement (as in the case of assonance) or disagreement (as in dissonance or cacaphony). Consequently, poetic structure or form has direct repercussions on the reader's involvement and intuitive perception. For example, whether one is conscious of it or not, rhyme transmits a sense of agreement, harmony, and cooperation. This is true especially in adjacent lines.

In the seventeenth century, the world was going through rapid change; England in particular was torn by unrest and internal strife. Samuel Butler, a convinced pessimist and skeptic, ridiculed his contemporaries for continuing to write poetry that implied harmony and accord in the midst of such turmoil. Any system, political or poetic, consists of different elements which relate to one another in either a concordant or discordant fashion. Some theorists have even argued that form in poetry offers a direct reflection of surrounding political, social, and religious forces. Whether one agrees with this or not, it is useful to recognize that the formal or abstract constructs of literature, visual art, and music often correspond to existing structures. In **Hudibras,** Butler is making fun of those who use the harmonious effect of rhyming heroic couplets to reflect a world in transition. He highlights this inappropriateness by juxtaposing his use of rhyme with harsh, discordant sound patterns in phrases such as "pike and gun", "blows and knocks", or "odd perverse antipathies".

In an age of great and frequently violent antagonism between Puritans, Anglicans, and Catholics, Butler described the hypocrisy of those who professed religious conviction but did not live according to basic spiritual principles. The character described in the first part of **Hudibras** is one who mixes religion with violence:

> He was of that stubborn crew
> Of errant saints whom all men grant
> To be the true church militant;
> Such as do build their faith upon
> The holy text of pike and gun...

As we can see, Butler had no patience with hypocrites who aligned themselves with a creed but did not practice it; he despised those who were "...perverse and opposite / As if they worshipped God for spite".

Butler mixes direct and earthly images such as

> More peevish, cross and splenetic
> Than dog distract, or monkey sick

with more intricate constructions such as

> A godly, thorough Reformation,
> Which always must be carried on
> And still be doing, never done;
> As if religion were intended
> For nothing else but to be mended.

Throughout **Hudibras,** Butler uses language drawn from different and contrasting realms of experience, mixing common monosyllables ("knocks", "sick", or "spite") with more elevated, sometimes outright religious or ecclesiastical terminology ("Reformation"). Unlike many poets, Butler does not limit himself to the homogeneous lexicon of this time but develops a rather unconventional conglomerate of seemingly unrelated words and phrases. This technique no doubt originates in a private frustration—the poet's eternal search for sublime order and spiritual satisfaction.

Like T.S. Eliot in **The Wasteland** or Sinclair Lewis in *Elmer Gantry*, Samuel Butler was outraged by the self-delusion and superficiality which characterized certain religious authorities of his day. The discordant features of **Hudibras** are of interest to the modern reader because they anticipate twentieth-century norms; they shed light on the curious techniques used to express contemporary agnosticism and distrust of organized religion.

William Wordsworth
(1770–1850)

Ode

"Intimations of Immortality from Recollections of Early Childhood"

The title of the poem, also known as **The Intimations Ode**, suggests that memories of early childhood can lead to the awareness of a unique spiritual realm which is normally not part of adult consciousness. Wordsworth chooses the subject for a specific reason: he is responding to popular sentiment. The early nineteenth century already showed signs of reaction to modern trends in society. Many people at the time expressed profound nostalgia for the kind of existence which was possible prior to the takeover of science, industry, and flagrant materialism. They yearned for the revival of religious values and a return to a state of "natural" or "child-like" innocence. Wordsworth embraces this sentiment but shows a breadth of intellect and poetic understanding that does not indulge in excessive sentimentality. The structure of the poem can be examined as having a "longitudinal" range of eleven interrelated but different sections, much like the separate movements of a musical composition. By contrast, the poem's subject, or "inner" content, offers a different diapason and can be analyzed in terms of a "latitudinal" range of emotions including simple, naive pleasure as well as deep philosophical meditation.

Any attempt to analyze a poem must begin with basic structural observations. This applies especially in cases where the work is lengthy and extends beyond the confines of a single printed page. Such works usually contain an abundance of material which is particularly difficult to grasp. Wordsworth's **Ode** is a good case in point. A beginner should start by focusing on the "big picture" and then attempting to distill the essential content of the poem's individual sections. The musical analogy will then become evident as the student begins to see the emergence of a pattern of "thematic" or "tonal" relationships, i.e. expositions, developments, variations, contrasts, extensions, repetitions, recapitulations etc. In the end, this will also lead to further investigation into other realms and should expose the existence of a common motif—a connective tissue, fabric, or thread of thought—which ties the work together as a whole.

A brief glance at Wordsworth's poem immediately suggests a number of things. The first, second, and eleventh sections all wistfully consider the subject of "former closeness to nature" and directly refer to images of streams, rainbows, valleys, hills, and groves. Section eleven, as a result, serves as a kind of recapitulation of fundamental ideas. The third section uses the pastoral sound of the shepherd's tabor (small drum) as the initial motif to express the speaker's sense of distance from the state or condition he longs to experience:

> Now, while the birds thus sing a joyous song,
> And while the young lambs bound
> As to the tabor's sound
> To me alone there came a thought of grief

The theme of estrangement prevails up to section ten when
the sound of the tabor is transformed into a cause for joy:

> Then sing, ye birds, sing, sing a joyous song!
> And let the young lambs bound
> As to the tabor's sound!
> We in thought will join your throng

The reality of this transformation is emphasized through a
clever use of the words "now" and "then", both of which
appear to have a special function; they articulate events "in
time" and impart a narrative quality to the poet's treatment
of basic psychological processes.

Sections four through nine, therefore, draw the poet
into a detailed study or contemplation of certain ideas
emanating from his subject. To return to our musical analogy, this span of six sections might be associated with
what is called "development" in a movement of the classical symphony or sonata. Section four sets up and defines
the tension between the speaker's feelings of alienation and
the joy he sees around him; sections five through eight take
the reader on a kind of episodic journey through various
panoramas and highly descriptive metaphors representing
"alienation". In effect, this portion of the poem represents
a climax during which the poet takes the opportunity to
give fullest expression to his feelings on the subject. Section five, as a result, serves as a kind of pivotal area towards a state of heightened emotion. As it unfolds, it
moves from nighttime, when the heavens are visible, into
the daylight of adulthood, when the soul's star fades "into
the light of common day". Parallel to this, however, is the
image of the prison house where the child—who is "nature's priest"—is entrapped. As the child matures, he is increasingly removed from an original state of deep spiritual
self-awareness. In section nine, the poem nears completion;

the poet gives us the first hints of a triumphant conclusion and invokes the image of a "perpetual benediction" of childhood which is the "fountain-light of all our day...of all our seeing".

Finally, like the so-called "recapitulation", or return of the major motif in a musical composition, the sound of the tabor in section ten signals the end or finale. The poet recalls the beginning material and brings the reader back to the pleasures of nature which were believed to have been lost. Then, in section eleven, the poet indulges in a reflection on what has happened; he takes the time to extend—and, once again, confirm—his belief that the experience of child-like pleasure is indeed accessible. This technique is similar to what is known in music as a coda ("tail" in Italian).

There are many levels on which this complicated poem can be experienced. The actual subject is the betrayed, grieving lover who searches for the cause of a breach and longs for healing. Detailed study of the poem, however, also leads to an appreciation of the poet's intimate feelings. This, in turn, gives meaning to his creation and evokes sympathy towards an underlying substance. The "substance", the reader finally realizes, is true-to-life and has a direct bearing on a universal spiritual state or condition.

John Milton
(1608–1674)

Paradise Lost

Milton's **Paradise Lost,** one of the most important works of literature in the English language, offers a detailed account of the Old Testament story of Adam and Eve. The poem is of monumental proportions and has much to reveal about the author and the historical period in which it was written. Milton first published the poem in 1667.

By the age of twenty, John Milton was already a sophisticated scholar with considerable education. In particular, he demonstrated a precocious knowledge of languages; during his early school years he mastered Greek, Hebrew, Italian, French and was able to write excellent verse in Latin. Milton's eventual blindness (he wrote the entire **Paradise Lost** when he was blind) is often attributed to the long hours he spent at reading and writing as a young student. The erudition acquired early in the poet's life had a great influence on his subsequent creative output. His mature writing reveals an extraordinarily powerful intellect and an ability to draw on a broad range of sources from a variety of literary traditions.

In particular, **Paradise Lost** shows a rich use of thematic material with numerous allusions to pagan mythology as well as New and Old Testament scripture. As a result, it frequently involves an intriguing blend of diverse

motifs. For example, Scott Elledge, a renowned expert on
the work, suggests that the "muse" in line 6 of Book I is
not one of the nine pagan muses, but a poetic metamorpho-
sis of an inspired Hebrew prophet—probably Moses who
received the Ten Commandments on Mount Sinai (Exodus
XIX: 20) and wrote the first five books of the Bible.* Milton encourages association with pagan Greek tradition
throughout the work. This hallmark of his literary technique reveals an intimate knowledge of ancient mythology.
For example, in Greece, it was known that the muses lived
near the Hippocrene spring on the side of Mount Helicon.
Consequently, in lines 10 through 15, Milton suggests that
his "muse" may prefer to dwell on Jerusalem's Mount
Zion, which is known to be situated near Siloa's brook.
This kind of allusion to pagan themes is intended to have a
particular effect; it is a delight to the reader and injects an
element of surprise into an otherwise familiar story. Fur-
thermore, it gives the poet a legitimate opportunity to dwell
on peripheral considerations. Thus, in lines 14 and 15,
Milton says that he intends "with no middle flight. . .to
soar / Above the Aonian Mount". Here he is referring to
the popular belief that the earth was at one time covered
with three layers of atmosphere and that the "middle" or
second layer reached only to the tops of mountains. According to the pagans, the territory of "middle air" was at
the level of the highest dwelling place of the gods, Mount
Olympus.* Therefore, Milton makes the point that in his
poem he will climb even higher and will attain the "true"
or "Christian" heaven beyond time and space. A straightforward treatment of the Biblical subject would probably
not have allowed him to make such a statement.

---

*Scott Elledge, ed., *Paradise Lost,* by John Milton (New
York: W.W. Norton & Company, 1975), p. 6 (footnotes).

The use of mythology in Milton's poem has other explanations as well. The unusual length of **Paradise Lost** suggests that the work is conceived in the form of an epic—a poem in the "narrative" tradition usually involving an extensive account of a particular historical or legendary subject. Since, however, the original Biblical story of the Fall is comparatively short, the poet must resort to liberal embellishment. To achieve the desired effect, he develops a new version of the old story and provides a fresh context for highly personal interpretation. At the same time, he skillfully uses numerous additions to create a coherent whole. Milton's repeated invocation of the muses is particularly revealing in this regard. As one of the recurring themes in the poem, it reflects the poet's wonder and amazement at the task before him. Milton understands that he has set out on a very responsible mission—the retelling of a sacred account from the Bible. He realizes that this could lead to serious challenges and might require divine intervention; hence, he calls upon the muses, the ancient pagan deities associated with artistic inspiration. If we think about it, however, this approach is somewhat surprising. What it implies is that the Christian God is expected to be of little help in the undertaking.

We know that, in the course of writing the poem, Milton struggled with blindness. In the evening, sitting at home before a fire, he would compose sets of lines and commit them to memory. Upon waking the next morning, he would review the previous night's work and dictate the final results to an assistant—usually one of his daughters. Against this kind of biographical background, the poet's repeated appeal to the muses also seems to represent an inner quest and the deep sentiments of an artist searching for a new kind of "sight" or source of inspiration. This is made explicit in lines 22 and 23 of the first invocation

where Milton writes: "What in me is dark / Illumine...".
Although recourse to mythological themes is known in
numerous works of European literature, **Paradise Lost**
represents an extraordinary achievement. In adopting a familiar technique, it attains especially pleasing results. It is
a recognized masterpiece on account of the unique power,
vigor, and virtuosity displayed by the author. Its special
achievement lies in the brilliant fusion of the disjunct
Christian and pagan worlds so that the poem ultimately
bears clear testimony to the validity of humanism and free-
masonry, as well as the prominent role of these intellectual
approaches in the evolution of Western, so-called "religious" thought. We should note that throughout his life
Milton remained a faithful Christian; he outwardly espoused the essential teaching of Protestantism and ascribed
especially to the peculiarities of Puritan doctrine. This
seems somewhat inconsistent with the aesthetic principles
displayed in his poetry. For example, the use of mythology
in **Paradise Lost** is ornamental and may appear removed
from a true understanding of the straightforward and simple values expressed in the Gospel.

Milton's account of man's expulsion from Eden focuses on the fundamental problem of "free will". The fall
of Adam and Eve was the direct consequence of a decision
to exercise free will beyond the measure decreed by God.
Consequently, the highly complex philosophical issue is essential.

In the poet's understanding, the existence of free will
is delimited by a sense of duty, obedience, or calling
which emanates from God's law and is observed in all of
Creation. Accordingly, everything in the universe is related
and connected through a hierarchy, or a specified structure
of authority descending from God to man and, in turn,
from man to the rest of the world. Thus, in the middle of

page 265 of volume IV of *The World's Best Poetry*, Eve's relationship to the animals in the Garden is described in the following terms:

> ...she busied, heard the sound
> Of rustling leaves, but minded not, as used
> To such disport before her through the field
> From every beast; more duteous at her call
> Than at Circean call the herd disguised

In these lines, Eve is endowed with a power which surpasses that of the mythical enchantress Circe, whose uncanny spell and ability to change men into subservient, docile creatures is well-known in passages from Homer's *Odyssey.** The key word, however, is "duteous". We know that man is duty-bound to God because he has been ordered by God not to eat of the Tree of Knowledge. According to Milton, this concept of "duty" lays the groundwork for a proper understanding of the Biblical events in the poem.

On the other hand, Milton repeatedly stresses that the existence of free will is essential and that God acts uniformly in the interests of maintaining man's freedom. God foresees all that is to come and is grieved by the prospect of the Fall. Yet, He is not willing to coerce man into obedience. Like someone perched on a mountain, He observes the path of man's journey below, but refuses to deprive that person of independence in selecting the path ahead. Man is made to be free; this was God's intention from the start. Without freedom, man loses his true identity as a unique and beloved creature of the Almighty. As Milton

---

*Homer, *The Odyssey,* trans. E.V. Rieu (Baltimore: Penguin Books, 1973), pp. 155-170.

writes: "Not free, what proof could they have giv'n sincere / Of true allegience...". In other words, it is only in the context of freedom that man can fulfill his duty towards the Creator and remain fully responsible for all of his actions. In Book III, Adam and Eve complete the tragic fall, and God remarks:

> ...They therefore as to right belonged,
> So were created, nor can justly accuse
> Their Maker, or their making or their fate,
> As if predestined overruled
> Their will, disposed by absolute decree
> Or high foreknowledge; they themselves decreed
> Their own revolt, not I: if I foreknow
> Foreknowledge had no influence on their fault,
> Which had no less proved certain unforeknown
> So without least impulse or shadow of fate,
> Or aught by me immutable foreseen,
> They trespass authors to themselves in all
> Both what they judge and what they choose; for so
> I formed them free, and free they must remain,
> Till they enthrall themselves; I else must change
> Their nature, and revoke the hight decree
> Unchangeable, eternal, which ordained
> Their freedom, they themselves ordained their fall.

The subsequent portion of Milton's poem deals with the consequence of Adam's action. This begins with a description of Eve's despair and her final confession to Adam. As a result, in Book IX, Adam is confronted with a classic dilemma and is forced to choose between loyalty to God or to fellow man. He decides:

> ...I with thee have fixed my lot,
> Certain to undergo like doom; if death

> Consort with thee, death is to me as life;
> So forcible within my heart I feel
> The bond of nature draw me to my own
> My own in thee, for what thou art is mine;
> Our state cannot be severed, we are one,
> One flesh; to lose thee were to lose myself

The decision to remain faithful to Eve lays the cornerstone for everything that follows. Adam chooses his mortal lot and thus relinquishes idealistic spirituality and religion in favor of a basic commitment to human companionship. At the same time, Eve appears to be bound by a similar decision:

> ...with thee I go,
> Is to stay here; without thee there to stay
> Is to go hence unwilling; thou to me
> Art all things under heaven, all places thou,
> Who for my willful crime art banished hence.

Eve realizes that she is to be banished for her "willful crime"; hence, she clings to Adam, her husband and only remaining source of comfort and solace. The passages describing Adam and Eve's resolution to accept the consequences of sinful action are among the most poignant in all of Milton's poetry.

Paradise Lost was written at an important time in British history. While Milton wrote the poem, England was in the midst of political and spiritual upheaval. The bloody Civil War, lasting from 1642 to 1649, ended with the execution of the monarch, Charles I, and the institution of a dictatorship by Oliver Cromwell, a Puritan military leader. Milton took active part in this conflict and held a position of government secretary up to the time when parliament reinstated the monarchy. Although he was sympathetic to Cromwell's ideals, Milton retained many traditional views and saw the need for political stability along usual lines. Unlike the increasingly materialistic philosophers of the time, throughout his life he clung to spiritual vision and retained a medieval or "hierarchic" understanding of the universe.

The seventeenth century in England was also a time of burgeoning political views. For example, Thomas Hobbes (1588-1679), another prominent intellectual of the period, was known primarily for his philosophy of government. The solution he set forth in *Leviathan* (1651), however, contains many elements diametrically opposed to Milton. Although Hobbes agrees on the need for popular sanction in monarchy, his underlying assessment of human society is pessimistic and describes mankind as embroiled in a state of constant war. As a result, his approach to the political problem is different from Milton's; it appears to reject the validity of traditional religious values and the promise of salvation through Christianity. In describing public reaction to Hobbes' ideas, the commentator J.W.N. Watkins wrote:

> What aroused hostility was /the/ realization that he (Hobbes) was attempting to transform their God-supervised, man-oriented, law-bound and comfortably articulated cosmos into something quite alien: into a material expanse within which lonely individuals are driven by terror to manufacture a Leviathan whose definitions will create an artificial morality for them, and whose sword will impose an artificial unity on them.*

---

*J.W.N. Watkins, *Hobbe's System of Ideas* (London: Hutchinson & Co. Ltd., 1965), pp. 9-10.

Thus, in many ways Thomas Hobbes was far in advance of Milton and anticipated the work of atheist philosophers from the eighteenth-century Enlightenment.

Nevertheless, John Milton occupies a leading place in the history of European letters, and his magnificent poem **Paradise Lost** has all the elements of an enduring masterpiece with universal appeal. Milton was a man thoroughly representative of his time. Throughout his life, he remained abreast of current thought and developed his own convictions on the basis of a broad sphere of knowledge. His religious views therefore represent the conservative position of a serious scholar with liberal training. At other times, the poet's unusual intellectual curiosity resulted in thoroughly astonishing conclusions. Thus, for example, Milton became the author of a unique publication in seventeenth-century Europe—a pamphlet defending the individual's right to divorce. The ideas expressed in this document are revolutionary. But Milton also expressed fascination with many other "modern" concepts and was well aware of the level of scientific advancement during his lifetime. In **Paradise Lost** he even alludes to Galileo and his research connected with the telescope. In general, we might say, Milton has none of the "narrow" views often associated with persons of traditional religious belief. On the contrary, he conveys complete balance. He expresses generosity as well as conviction. His work is solid, sober, and at the same time open to sensuality. In this context, we might note that Milton was also a talented musician and inherited a musical sensitivity from his father. As a result, many passages in his work display unusual attention to the sound quality of words. Consider, for example, the following description of a scene from nature:

> O flowers
> That never will in other climate grow,

My early visitation, and my last
At even, which I bred up with tender hand
From the first opening bud, and gave ye names!
Who now shall rear ye to the sun, or rank
Your tribes, and water from the ambrosial fount?

One can also compare the passages on pages 30 and 56 in volume V of *The World's Best Poetry.*

If **Paradise Lost** by John Milton is considered a landmark of seventeenth-century letters, the claim rests with the particular strain of religiosity expressed in the work: it is a religiosity of enormous spirit and intellect. Milton was fully aware of rapidly developing trends in European culture and wanted to articulate a measure of caution towards the unsettled and increasingly secular atmosphere of his day. In the process, however, he did not attempt to reject or condemn modern developments. Rather, his approach was to infuse traditional understanding into the consciousness of the contemporary person and to reaffirm that (1) Evil is a reality; (2) Man is a fallen creature and has been expelled from Paradise; (3) one must not become overly optimistic about scientific, cultural, and social advances, no matter how great they may seem.

V
Nature

Preface

Nature, a universal theme in poetry, has inspired numerous poets in seemingly countless ways. It is an inexhaustible theme which lends itself to the treatment of a wide variety of moods and ideas. Nature is a live force. It is dynamic; it has a rhythm and energy of its own. Throughout history, civilized man—the artist—has been challenged to express its unique marvel.

Yet, in the tradition of the great poets, a "nature poem" is not simply descriptive and must go beyond an objective treatment of outside or external phenomena. In other words, good poetry about nature cannot be superficial and must offer the reader an element of insight. The natural world is observed through the five senses. At the same time, it is attractive for inner or hidden reasons and, most of all, for the profound mystical feeling conveyed by its power and beauty. There is an intrinsically human realization that the natural environment constitutes man's rightful domain. As a result the nature poet will always adopt a philosophical vantage point and will always aim to instill an appreciation of man's relationship to lakes, trees, flowers, animals, etc.; in Shakespeare's words, his objective will always be "to hold, as twere, the mirror up to nature".* In the past, poets have done this in different ways. Some have chosen to express a oneness with the surrounding world; others have dwelt on "alienation." John Milton, for example, has described a state of human estrangement, a condition which he explains in terms of the Biblical story of Adam and Eve (see **Paradise Lost**). On the other hand, two centuries later, the Romantic poets found less conventional ways to stress generally optimistic ideas about a return to pastoral bliss. In more recent times, Dylan Thomas wrote: "The force that drives the water through the rocks / Drives my red blood."** Today, however, feelings of true communion with nature are rare, and most contemporary poets would rather emphasize a profound sense of loss or distance. The latter condition, anticipated in the nineteenth century by Matthew Arnold (see **Dover Beach**), was masterfully treated by T. S. Eliot in **The Wasteland** (1922), one of the most famous poems of the modern era.

---

*William Shakespeare, *William Shakespeare: The Complete Works*, ed. Alfred Harbage et al. (Baltimore: Penguin Books, 1972), p. 953. This is from *Hamlet*, III, ii, 20.

**Dylan Thomas, *The Collected Poems of Dylan Thomas* (New York: New Directions Books, 1957), p. 10.

John Keats
(1795–1821)

To Autumn

One way to enjoy poetry is to read it aloud. Poetry is meant to be heard, and much of what it has to say is communicated through oral declamation. The work of John Keats can help to illustrate the point. Always pleasing to the ear and never stiff or contrived, it is emotional, spontaneous, and often relies on the sheer luxury of diction.

In the first line of **To Autumn**, for example, the subject is portrayed by the use of three words: "mist" "mellow" and "fruitfulness". This establishes a tonality or musical mood for the rest of the poem. In particular, the poet's choice of words relies on what is called onomatopeia, or the description of a thing or action by a vocal imitation of associated sound. Thus, the recurring sibilant "s" evokes "mist" and "mellow"; it creates a sense of hushed silence associated with the two words. Similarly the use of "fruitfulness"—an important idea strategically placed at the end of the line—can be understood in the following way: the first syllable with the resonant "r" is sounded far back in the throat; the second syllable with the "l" affects the middle of the mouth; and the final double "s" is sounded near the front. The end result is a rich sonic aggregate bearing every connotation of the meaning of "fruitfulness".

The poet then continues to describe the season through the use of personification:

> Close bosom friend of the maturing sun!
> Conspiring with him how to lead and bless
> With fruit the vines that round the thatch eaves
>   run—

In other words, autumn is described as an agent of the sun whose role is to help bring about the completion of an annual cycle of seasons. These "bosom friends" go on to "bend", "fill", "swell", "plump", and "set budding" the fruits of the year including assorted vegetables, nuts, and trees. The second stanza introduces several images conveying the seasonal preoccupation of various individuals. Some people are at work bringing in the harvest; others are "sitting careless on the granary floor" or "on half reaped furrow sound asleep / Drowsed with the fume of poppies". Then, in the third stanza, the imagery of "sound" returns and the poet affirms that, despite the particular atmosphere, all energy is not yet depleted. In conjunction with this, he has a specific idea in mind. He states that there is abundant evidence of life in autumn's broad diapason of sounds including "a wailful choir the small gnats mourn", "lambs bleat", "hedge crickets sing", "redbreast whistles", and "swallows twitter". This endows the poem with vitality and affirms the essential underlying point that the somewhat relaxed, pastoral scenario is transient and constitutes an integral episode in a sequence of recurring natural phenomena. In short, what the poet wishes to convey is the ultimate understanding that nature never dies and is a powerful force capable of self-regeneration.

Keats died at the very early age of twenty-five. Yet,

by that time, his mastery of poetic form was complete and exhibited a thoroughly mature understanding of the main aesthetic currents of his day. In **To Autumn**, we can see all the elements of an ingenious synthesis signifying a transition between the Classical and Romantic periods. The basic tenet of poetry from the Classical period of the eighteenth century is to emulate the ancient writers such as Aristotle, Virgil, and Cicero; this involves the rational expression of beauty through the use of formal principles such as symmetry, harmony, and balance. Keats' poem exhibits this not only in the rhyme scheme and the recurring eleven line format of each section, but also in the way in which the poet concludes the final stanza. The ending refers to the ethereal image of "skies"—an idea which echoes the "mists" from the beginning of the poem and thus connotes rudimentary structural and cognitive symmetry. In the second and third stanzas, references to a "half reaped furrow" and "the stubble plains with rosy hue" perform a complementary function; they are strategically placed images which serve to anchor the poem and to give it a tangible, earthly point of reference. At the same time, **To Autumn** bears association with Romantic ideals and treats the realm of inspired emotional and intuitive feelings best known in the poetry of Blake, Wordsworth, and Coleridge. In line with this, the use of personification allows the poet an extended opportunity to treat human emotions. **To Autumn** also includes images such as "sitting careless on a granary floor", "drowsied with the fume of poppies", and "oozing". These, together with a strong tendency to idealize the beauty of nature, lend the poem a characteristically early nineteenth-century Romantic air. Indeed, the work ultimately breathes informality, freedom, and basic comfort.

In analyzing this poem, the reader can spend considerable time on a broad range of subtleties related to the
poet's intellectual orientation. The work's thoroughly integrated approach, however, never fails to achieve an ultimate end. It is somehow insistently focused on an imaginative and satisfying appeal to the beauty of sound. This
leads us to the essential realization that Keats, like all other
great poets of the world, grasped poetic technique through
an innate perception of the powerful "musical" ethos of
language.

William Blake
(1757–1827)

The Tyger

"Something else exists alongside the acknowledged above-board reality of everyday life." This intriguing statement by the contemporary French novelist André Gide (1869-1951) affirms an essential philosophical truth.* Man is given to ponder this truth; he yearns to explore the "hidden" realms outside material or physical being.

Since antiquity, the branch of philosophy called metaphysics has systematically investigated the nature of "first principles" and "ultimate reality". The discoveries of philosophers have, in turn, given shape to much of what is intellectual in the arts. **The Tyger** by William Blake shows some of the ways in which poetry is particularly suited for the treatment of metaphysical concepts. At first glance, the poem may appear simple, naive, and unassuming. But, in fact, when we look closer, it carries an important message; it urges the reader to consider the sum total of Creation and to assess the visible world and nature in respect to the background of eternal reality.

---

*André Gide, *Si le grain ne meurt* (Paris: Gallimard, 1969), I, 27-28. For a discussion of Gide's remark turn to Jean Delay's *The Youth of André Gide*, trans. June Guicharnaud (Chicago: University of Chicago Press, 1956-57), p. 31.

Blake begins by drawing attention to an image of light and to the startling contrast between the brilliant color of a tiger "burning bright" and the darkness "in the forests of the night". The initial image imparts an immediate sense of the extraordinary quality of the animate creature. According to Blake, this creature has a special "inner" source of energy which sharply distinguishes its existence from the cold and dark world of inanimate things. In the third line of the stanza, however, the poet introduces yet another category of being—the "immortal". This completes his description of an essentially "stratified" cosmic order against which one must learn to appreciate the unique qualities—"fearful symmetry"—of the living creature.

To develop a philosophical idea the poet takes a special approach. As a writer and thinker, he articulates his thoughts with the tool of language. Yet, his method is distinctive and is motivated by a highly personal and independent manner. Moreover, his results are separate from those of other writers and especially writers of prose. The beauty of **The Tyger** lies in the poem's forthright manner and the way in which potentially complex, intuitive understanding is espoused. The work is brief, to the point, and remains strikingly lucid in spite of its underlying objective. To achieve such results the poet adopts a rhetorical mode of speech. He offers no argument, but simply shares with the reader an acute sense of the existence of a fundamental philosophical challenge. As a poet, therefore, he takes the liberty to bypass the requirements of commonplace discourse and to elevate language beyond the realm of earthly polemics. This is evident, first of all, in the candid enthusiasm with which he structures his work: the poem, we see is "open ended" and consists of hardly more than a series of unanswered questions.

Nevertheless, the poem grows out of some fundamental premises, and it is the poet's express desire to communicate particular conviction. Here, again, we see traces of a unique craft. In discussing matters pertaining to the divine origin of Creation, the usual approach of a philosophical treatise is to begin with the assumption that "God exists". (In philosophy there can be no logical proof of the existence of God, so that any discussion of divine principles must rest on what is known as an axiom.) Blake's poem, however, shows that the poet can escape the requirements of logic and can rely on other equally powerful and effective means to express metaphysical understanding. In his poem, he selects a "natural" subject—the tiger—and suggests that if we examine it, we can approach divine experience. To lead us along, he hints at the existence of an "immortal" Creative Force and describes its attributes in human terms; he gives it hands, eyes, and shoulders, as well as an ability to work with hammer, chain, and anvil. This use of images allows him to stimulate the imagination and to make vivid, concrete, and humanly understandable something which is otherwise lacking form.

At the same time, the poet injects another dimension of personal interpretation; he endows his poem with an element of fear. In other words, in the final analysis, we learn that poetic vision is not necessarily comforting and, in the case of this work, requires resolute courage. In particular, the poem confronts the reader with an uncomfortable environment of overwhelming—"dizzying"— dimensions. There are the "distant deeps or skies" with airy heights where one needs "wings"; there are also the opposite realms of the underground with "furnaces". In addition, the reader is repeatedly assaulted with the use of threatening words such as "dread", "deadly demons", "spears", "tears", and "fearful". Why is Blake's world such a frightening place? It is difficult to say. But we can venture the possibility that the demonic feeling is a reflection of the poet's encounter with an immense, unfamiliar territory. Blake grew up in a family without conventional moral and social constraints. This gave him the freedom to make personal discoveries concerning the nature of the Divine. In developing his thoughts, therefore, Blake arrived at something entirely new and was inspired to use a vocabulary which he felt was suited to his particular experience. Moreover, it was only natural that he should choose to express ideas in terms of a visual sense of space; by profession, Blake was not only a poet, but also an artist and engraver.

The Tyger, published in 1794, is from the collection entitled *Songs of Innocence and Experience*. As such, it exemplifies the style and approach of Blake's early poetry. It is accessible, yet challenging and aims to transport seemingly mundane elements to a level of eternal or universal understanding.

Matthew Arnold
(1822–1888)

Dover Beach

In spite of its serene opening, the well-known masterpiece
by Matthew Arnold carries a message of threat and fore-
boding. It maintains that the world exists in a state of constant turmoil and that, in particular, human suffering is in-
extricably tied to a state of perpetual discord between
objective reality—as found in nature—and subjective or
"inner" feelings. Although such ideas are hardly new and
have been pondered by philosophers throughout civilization, Arnold's poem assumes a particular point of view. It
conveys the growing sense of despair and pessimism which
characterizes European intellectual thought in the modern
age. The poet, as a result, creates a short but intense dramatic scenario with an abrupt conclusion forecasting the
approach in many works by twentieth-century authors.

The first stanza establishes a basic feeling of apprehension and sets the stage for the action to come. It begins by
describing an impressive nocturnal landscape.—It is night
on the coast of England. The moon shines above, and the
poet stands surveying the cliffs of Dover. Words such as
"calm", "fair", "tranquil", and "sweet" help to impart
a sense of beauty, harmony, and peace. At the same time,
the poet focuses on the reality of geographical boundaries

and juxtaposes the cliffs of England which "stand / Glimmering and vast" to the French coast whose "light / Gleams and is gone". This becomes the metaphor for the sinister, brooding undercurrent which plagues the poet's private concerns. In other words, he tells us, the placid external appearance of the landscape does not account for the real existence of differences and for the possibility of hostility between neighboring factions. Nevertheless, at this point, he retains an initial element of optimism; he invites his companion to forget dark inner worries—to come to the window and to enjoy the sweet night air. We soon find out, however, that the invitation is futile because, in fact, the poet himself can have no peace and carries the painful burden of a deep psychological obsession.

Consequently, in the second stanza, he begins by immediately drawing our attention to the observation that not all is harmonious and that, if we look closer at the surroundings, we will undoubtedly observe a state of continuous motion and flux. Needless to say, this essentially concerns the sea, which "meets the moon-blanched sand" and signifies fundamental restlessness. In the first stanza, we were already told that "the tide is full"; now the poet tells us more:

> Listen! you hear the grating roar
> Of pebbles which the waves draw back and fling,
> At their return, up the high strand,
> Begin, and cease, and then again begin...

To make the point, however, the poet once again interjects a statement of subjective qualification; in the deepest recesses of his soul he fully realizes that the "tremulous cadence" of the sea carries with it an "eternal note of sadness." Why does Arnold do this?—It is difficult to say with certainty. But, in view of the particular imagery used in this stanza, we might assume that the ocean pebbles— which "draw back and fling"—are somehow unsettling to the mind; they are a disturbing reminder of the warfare which, according to the poet's beliefs, dominates the long chronicle of human history involving man's continual experience of error, disappointment, and failure.

By the third stanza, the poet arrives at an issue of central concern, and it becomes clear that the poem, which ostensibly deals with the description of landscape is first of all preoccupied with issues of momentous historical significance. The decidedly political overtones of the first stanza, therefore, gradually assume the proportions of a vast panorama. It is in this context that Arnold quizzically introduces the distant and somewhat surprising image of "Sophocles long ago". The point he wishes to make, however, is clear; his objective is to evoke the ancient Greek writer's famed portrayal of human misery and suffering. "The sea of faith", in turn, is the response of the fourth stanza which further advances the poet's notion about the process of world history and invokes an atmosphere of spirituality and devotion. In effect, this image reminds us of what might be called "the age of faith" or the era of Christian belief which followed in the wake of disillusioned pagan atheism. In other words, Arnold now tells us that there was a period when spiritual convictions prevailed and religion served as a unifying factor in man's daily experience; this is the idea behind his use of the "girdle" image which connotes propriety and respectable containment. Nevertheless, we are immediately told that this historical era is something of the past:

> But now I only hear
> Its melancholy, long, withdrawing roar,
> Retreating, to the breath...

In short, according to the poet, times have changed, and
man now stands at the threshold of an encounter with the
"naked shingles of the world."

The mounting tension of the poem finally culminates in
the fifth stanza where the poet concludes with a pronouncement of open hostility and combat. This is touched off by
an initial statement which makes us understand that the serene quality of "nature" and "being" is but a facade and
that the deep concerns of humanity have to do with an in-
sidious state of on-going gloom and despair. In view of
this, the poet's thought is put boldly and directly:

> ...for the world, which seems
> To lie before us like a land of dreams,
> So various, so beautiful, so new,
> Hath really neither joy, nor love, nor light,
> Nor certitude, nor peace, nor help for pain;
> And we are here as on a darkling plain...

Mankind, therefore, suffers an essentially meaningless, tor-
tured existence. Moreover, due to inherent sickness and
malaise, the world awaits impending disaster. Society's ultimate destiny is that of violent self-destruction:

> Swept with confused alarms of struggle and flight
> Where ignorant armies clash by night...

Although the poem is intensely personal and overtly
focused on individual experience, **Dover Beach** has far-
reaching ramifications applicable to a broad spectrum of
considerations in Western civilization. Indeed, this is the
work's most remarkable feature. The poem begins with the
private musing of an individual; no doubt, it is Arnold
himself who stands peering through the shadows of the

night. By the end of the poem, however, one no longer feels the solitude; it is as if the entire universe has come alive and joins in the chorus of a haunting lament. The conflict between material and spiritual understanding is of central importance in the development of philosophy. One might even say that by the seventeenth century the predicament begins to occupy an urgent place. Take, for example, the European thinkers such as Thomas Hobbes (1588-1679), Rene Descartes (1596-1650), John Locke (1632-1704), and others, all of whom gradually abandoned traditional religious insight. The materialistic approach accordingly reached a pinnacle in the middle of the nineteenth century. It was Friedrich Nietzsche (1844-1900), a contemporary of Matthew Arnold, who made the world-famous pronouncement: "God is dead!"

Dover Beach shows that Arnold was acutely aware of the intellectual predicament of modern man. He espoused a truly critical approach to history which allowed him to see beyond the superficial acclaim of comparatively small, insignificant cultural achievements. In particular, he was not corrupted by the burst of optimism which followed the agony of the French Revolution in the late eighteenth century; nor did he really believe in the ideas pertaining to radical social change and advancement. Rather, he was a prophet of tragedy and human "nakedness". He understood that nature is cruel—that man is powerless to change its forces—and, consequently, that any prospect for the future would have to rely on temporary, short-lived strategies for human survival.

William Butler Yeats
(1865–1939)

The Lake Isle of Innisfree

William Butler Yeats is characteristically referred to as a
modern poet. More specifically, his career spans the nineteenth and twentieth-centuries. Having lived over three decades on either side of the millenium, Yeats entered the
modern period with much of his ideology already shaped
by nineteenth century thought. In 1914, when World War I
shattered society's romantic illusions of war through the
chaotic destruction caused by such sophisticated weaponry
as poison gas, machine guns, and tanks, Yeats was already
in his forty-ninth year. However, so violently was the new
age ushered in that its impact upon the poet was quite profound. During 1919, the year after the Great War had
ended, the experience had been sufficiently moving for him
to write these powerful lines taken from "The Second
Coming":

> Things fall apart; the centre cannot hold;
> Mere anarchy is loosed upon the world,
> The blood-dimmed tide is loosed, and everywhere
> The ceremony of innocence is drowned.*

---

*William Butler Yeats, *The Collected Poems of W.B.
Yeats* (New York: The Macmillan Company), pp. 184-185.

This vision of world destruction is a notable departure
from the pastoral tranquility depicted in an earlier work,
"The Lake Isle of Innisfree":

> And I shall have some peace there, for peace comes
> dropping slow,
> Dropping from the veils of the morning to where the
> cricket sings;
> There's midnight all a-glimmer, and noon a purple
> glow,
> And evening full of the linnet's wings.

In this poem, written in 1890, his imagination of the world
still contains the possibility of softly lit beauty and spontaneous song. It was during this early period that Yeats'
poetics became so firmly entrenched in the lyric tradition
that, although the war experience would darken his songs
somewhat, they would nevertheless retain their haunting
musicality.

Yeats' inclination to emphasize the musical nature of
poetic language can be traced to the influence of the Pre-
Raphaelites, specifically William Morris* (1834-1986), on
the poet as a young man. The Pre-Raphaelites were a
group of artists and poets who shared the conviction that
art had become corrupt during the Renaissance, beginning
with Raphael (1483-1520), and was thereafter in decline.
This critical opinion led to an interest in old forms which
were typically neglected by advocates of the Classical
period: chants, integral to religious worship during the
Middle Ages is one such example; and, lyric poetry which
had been sung by troubadours, the wandering poet-
musicians of medieval Italy is yet another.

---

*Cf. "March" in *World's Best Poetry Volume V: Nature*,
p. 74.

The Lake Isle of Innisfree exemplifies Yeats' ability to place himself in the tradition of lyric poetry by the special attention he gives to *melos* (the Greek word for song) in his poems. In this particular poem, the reader is asked to share the joy of listening to the world through its many sound-related references, for example: "the bee-loud glade," "the cricket sings," and "lake water lapping with low sounds." However, the poet uses language in a way that more than merely describes sound; he also offers rhymes and repetitions so that his words may be heard as well as understood. A well-known effect illustrates this point: if any word is repeated any number of times, at some point its meaning drops away—leaving only a pure sound. The words "go," "bee," "peace," and "dropping" seem to be repeated to achieve that effect. Without falling into doggerel, Yeats shapes his poem into end-line rhymes in the pattern: *ababcdcdefef*, and he uses internal rhymes with great subtlety as well: "While I stand on the roadway, or on the pavement gray." Finally, the poet's choice of predominantly monosyllabic and bisyllabic words minimize any distractions away from the rhythm he has so carefully constructed.

Yeats' poetics is thus shown to be quite different from that of Thomas Stearns Eliot (1888-1965), a modern poet twenty-three years Yeats' junior, who is best known for his startling expression of the modern spirit through the breakdown of the lyric in **The Wasteland.** This poem was considered highly innovative for successfully mirroring its theme within its fragmented structure. Surprisingly, in its original form it had been flawlessly metered and rhymed; but, upon revision with the help of close friend and poet, Ezra Pound (1885-1972), the poem was transformed into a perfect ruin. The critical decision to distort the lyric, as opposed to dropping the form completely, is the issue that separates Yeats from the later moderns. The important role of music in poetry was Yeats' inheritance from the nineteenth-century which he carried into his twentieth-century works. Returning to the early poem, **The Lake Isle of Innisfree**, we may now begin to understand the poet's commitment to capturing the music of the world in his lines; as he so elegantly explains, "I hear it in the deep heart's core."

VI

Fancy and Sentiment

Preface

The broad categories traditionally known as fancy and sentiment stand for different creative instincts of the poet. While poems of fancy generally involve expansive free-flight of the imagination, poems of sentiment are characterized by introspective, focused meditation. The distinction is also made on the basis of opposing intellectual and sensual realms of experience. Thus, fancy will normally tend towards abstract play of the mind; it is the process and the faculty of forming a mental image or fantastic invention of things not present to the senses. Sentiment, on the other hand, always connotes a state or disposition aroused by human feeling and emotion.

Samuel Taylor Coleridge
(1772–1834)

Kubla Khan

The title of Coleridge's poem has a specific and immediate impact. In the first place, by referring to Kubla Khan (1216-1294), the founder of the Mongol dynasty in China, it transports us to a distant, unfamiliar time and place. Secondly, it suggests that whatever follows will fall within the boundaries of a unique biography—one with certain elements of adventure, mystery, and Oriental romance. (We might note that the ominous sound of the "k" reinforces the brute sense of primitive, war-like demonic force suggested by the title.) In short, **Kubla Khan** evokes the two dimensions we usually associate with the names of well-known figures—the "legendary" and the "historical". The "legendary" is mythical and therefore amorphous, while the "historical" is factual and therefore concrete. Of course, the implications here are that the names of all human individuals reveal an identity with elements in both of these dimensions.

The poem's first eleven lines evoke a specific landscape; they place us within a defined setting. To achieve this, the poet uses words such as "in", "where", "through", "down", and he qualifies the location in terms of "pleasure", "bright", and "sunny". "Pleasant", however, only applies to the limited territory of the "pleasure-dome" because the space the poet wishes to deal with—

"Where Alph, the sacred river, ran,/ Through caverns
measureless to man,/ Down to a sunless sea"—is somehow
ominous. Coleridge thus gives a dual nature to the landscape which is, on the one hand, "sunny" and filled with
light and, on the other, sunless and "dark". In Christian
terms, this reference to opposite aspects of a single world
immediately evokes the concept of heaven and hell. A
more modern or secular interpretation in Freudian terms
might be articulated in the "outer" physical and "inner"
psychological spheres of consciousness.

Coleridge's **Kubla Khan** is a poem written in the
Romantic tradition of the nineteenth century. Thus, the
"psychological" approach to its interpretation seems especially appropriate because prior to this aesthetic movement
in poetry, there was little direct expression given to the
poet's subjective, interior world. In fact, it has been suggested that William Wordsworth (1770-1850), a close
friend of Coleridge, did for literature what Sigmund Freud
was to do for psychology nearly a century later. Wordsworth devoted attention to an aspect of internal and private realms of human experience which former poets never
consciously acknowledged. Needless to say, feelings had
always been part of poetry, but it is generally agreed that
aesthetic beauty prior to Wordsworth was discussed in
reference to objectively verifiable standards such as symmetry and order. In a sense, it was assumed to be more a
theme resting on intellectual rather than intuitive perception. In the hands of Wordsworth and his associate
Coleridge (they collaborated on an important book published in 1798 called *Lyrical Ballads*), poetry was steered
into a self-conscious, emotional direction which prevails to
the present. With this much in mind, we can now understand why Coleridge would be inclined to stress in **Kubla
Khan** a duality between the mind and body, or the soul

and the intellect. This approach emanates from the historical trend in poetic thought during the author's life. The
first eleven lines also introduce another theme of the poem;
the name "Alph" is an allusion to the ancient Greek river
Alpheus which, according to fable, flowed into the Ionian
Sea and surfaced again in Sicily as the fountain of
Arethuse. The reference, as we shall see, anticipates the
next section of the poem.*

In the word "But" of the twelfth line, we have what
seems to be an immediate retrospective allusion to the
pleasant aspects of the "pleasure-dome" as well as to the
ominous and somehow "romantic" and "savage" qualities
of the "chasm". The following lines demonstrate the use
of odd diction, or word choice, which characterizes this
section of the poem:

> A savage place! as holy and enchanted
> As e'er beneath a waning moon was haunted
> By woman wailing for her demon lover!

The words "holy" and "enchanted" are roughly synonymous though "holy" is a Christian adjective while
"enchanted" is pagan. How can Coleridge mingle these
two opposed traditions? The answer is probably found in
terms of the explosive miracle taking place in this section
("Huge fragments vaulted like rebounding hail"); the
miracle would be Christian if it were not in fact attached to
the pagan image of "daemon lover".

The simile evoked in the line "As if this earth in fast
thick pants were breathing" uses personification to attribute

*M. H. Abrams, Gen. Ed., *The Norton Anthology of English Liter-
ature, 4th Ed.* (New York: W. W. Norton & Company, 1979), II, p.
354 (footnote).

human qualities to the earth. This reference recalls the psychological insights mentioned earlier; the earth's surface (where the "pleasure-dome" lies) becomes analogous to the human body while its interior (the "measureless caverns") is to be associated with the individual's "measureless" inner life. It is precisely the poet's use of personification that leads to such an interpretation. Then, there is also the iteration of dualities; the opposites "sunless" and "sunny" are now articulated in terms of "holy" and "enchanted". Similarly, towards the bottom of page 163, we find "From the fountain and the caves"—"fountains" being surface phenomena while caves are always an interior space. We also learn that interior spaces themselves are prone to opposite conditions, and that the poet's mind has realms of "sunny pleasure domes" and "caves of ice".

Towards the end of the poem there occurs an important transition signifying the poet's conscious intention to move from objective to subjective verse. In "A damsel with a dulcimer / In a vision I saw" the poet abruptly shifts the reader's attention away from the "pleasure-dome" and "caves of ice" to his own private "vision". Thus, when the poem opens with the lines "In Xanadu did Kubla Khan / A stately pleasure-dome decree", the poet assumes a kind of objective, journalistic tone in order to instill a sense of confidence. But in the final section, he withdraws from pseudo-narrative to a totally new dimension of experience. He describes "a vision I once saw".

In addition, the poem's final section has two noteworthy technical points. First, "Abora" (in the line "Singing of Mount Abora") is an allusion to John Milton's *Paradise Lost*, Book IV, lines 280-283; "Nor where Abassin kings their issue guard, / Mount Amara, though this by some supposed / True Paradise under the Ethiop line."* Second, the poet introduces the use of a special technique known as synaesthesia which involves a mingling of the senses, i.e., the sound of the dulcimer's music is depicted as capable of ushering in sight or vision of the "pleasure-dome" ("And all who heard should see them there").

In the course of straying away from the poem's original path, the poet also makes a peculiar shift in the use of the possessive pronoun; thus, the sudden appearance of the third person singular "his" seems to have no antecedent. This was no doubt a calculated effect in the poet's conception of the verse. "His" may refer to the personified earth, the "dome"—or, perhaps, the poet himself. The latter, in particular, seems likely because it echoes a passage in Plato's *Ion* (533-534) where inspired poets are seen to be "like Bacchic maidens who draw milk and honey from the rivers when they are under the influence of Dionysus but not when they are in their right mind."** In telling his readers that the poem is the product of an opium dream, Coleridge himself seems to support Plato's argument that poets make poor citizens in the ideal "republic" because, subject as they are to passions, they are untrustworthy.

---

*M. H. Abrams, Gen. Ed., *The Norton Anthology of English Literature, 4th Ed.* (New York: W. W. Norton & Company, 1979), II, p. 355 (footnote). For a look at this passage in *Paradise Lost* one can turn to John Milton, *Paradise Lost*, ed. Scott Elledge (New York: W. W. Norton & Company, 1975), p. 86.

**M. H. Abrams, Gen. Ed., *The Norton Anthology of English Literature, 4th Ed.* (New York: W. W. Norton & Company, 1979), II, p. 355 (footnote). For a look at this work by Plato one can turn to the *Collected Works of Plato* (Cambridge MA: Harvard University Press, 1962), 8, pp. 401-448.

(Plato indicated that philosophers, who emphasize the control of reason over emotion, would be the best participants in a republican society.)

With the "synaesthetic" mixing of the senses at the end of the poem, Coleridge indicates that a purely sensual experience of the work—without the intrusion of the intellect—is not inappropriate. Both Milton, with his religious emphasis on original sin, and Plato, with his pre-Christian understanding of the unfortunate side of the poet's passions, would argue against the possibility of any redeeming use to the human senses. Coleridge, however, disagrees, and by showing us the complexity and depth of man's sensual nature, he leads to an ultimate vindication of subjective experience—one can indeed trust feelings in the personal quest for truth.

Kubla Khan is a work of fantasy. But it is nevertheless firmly grounded in the intellectual changes which took place towards the end of the eighteenth and beginning of the nineteenth centuries. In particular, these were changes concerning the idea of "beauty" whose intellectual and rational dependency on the mind to the poet's private world of emotional response.

Alfred Lord Tennyson
(1809–1892)

The Lady of Shalott

In 1850, Alfred Lord Tennyson became England's Poet
Laureate. Like many other poets of the later Romantic
period, he had a nostalgic attraction for the poetry of the
Middle Ages when romance, love, and death were popular
themes. A glance at the titles of his well-known works at-
tests to the fact: "Idylls of the King, "Merlin and the
Gleam," "The Lady of Shalott," etc., The so-called high
Romantics—Blake, Wordsworth, Coleridge, Byron, Shelley, and Keats—represented an early stage of Romanticism
associated primarily with the treatment of rather unconventional, revolutionary concepts. Unlike his predecessors,
Tennyson saw the need for a revival of formal concerns
and turned to ideals of the mannered court in the Middle
Ages.

In the **The Lady of Shalott**, this is first evident in
terms of structure. Each stanza of the poem adheres strictly
to the rhyme pattern aaaabcccb according to which, as we
see, there are two large families of verse lines ("a" and
"c") separated by a distinct and apparently unrelated
rhyme ("b"). This turns out to be significant because the
rhyme scheme in fact reflects the main subject of the
poem—the isolation of the lady on the island and her sepa-

ration from Camelot. Tennyson's use of the particular
rhyme scheme is "descriptive" in other ways. As we see,
the "b" lines consistently terminate in the words "Camelot" and "Shalott" thus repeatedly stressing a sense of re-
moteness focused on an opposition between the community
of the castle and the complete loneliness of the individual.
Similarly, the grouping of verse lines around the middle
verse can be interpreted as a kind of metaphor for the
"forest" separating Shalott from Camelot.

A different dimension of the concerns exhibited in this
poem is inherent in the association of Lady Shalott with
"horizontality"; her condition of isolation is dictated
primarily by the winding river on which her island is situated. Camelot, on the other hand, with its "many-
towered" walls immediately surrounded by the forest, is
replete with "verticality". To further support this interpretation, we might note that at the end, when the lady floats
down the river, she is found lying in the boat; on the other
hand, when Lancelot passes, he always remains mounted
on his "war-horse".

In much the same way, a considerable preoccupation
with formal concerns is found in Tennyson's distinction between images of "stasis" and "motion". Thus, in the first
stanza of Part II, the lady hears a whisper which tells her
that (a curse is on her if she stays). In a sense, this trig-
gers the beginning of the drama. By the third stanza of
Part III, the poet gives an essential summary of his subject
and sets up the following simile (a comparison using
"like" or "as") to give a fundamental description of the
relationship between the Knight Lancelot and the Lady of
Shalott:

> All in the blue unclouded weather
> Thick-jewelled shone the saddle-leather;
> The helmet and the helmet-feather

> Burned like one burning flame together,
>   As he rode down to Camelot:
> As often, through the purple night,
> Below the starry clusters bright,
> Some bearded meteor, trailing light,
>   Moves over still Shalott.

The key images here, of course, are the "motion" associated with Camelot and Shalott's "stillness". This contrast has already been anticipated in the description of river traffic—events and people flowing past the island:

> And up and down the people go   (Part I, stanza 1)
> By the margin, willow-veiled,
> Slide the heavy barges...   (Part I, stanza 3)
> And moving through a mirror clear
> That hangs before her all the year,
> Shadow of the world appear.   (Part II, stanza 2)

In these and many other ways, Tennyson develops a thoroughly picturesque and dramatic scenario based on the classical aesthetic of proportion, symmetry, and balance: Camelot is associated with community, motion, verticality and sunlight, while Lady Shalott exists in isolation, stasis, an essential horizontality, and lives in a shadowed world. The main focus of the drama, however, is always the lady herself. In some mysterious way, we might say, she is the very embodiment of the opposition between symmetrically opposed elements.

Color is also an important component in the poem, as we see from the descriptions: "willows whiten", "gray towers", "red cloaks", "crimson clad", "a red-cross knight", "yellow field", "blue unclouded weather", "purple night", etc. The Lady of Shalott "weaves by

night and day / A magic web with colors gay''. But the
only way the lady can see these colors is as ''shadows'' in
a ''mirror...that hangs before her all the year''. Thus, she
is confined to ''shadows of the world'' and not to the
world itself. As Tennyson makes evident, however, this is
somehow inherent to her character for, as we read in Part
II: ''in her web she still delights / To weave the mirror's
magic sights''. It is here that lies the key to the ''curse''
whose realization comes with the arrival of Lancelot in
Part III.

The stanza from this section already quoted above is
one of the most appealing passages in the poem. Its
straightforward beauty lies in the following: (1) internal
rhyme of words such as ''shone'', ''one'', ''rode'', ''below'', and ''over''; (2) emphasized euphony (the pleasing
combination of sound and image in the repetition of certain
words) in the line ''The helmet and the helmet feather /
Burning like one burning flame together''; and (3) use of
contrasting images, i.e., the ''thick-jeweled...saddle-
leather'' and the ''purple light'' with ''bearded meteor
trailing light''. Thus, Tennyson exhibits his mastery in the
brilliant use of word textures, color, image, rhyme, assonance, and rhythmic effect. All of these are an important
part of his technical skill as poet.

The climax of the poem comes in the first stanza of
Part IV when, as a result of the lady's encounter with the
world (Lancelot ''flashed into the crystal mirror''), she
dies and moves away from the island. It is ironic that she
was previously told by the ''whisper'' that ''A curse is on
her if she stays / To look down to Camelot'', in other
words, that the very proximity of Camelot is a threat to
her and that she should move away.

In the final analysis, **The Lady of Shalott** is a strange
and paradoxical work. The most commonly accepted in-

terpretation of the poem suggests that Shalott stands for the ideal artist whose subjective interpretation of events is the mirror which allows a translation of experience into art (the "web with colors gay"). In this way, Tennyson's point seems to be that the artist and the work of art have a fateful union because, once Shalott leaves the "web" to join the world of Camelot, she dies. To put things another way, the artist's world, for all intents and purposes, should remain remote from reality and dedicated strictly to the creation of art. In this regard, Tennyson displays a conviction characteristic for his time. Prior to the nineteenth century, all artists—painters, sculptors, musicians, etc., were generally part of the community at large; they dealt with images, ideas, and themes which substantiated existing social values in an accessible and constructive way. Later on, however, this situation changed considerably. Prevailing trends placed increasing emphasis on the personal feelings of an individual, and a movement away from classical and objective interpretations of beauty gradually resulted in a social alienation of the artist.

In spite of its rigid structure, Tennyson's poem is faithful to quintessential views of the Romantic era. In other words, it is within the context of a fixed mold that the lady's attempt to discard her role proves fruitless and Tennyson is able to attribute a kind of determinism (the doctrine that all facts and events exemplify natural laws) to the environment depicts. Appropriately enough, the drama takes place during the Middle Ages when, according to the feudal structure of society, a "commoner" could never become a member of the "nobility". Today, Tennyson's **The Lady of Shalott** is a universally acclaimed work. As a masterpiece of beauty, however, it is also one of the most controversial poems in the English language.

Walt Whitman
(1819–1892)

The Song of Myself

The poem by Whitman was published as part of *Leaves of Grass*, the author's famous cycle of 1855. It is of some interest that the poem belongs to the same year as Henry Wadsworth Longfellow's *Song of Hiawatha*.

When they first appeared, the two masterpieces evoked quite different public response. While Longfellow's work responded to a popular nostalgia for Indian lore, Whitman's book, at first, attracted only a small circle of elite. For example, in *Walt Whitman: A Life*, Justin Kaplan reports that the poet's brother, George, "inspector in a Camden, New Jersey pipe foundry", did not at all approve of the book; he dubbed it's celebration of love— "a muddle...of the whorehouse variety."*

Today, however, more than a century has elapsed, and attitudes towards the two works have changed drastically. Ironically, *Song of Hiawatha*, with its predictable meter and rhyme scheme, has been demoted to the rank of a child's poem, while all of the poems in *Leaves of Grass* are listed among the most important poetic creations in American history. How is this possible? And why wasn't

---

*Justin Kaplan, *Walt Whitman: A Life* (New York: Simon and Schuster, 1980), p. 11.

the significance of Whitman's work immediately recognized? Let us examine these crucial questions in a number of different contexts.

A proper understanding of Whitman's poetry, we might say, hinges on a sense of the historical flow of ideas dating back to the times of the earliest European settlers in America. The original settlement of Puritans was inspired by an intensely religious mission which regarded the landing in Massachusetts (1603) as nothing less than the discovery of "a new Jerusalem". In other words, in the minds of the early Americans, the task of survival on new territory was entirely motivated by the ideal of spiritual rebirth, that is, a new religious beginning for mankind. Toward the end of the seventeenth century, rigid Puritanism began to disappear, and fanatical spirituality in America yielded especially in the face of public dismay over the Salem witch trials in 1692. With Jonathan Edwards and the "Great Awakening" of the early eighteenth century, a return to Puritan values was attempted but with a kind of emotionalism that would have been scorned in earlier times. Finally, the Puritan focus on the Bible as the single criterion of truth was challenged in the late eighteenth century by deism, a philosophy set forth especially by Thomas Paine. In the treatise entitled *The Age of Reason*, Paine argued that nature and man's reason—*not the Bible*—offer the means for a true spiritual union between God and man.* Other thought along the same lines finally came to fruition in the American Constitution as well as in the work of Benjamin Franklin, Thomas Jefferson, and other thinkers of the time.

---

*Thomas Paine, *The Age of Reason*, Part I, ed. Alburey Castell (New York: The Bobbs-Merrill Company, Inc., 1957), p. 4: "My own mind is my own church."

Consequently, by the early nineteenth century, the ideal of complete submission to the arbitrary will of a "Calvinistic" God was virtually replaced by an emphasis on the individual's power to build, create, and invent. Emerging from a background and training as Unitarian minister, Ralph Waldo Emerson took the lead and, in view of the increasingly individualistic society of the time, suggested that each person had great potential and a special ability for spiritual growth. Needless to say, it is not surprising that such an idea immediately took root, and a period of fervent social idealism followed. Americans at this time witnessed the start of "socialist" communities such as Brook Farm. In addition, the slave question—a difficult moral issue—became the source of an increasingly intense polemic. Thus, the young nation, one of the first to ever challenge slavery, once again emerged as a kind of leader on the arena of universal spiritual concerns. Whitman, born in 1819, was a close observer of these pathbreaking developments.

The English-speaking public of the mid-nineteenth century, largely accustomed to poetry in *iambic pentameter*, had substantial difficulties with the sprawling, free verse published by Whitman. Yet, if we examine it, the poet's style did not emerge without precedent, for Whitman worked primarily with long, loosely cadenced lines reminiscent of the Bible. As a possible example, one can compare the following lines from the King James translation, Song of Solomon 8:6 and 7, with the opening section of Whitman's poem printed in volume 7 of the *The World's Best Poetry* (p. 198):

> Set me as a seal upon your heart, as a seal upon
>   your arm;

> For love is strong as death, jealousy is cruel
>   as the grave.
> Its flashes are flashes of fire, a most vehement
>   flame.
> Many waters cannot quench love, neither can floods
>   drown it.
> If a man offered for love all the wealth of his
>   house, it would be utterly scorned.

Certainly, there are many reasons why Whitman found the long line a suitable form. In some respects, we might say, his intention was to reflect the American spirit, the vast size of the country, and generous ideals of democratic freedom. But, at the same time, the origin of the verse is in the Bible. Take, for example, the central Christian theme evoked by the initial words "A child", and consider the following representative passages from the New Testament:

> Except ye be converted, and become as little children,
> ye shall not enter into the kingdom of Heaven. (Matt.
> 18:3)

> Blessed are the peace makers: for they shall be called
> the children of God. (Matt. 5:3-9)

The disarming opening and innocent simplicity of the first two lines of this section of *The Song of Myself* are reminiscent of William Blake's poem *The Tyger*; the naive speaker in this latter poem ("What immortal hand or eye / Could frame thy fearful symmetry?") is echoed by Whitman's child who asks "What is the grass?"—the quintessence of an impossible, yet simple-minded question. The author follows this with: "How could I answer the child? I do not know what it is anymore than he." This, of course, is feigned ignorance on the part of the poet, who, ultimately discloses how much he actually *does* know about such difficult questions.

In line 3, the author ventures an initial response with the appropriately hesitant "I guess it must be...". The first image he gives ("...the flag of my disposition, out of hopeful green stuff woven") is a curious mixture of nationalistic and spiritual elements. This, in fact, stands for one of Whitman's fundamental concepts: the union of self and democratic purpose. The next three lines, however, are only indirectly religious:

> Or I guess it is the handkerchief of the Lord,
> A scented gift and remembrancer designedly dropped,
> Bearing the owner's name someway in the corners,
>   that we may see and remark, and say *Whose*?

Here, Whitman uses a speculative mood to launch one of his famous lists; he discusses first one possible meaning of "grass", then another, and yet again another. In the course of things, his imagery is astonishingly bold, leaping about, here and there, like an acrobat into unexpected territory of the imagination. In the next line, for example, Whitman goes full circle, leaving the ideal of the "Lord's handkerchief" and coming back to an assessment of the grass as "a child" of some kind, "the produced babe of the vegetation". As we shall see, he thus makes an early allusion to one of the main ideas of his poem.

It is likely that in the hands of a less gifted poet this image would not have appeared in the middle of the poem and would have offered an opportunity simply to tie things up at the end. In a style characteristic of Whitman, however, it is just another way-station in a journey towards a philosophical conclusion. The point is that Whitman is neither an amateur nor a poet interested in formal symmetries, but a true example of the sensitive "Romantic" with far-reaching, private goals from which he will not be distracted by popular poetic trends. (To reinforce this point, compare the opening lines of Longfellow's *Song of Hiawatha* with *The Song of Myself*, keeping in mind that the style of the former poem was typical of its time.)

The next four lines of the poem strike a distinctly "democratic" note:

> Or I guess it is a uniform hieroglyphic,
> And it means, Sprouting alike in broad zones
>   and narrow zones,
> Growing among black folks as among white,
> Kanuck, Tuckahoe, Congressman, Cuff, I give them
>   the same, I receive them the same.

Here Whitman casts his vote for anti-slavery and for a country which is democratic and open in every sense of the word.

The next line ("And now it seems to me the beautiful uncut hair of graves") turns from the political to the spiritual. With the metaphysical meditation on death which begins here, it is appropriate to mention a few points about the role of certain religious and philosophical ideas among poets of the time. In the first place, like Emerson and Thoreau, Whitman was quite aware of popular concepts drawn from Eastern religion. For example, he knew Hinduism and was influenced by its emphasis on the brahman, the idea of universal spiritual oneness. (See the discussion of the poem by Emerson on page 59.) More importantly, however, are the roots of Whitman's thought in Puritanism from which he inherited a distinctly optimistic attitude—the idea that the experience of a spiritual rebirth in America was destined to be the driving force behind a world-wide abolition of slavery.

With a style similar to Scripture and ideas akin to Emerson's *transcendentalism* (and *Romanticism* in general), *Leaves of Grass* (including *Song of Myself*) becomes, in a sense, "the American Bible"—the political, social, and ultimately spiritual testament of democracy. As Kaplan writes:

> Like "Song of Myself", the earliest editions of *Leaves of Grass* both celebrated and reenacted the act of becoming...In Biblically cadenced, unrhymed verse he celebrated a psychic revolution: the single self, happy merely to exist, enjoying "the ecstasy of simple psychological Being" and changing "the chant of dilation or pride". Other masters singing the wrath of Achilles and man's first disobedience had created an epic literature out of war, pain, denial, and oppression and enforced belief.*

Like the child who in the beginning asked "What is the grass?", Whitman in the last part of this section asks about those who have died:

> What do you think has become of the young and
>   old men?
> And what do you think has become of the women and
>   children?

His answer is that "They are alive and well somewhere, / The smallest sprout shows there is really no death...".

---

*Justin Kaplan, *Walt Whitman: A Life* (New York: Simon and Schuster, 1980), pp. 186-187.

This idea breathes the freshness and optimism so readily associated with Whitman.

Song of Myself, like the whole of *Leaves of Grass*, is a milestone in American letters. Against the background of the Civil War (1860-62) and a declining interest in religion, Whitman's book marks a climax in American nationalistic fervor and optimism. Whitman himself said, "Test of a poem /is/ how far it can elevate, enlarge, purify, deepen and make happy the attributes of the body and soul."* Whitman's book allows us to observe the nature of American consciousness dating back to the time of the Puritans. It serves to remind us that hopes and dreams of a spiritual awakening are a consistent and deeply human reality.

In conclusion, we might say, the publication of *Leaves of Grass* was slow to capture attention because the author, like Emerson, was an idealist who would not conform to fashionable literary trends. Both the form and content of his poetry were totally unconventional in his day and expressed a highly personalized view of the "American Dream". In 1855, Emerson wrote a letter to Whitman in which he praised his work with the following words:

> I find it /*Leaves of Grass*/ the most extraordinary piece of wit and wisdom that America has yet contributed. I am very happy in reading it, as great power makes us happy. It meets the demand I am always making of what seemed the sterile and stingy Nature, as if too much handiwork or too much lymph in the temperament were making our western wits fat and mean. /.../ I greet you at the beginning of a great career,

---

*Emory Holloway, ed., *The Uncollected Poetry and Prose of Walt Whitman*, 2 Vols. (Garden City, NY, 1921), p. 75.

which yet must have had a long foreground somewhere,
for such a start. I rubbed my eyes a little to see if this
sunbeam were no illusion; but the solid sense of the
book is a sober certainty. It has the best merits,
namely, of fortifying and encouraging.*

Subsequent criticism of Whitman's poetry has continually
stood behind Emerson's positive evaluation.

---

*Edwin Haviland Miller, ed., *The Correspondence of Walt
Whitman* (New York: New York University Press, 1961-1977),
I, p. 41.

William Shakespeare
(1564–1616)

Sonnet XII

"When I Do Count The Clock That Tells The Time"

In **Sonnet XII,** Shakespeare endows calculated neo-
classicism with a peculiar intellectual twist. To understand
the nature of this approach, it is essential to carefully examine his particular treatment of poetic form. Only through
the observation of the genial manipulation of structure and
proportion can one hope to understand the poet's fundamental idea and to recognize his treatment of related
concepts in other works. Shakespeare's mastery is unsur-
passed on this account; his poetry, as a result, is acclaimed
for those rare, intimate moments when language rises to
lofty heights of uncharted space and the bare rudiments of
poetic technique seem to vanish. In achieving this effect,
however, the poet's blending of form and content is not exclusively rational but seems to be rather intuitive.

Broad structural analysis shows that the poem falls into
two sections standing for a logical temporal distinction on
the basis of the opening words "when" and "then". The
first eight lines therefore represent an antecedent or conditional thought; they are the part "before". The final six
lines are the consequent or resultant conclusion; they are
the part "after". This bi-partite structure gives an essential

framework for the development of the poet's idea that "time" is a transforming force. The thought is immediately reflected in the first two lines. Although iambic pentameter (five alternating unstressed and stressed syllabic pairs or verse feet) is a standard verse meter in English poetry, variations are used for special effects. Thus, in the first line of the poem, Shakespeare maintains the pattern and brings out the idea of the "clock" by applying the strict beat with a metronome-like quality:

"When I do count the clock that tells the time": the effect of this line is heightened by alliteration so that the use of monosyllabic words with the hard "c" and "t" sounds remind us of a clock. The second line, by contrast, not only emphasizes soft consonants (the repeated "s"), but also offers an interrupted rhythmic pattern. (Note the break introduced by "hideous" which, as we shall see, is a key word in the poem.) Shakespeare also establishes an emotional distance; the first line is neutral, abstract, and non-commital, while the second describes the personified "brave" day as "sunk in hideous night"—as if night were a hellish, horrible condition.

The theme of thesis and antithesis—or anticedent and consequent—is further developed in the use of "mirror" or "echo" images which involve the poet in a conscious shifting of his reader's attention between opposites. In the first two lines, for example, the alternating effect is produced by the words "day" and "night"; similarly, in lines 3 and 4 we read "sable" (or black) and "white". At another point in the poem, however, the poet lists images which "mirror" or "echo" each other in a more complicated way. Thus, the words "leaves", "herd", "sheaves", and "beard" are images terminating lines 5 through 8; they all convey the concept of a common bond in the union of a group. For example, the leaves are united by the tree, the herd by instinct, the sheaves by the gird, the beard by the chin. But, whereas beard, leaves, and herds share a common element because they represent collectivity in nature, sheaves probably refers to Shakespeare's pessimistic notion that the bond which unites people is artificial and becomes discernible only when "Time's scythe" (see the poem's penultimate line) reaps them unto death.

The poet's craft is further exhibited in the use of "barren" and "borne". It is clear that both words have double meanings and that Shakespeare's intention is to create a pun: "barren", used in the sense of "empty", also means "unable to bear children"; "borne", on the other hand, has the sense of "carried" as well as "brought into existence by birth". Thus, in the secondary meaning of the two words, we find reference to what are opposite conditions in procreation. There is, however, another subtle twist in the line "Borne on the bier with white and bristly beard". In addition to the use of alliteration, Shakespeare plays on the double meaning of "bier" which in his day was commonly used to designate both a handbarrow or cart for carrying objects as well as a platform on which a corpse is placed for funeral procession. The image therefore reinforces our previously stated interpretation of the "sheaves"; it applies not only to the harvest but also to the process of death and dying.

Earlier we noted an emotional contrast in the first two lines of the poem. Now this contrast can be seen to have also a broader application. The description of a "violet past prime" in line 3 is optimistic and positive in comparison with the morbid, "black", and final vision of a metaphorical corpse being carried away with "bristly beard" in line 8. What makes the latter image all the more "hideous" is the following: unlike the single violet which has harmlessly faded, the dead corpse in fact stands for the harvest of an entire "summer's green". One facet of Shakespeare's technique, therefore, is to create a contrast

between relatively mild or "white" images of time passing
(or the fading of youth and beauty) and definitive or comparatively strong images signifying death. Thus, the emphasis on visual imagery in the first section of the sonnet
touches off an internal self-questioning. In the second section we ultimately find the poet's philosophical meditation
on "thy beauty" which no doubt concerns the person to
whom the poem is addressed.

The points Shakespeare makes are: (1) the cherished
object of "beauty", like the rest of nature, is transient and
"must go"; (2) the "sweets and beauties" in nature actually self-destruct; (3) dying is a natural and quick process
which simply mirrors the process of growth; and (4) taking
into account the destructive forces of time, the only hope is
in the coming of new generations. (Note that, in the final
line, "breed" means "offspring" and "brave" means
"defy".)

Thus, Shakespeare's overall conclusions appear somewhat ironic: anyone who considers someone's beauty as the
exclusive object of his interest should not despair at the
prospect of its gradual disappearance. Instead, there is consolation in the fact that decay plays a predictable role in
the cycle of death and rebirth. In other words, according to
the poet, there is no cause to fear the power of Time's
ruthless destruction because there also exists an opposing
force in Nature which brings new life and makes "dying"
practically synonymous with "procreation".

In conclusion, we might say, the special use of mirror
images in **Sonnet XII** is the focal expression of
Shakespeare's deep concern with Nature and the universal
"mirror-like" process which constantly restores, replaces,
and compensates for the annihilation brought on by Time.
In the hands of a master, this technical device is thus
thoroughly integrated into the poem's intellectual substance
and serves to advance principal ideas.

VII

Descriptive and Narrative

Preface

The categories descriptive and narrative are related to each other in a curious way. In fact, drawing a sharp distinction between them could be misleading. Neither one delimits a theme or subject. Instead, both indicate that the poet will adopt a particular manner of speech and that the mode of delivery will conform to basic requirements of rhetoric. In both kinds of poetry, moreover, the focus is on a presentation of supposedly reliable or time-tested information. In delivering this data, the poet deals much like a historian or scientist: to convey creative insight into the material is the main goal. Facts, we should remember, are meaningless outside of a specified context; they have no value unless they are analyzed and interpreted. This is the conviction of philosophers. It is a popular misconception that history is written objectively or that scientific knowledge comes in the form of sheer quantitative measurement.

Nevertheless, one can expect that a special kind of subject will best suit the requirements of each category. Thus, descriptive poetry will address the still life; it will convey a state of being. Narrative, on the other hand, will have to do almost exclusively with the dynamic; it will usually give account of a series of related events. In conveying such material, the poet's power of interpretation hinges on a key portrayal of two temporal dimensions. The descriptive mode will tend to speak in definitive terms admissible mainly in the absolute context of eternity, while the narrative will always strive to remain true to historical time, even at the expense of ascribing mortal attributes to the gods in heaven. We should note that quintessential narrative comes in the ancient form of poetry known as the epic. Such poetry usually betrays its origin in oral forms of declamation. Famous examples of the epic are Homer's *Iliad*, Virgil's *Aeneid*, and Dante's *Inferno*.

Elizabeth Barrett Browning
(1806–1861)

George Sand

Elizabeth Barrett Browning gleaned enormous popularity during her lifetime. As one of the few successful woman writers in the mid-nineteenth century, she managed to portray ideals which evidently elicited a response among a wide readership and especially among other women. Before her marriage to the renowned English poet Robert Browning, Elizabeth Barrett was already a well-known literary figure. A remarkable education, including thorough training in ancient Greek and classical philosophy, inspired her to undertake the writing of verse; her first volume was printed when she was 13. Among other works, the long poem "**Aurora Leigh**" (1857) quickly became a universally acclaimed best seller.

In an effort to promote forward-looking, liberal causes, Elizabeth Barrett did not stop short of expressing deep admiration for other women with similar outlooks. Among these, perhaps the most famous was the novelist Amandine Aurore Lucie Dupin, Baroness Dudevant (1804-1876), a striking personality known in French literary circles by the pseudonym "George Sand". Sand was famous for a liaison with the Polish composer and pianist, Frederic Chopin (1810-1849) and for her many successful novels. At the same time, her appearance in public always evoked outrage; she took it upon herself to express personal convictions not only through the use of a masculine-sounding name, but also by wearing pants and smoking cigars. Women in those days did not do such things.

The poem "George Sand", therefore, offers an occasion to view Elizabeth Barrett's sympathy for a somewhat controversial personality. In particular, the poet's object of attention is the figure of another writer, moreover, another female writer whose wide reputation rides on unquestionable talent accompanied by somewhat bizarre behaviour in society. Written in the form of a Petrarchan sonnet (rhyming abbaabba cdcdcd), the work appropriately deals with a serious predicament. At the time, women were not expected to be influential or to have careers; living in a traditional, male-dominated society, they generally held to established norms of appearance and behavior. In expressing admiration for George Sand, Elizabeth Barrett raises the question of a contrast between outward looks and inward purpose.

The poem begins with the form of a vocative preface. Elizabeth Barrett addresses her literary colleague: "True genius, but true woman!" The thought behind such an exclamation may seem strange to us today. Nevertheless, at the time the poem was written, it had potent implications. The conjunction "but", in this context, suggests that "genius" is something quite extraordinary. But, in the eyes of society, the phenomenon of female genius is especially surprising, unconventional, and requires not a small measure of apology and explanation. What follows in the next three lines reveals the main evidence for this opening claim. George Sand has apparently met with a strange fate: in the face of true genius, she has had to deny her own womanhood. In other words, she has come to embody radical rebellion; she has had to break with convention and to shed "the gauds and armlets worn / By weaker women in captivity". What is more, in the process, she has had to assimilate certain "manly" attitudes. The trivial idiosyncracies behind George Sand's reputation, of course, do not interest Elizabeth Barrett; these are not the essential manifestations. Sand's "manliness" is manifest primarily in the "scorn" with which she has come to part with conventional womanhood.

In the next four lines, however, Browning proceeds to delineate an essential difficulty. Sand's action is immediately termed a "vain denial", that is, a denial which is bound with problems and frustration; it is a denial of "Nature" itself. Accordingly, there is also an element of tragedy; Sand's sentiments are ultimately internalized ("sobbed in") and inherently remain the utterance of "a woman's voice forlorn." In Browning's view, this is inevitable; this is the result of Sand's true womanhood. Thus, by lines seven and eight, or about midway through the poem, the reader is prepared to accept Browning's first crowning point:

> Thy woman's hair, my sister, all unshorn,
> Floats back dishevelled strength in agony,
> Disproving thy man's name;

The image of Sand's hair evokes the character of true personal testimony. Echoing the familiar Biblical story of Samson and Delilah, it points to an essential source of sexual prowess and to the way in which external appearance carries strength and conviction. The implication is that the woman's hair, just like any man's (i.e., Samson's), can symbolize a chosen path even in a state of weakness and oppression.

In the ninth through twelfth lines, the poet creates images of George Sand's "poet-fire" (which corresponds to the initial "true genius") and "woman-heart" (which corresponds to "true woman"). These suggest the coming together of forces that Browning had previously thought might be mutually exclusive. In suggesting that Sand's genius is intact, therefore, the poet praises its unique qualities which are obvious to everyone: "We see they woman-heart beat evermore / through the large flame." The final lines, in which the Almighty God "unsexes" the human creature "on the heavenly shore", place special emphasis on the theme of outward appearance and inward purpose. The repeated word "pure" in lines twelve and fourteen suggests that everyone—man or woman—has potential purity and an element of moral, aesthetic purpose. In the case of women, however, this is often difficult to realize; circumstances usually offer men an advantage and greater opportunities for personal expression. Browning's assessment of George Sand, therefore, is essentially the following: beneath the manifestations of a peculiar external appearance, there is the "woman-heart" and all of its "purer" aspirations. This is the ultimate triumph of female genius; it brings together otherwise seemingly irreconcilable spheres.

Women writers other than George Sand were no doubt known to Browning, famous literary names such as Sappho (7th century B.C.), Mary Wollstonecraft (1759-1797), Jane Austen (1775-1817), George Eliot (1819-1880), Christina Georgina Rossetti (1830-1894), and others. Nevertheless, Sand evidently appealed to the poet in a very special way. Her embodiment of "female greatness" was something especially attractive; to the sensitive, intellectually developed, and free-thinking woman of the 19th century, it offered curious proof of the way in which genius transcends mundane boundaries and forges ahead towards new horizons of achievement.

Percy Bysshe Shelley
(1792–1822)

Ozymandias of Egypt

The period of English letters known as the "Augustan Age" encompasses the work of early eighteenth-century authors such as Alexander Pope, whose main interest lay in the development of literary standards based on a classical sense of form and proportion. By the turn of the century, however, intellectual thought turned to a radically different set of principles. Following in the footsteps of the Romantic school which included Blake, Wordsworth, Coleridge, and others, the generation of poets led by Shelley (1792-1822) and Byron (1788-1824) was little interested in pursuing the ideals of classicism and began to produce a poetry based on a new aesthetic. A brief glance at Shelley's personal life reveals a revolutionary fervor. The grandson of a Baronet, Percy Bysshe Shelley belonged to a family of squires from Sussex. Nevertheless, in 1811, he was expelled from Oxford for publishing an essay entitled "The Necessity of Atheism". Upon insistence from his relatives that he undergo religious instruction, Shelley refused to return home; a further dispute with his father resulted in the rejection of a sizeable family fortune.* While married, Shelley led a promiscuous life and even wrote about his

---

*Richard Holmes, *Shelley: the Pursuit* (London: Weidenfeld and Nicolson, 1974), pp. 51-60.

love for Mary Godwin (who eventually became the author of the well-known novel *Frankenstein*). In 1816, as a result of marriage-related tensions, his wife, Harriet, committed suicide.** In summary, we might say, Shelley was the arch-Romantic showing little concern for the conventional life-style of his day. It is not surprising, therefore, that **Ozymandias of Egypt** reflects a spirit of aesthetic abandon.

Although Shelley adheres to some features of the sonnet (i.e. fourteen lines in iambic verse), the structure of his poem does not conform to an appropriate rhyme and makes occasional use of verse lines with nine or eleven syllables instead of the usual ten associated with iambic pentameter. Moreover, it tends to disregard another routine procedure. To make the point, we can contrast the poem to Alexander Pope's **Rape of the Lock** (*The World's Best Poetry*, vol. VI, p. 135) where the end of each "sense-unit" (i.e. clause, phrase, or sentence) always coincides with the end of a poetic line. Looking at Shelley's poem, however, we find the following:

> I met a traveller from an antique land
> Who said: Two vast and trunkless legs of stone
> Stand in the desert. Near them on the sand,
> Half sunk, a shattered visage lies, whose frown
> And wrinkled lip and sneer of cold command
> Tell that its sculptor well those passions read
> Which yet survive, stamped on those lifeless things...

Thus, while the first line can be termed "end-stopped", the majority seem to break quite arbitrarily; they comprise sense-units which span several lines. This is another important indication of Shelley's break with neo-classicism.

**Richard Holmes, *Shelley: the Pursuit* (London: Weidenfeld and Nicolson, 1974), pp. 352-359.

However, it is the poet's choice of subject that really makes the point clear. The focus on the first five lines of the poem is on a demolished statue, which, in Shelley's understanding, is a symbolic ruin: the remains connote the downfall of antiquity. Thus, the number "two" in the second line implies "balance" or "symmetry" not only because it constitutes the minimum number of parts required in a "classical" composition, but also because in the visual arts the ancient standard for proportion and order is the human body. The word "antique" in the first line reinforces a specific association of the poetic image with classicism, which the poet tells us still has "legs", but "a shattered visage" that has lost integrity and, in fact, stands "half sunk" in the sands of a desert. Following the initial section, the poet introduces a basic three-fold sequence of images: (1) the artist who created the crumbling statuary ("The hand that mocked them and the heart that fed..."); (2) the inscription on the pedestal ("My name is Ozymandias, king of kings: Look on my works, ye Mighty, and despair!"); and (3) again, the setting defined in the first two and a half lines i.e., the "boundless and bare" desert whose "lone and level sands stretch far away". We should note that, by ending where he began, Shelley gives a sense of order to the work—an order, however, which is dismantled by a freely handled rhyme and meter.

Against the background of what he describes, Shelley also conveys a sense of the poet's predicament. The line "The hand that mocked them and the heart that fed" describes an artist who outwardly "mocks" the world but nevertheless feels in his "heart" an identification with the "wrinkled lip and sneer of cold command". To "mock" and "feed" at the same time is to be committed to an essentially self-indulgent process in a rebellious and ungrateful way. What Shelley describes is an alienation and breakdown in the relationship between artist and society. In traditional Christian society, artists were predominantly in the employ of a ruling class; they created works which reflected the values associated with the church and state. Thus, for example, just as Michelangelo once painted the inside of the Sistine Chapel, in the present poem, the sculptor creates a likeness of the "king of kings". But by the nineteenth century, many artists—including Shelley— felt a distance from established social, political and religious values; thus, in their work, they began to flaunt a sense of separation. In **Ozymandias of Egypt**, the true emotions expressed in the line "The hand that mocked..." refer to someone who feels the need to maintain the false appearance of continued belief.

In expressing this emotion, however, Shelley also describes a related state of mind. To do so, he introduces the openly defiant remark on the pedestal of his defunct statue, where a supposedly powerful leader (the "king of kings") invites "ye Mighty" to "look on my works...and despair". In other words, the poet wishes to convey that, in view of the surrounding desert, it is precisely "despair" that is the only appropriate emotion. Moreover, the point is that the "desperation" is applicable not only to his own day. It has universal ramifications. For the ancient ruler himself, like the sculptor, already shared a similar intuition concerning the fleeting, temporal nature of a seemingly stable or fixed universe. The poet's special preoccupation is evident in the poem's diction and is exemplified in the use of words such as "despair", "lifeless", "mocked", "wreck", "bare", "sunk", "shattered", "wrinkled", and "sneer". Shelley's interest in a dissolute movement away from classical values was a central theme of his literary output. Thus, in an early poem entitled **Queen Mab**, the poet wrote:

How Wonderful is Death,
Death and his brother Sleep.

* * *

Power, like a desolating pestilence,
Pollutes whate'er it touches; and obedience,
Bane of all genius, virtue, freedom, truth,
Makes slaves of men, and, of the human frame,
A mechanized automation.*

As a fundamentally creative genius, Shelley was interested in aesthetic anarchy and in the new modes of expression. Inherited forms and values meant little to him. In **Ozymandias of Egypt**, Shelley also suggests that an alienation of "the arts" from the mainstream of society is unfortunate and signifies a general downfall of the human spirit.

---

*Percy Bysshe Shelley, *The Complete Works of Percy Bysshe Shelley* (New York: Charles Scribner's Sons, 1927), I, pp. 67, 88.

Geoffrey Chaucer
(1340–1400)

"The Prologue" to
The Canterbury Tales

There is good reason to consider **The Canterbury Tales**
by Geoffrey Chaucer among the most important literary
works of the English language. Both in spirit and content,
it stands at the crossroads between the Middle Ages and
the Renaissance. Traditionally called "the father of English
literature", Chaucer began work on the masterpiece late in
life, around 1386.

During the Middle Ages (ca. 400-1400 A.D.), there
were two basic kinds of literature, religious and secular.*
Religious works stressed a standard belief in God; they
conveyed the fact that spiritual life is an important, traditional component of prosperity and welfare. Secular works,
on the other hand, had a less ponderous purpose; they
generally contained lighter and even humorous material
aimed at amusing the gentry. As time went on, however,
this division between "the sacred" and "the profane" became less prominent, so that by about the fifteenth century,
the epoch later identified by historians as "the Renais-

*John Gardner, *The Life and Times of Chaucer* (New
York: Alfred A. Knopf, 1977), p. 53.

sance'' began to flaunt an open, candid intermingling of
seemingly disparate spheres. England, an island somewhat
removed from the European continent, absorbed this approach in its own way and at its own pace. This was
thanks to creative individuals such as Chaucer who made
deliberate and concerted efforts towards an implementation
of new trends.

A commoner born into a wine merchant's family,
Chaucer in his early teens was offered the role of ''page''
in one of the great households of the English aristocracy,
that of Lionel of Antwerp, son of the reigning monarch,
Edward III. The young man was very attractive, bright,
and quickly rose in rank. In 1359, working as a soldier for
the king, Chaucer was captured by the French; after a
clever bargain with the captors, he eventually returned to
his homeland. Thereafter, his life was distinguished by
good fortune; he once again became a favorite in the court
of both Edward III and, afterwards, John of Gaunt. The
latter seemed especially appreciative of his many talents
and sent him on official missions to Italy and France. In
1366, Chaucer met and married Philippa Roet, a lady from
the court of Queen Philippa. Civic duties of his later life
included membership in parliament for the County of Kent.

However brief and sketchy, this account can help us to
put Chaucer's work into perspective and to clarify the personal concerns exhibited in the famous author's writing.
The biography reveals an enormous breadth of experience;
at the time, such exposure to different lifestyles, nationali-
ties, situations, and people was rather exceptional. Travel
was difficult and fraught with perils. Chaucer's work, as a
result, is a kind of catalogue, a record of impressions
reaped over decades of active life. Paradoxically, however,
the setting he selects is typically a limited one. In **The
Canterbury Tales**, for example, the author does not go

beyond the confines of a parochial English landscape; he conveys the complete message within the bounds of specified and restricted geography. The focus of attention is on the environs of "The Tabarde Inn, by Henry Baillie, the lodgynge-house for Pilgrims who journey to Saint Thomas's Shrine at Canterbury."

It is in this seemingly narrow setting that unfolds the magnificent panorama of **The Canterbury Tales**. But, how is the author able to capture so much of what is still meaningful today? What is it that endows the work with the status of "world classic"? How does this masterpiece speak to the modern reader?

There is no doubt that the answer lies in Chaucer's extraordinary understanding of human nature and insight into man's behavior. The author's special way of life brought him into contact with a broad spectrum of personalities. He himself was not a born noble. Yet, early in life he acquired unique experience with the idiosyncratic behavior of people at all levels of society. Indeed, how could this be otherwise? As a seventeen-year-old, he was not only aware of his own home environment, but was also making beds, carrying candles, and running numerous errands for royalty visiting from the world over.*

> The characters of Chaucer's Pilgrims are the characters which compose all ages and nations. As one age falls, another rises, different to mortal sight, but to immortals only the same; for we see the same characters repeated again and again, in animals, vegetables, minerals, and in men. Nothing new occurs in identical existence; accident ever varies, but substance can never suffer change nor decay.

---

*John Gardner, *The Life and Times of Chaucer* (New York: Alfred A. Knopf, 1977), pp. 90-126.

> Of Chaucer's charactes, as described in his **Can-
> terbury Tales**, some of the names or titles are altered
> by time, but the characters themselves forever remain
> unaltered; and consequently they are the physiognomies
> or lineaments of universal human life, beyond which
> Nature never steps. Names alter, things never alter. I
> have known multitudes of those who would have been
> monks in the age of monkery, who in this deistical age
> are deists. As Newton numbered the stars, and as Lin-
> naeus numbered the plants, so Chaucer numbered the
> classes of men.*

This concise yet thoroughly accurate statement belongs to
the pen of none other than William Blake (1757-1827),
Chaucer's famous compatriot of several centuries later.

Chaucer's life is divided into three periods. The first
period focuses on his involvement with French literature
and especially on his translation of *Le Roman de la Rose*, a
famous medieval allegory of youthful, chivalric love. The
second period, lasting from 1372-86, is marked by association with Italian literature; during these years Chaucer
wrote *The Parlement of Foules, The House of Fame*, and
Troilus and Cressida. The third period lasts from 1386 to
the author's death in 1400; it focuses on the appearance of
The Canterbury Tales.

In view of this, no one would have to be convinced
that Chaucer was hardly an insular writer; he comes from
a broad literary background which is unconstrained by the
moralistic and superficial nature of early English literature.
Italian masters of the early Renaissance had an especially
important influence on Chaucer. For example, it was from

---

*W. Blake "The Canterbury Pilgrims" (1809) in Edmund
D. Jones, ed. *English Critical Essays* (Oxford, 1916), pp.
86-7.

Boccaccio (1313-1375) that the author learned to tell a good story, and from Dante (1265-1321)—to embrace the "unembraceable", the ever-expanding and changing dimension of human expression. It is the depth of Chaucer's cultural insight that paved the way for a new direction among subsequent English writers. In addition to being well-travelled and experienced in the ways of the world, however, Chaucer was an omnivorous reader. Reading is among the best paths to a thorough education. Chaucer knew Latin, French, Anglo-Norman, Italian, and cultivated serious interest in subjects such as astronomy, medicine, physics, and alchemy. This active interest in learning and ideas also qualifies him as a harbinger of the English Renaissance.

The Canterbury Tales, Chaucer's finest work, comes to us in unfinished form. The original plan was to include one hundred and twenty tales, two told by each of the thirty pilgrims, one on the way to the cathedral and one on the way back. Of these, only twenty-two were completed. Some critics have expressed regret concerning the author's busy life and have even suggested that an overwhelming schedule may have been an obstacle to the writer's true calling. Such an assessment is not necessarily valid. We must remember that the experience of an artist's lifetime never stops and that limitations placed on any aspect of reality may, in fact, endanger the quality of an individual's creative output. Throughout history, masterpieces of art have commonly emerged as a result of "the human condition", i.e. suffering and hardship. In short, true genius has always created in spite of the surrounding world.

The pilgrims in Chaucer's prologue have set out on a journey from London to the shrine of St. Thomas at Canterbury. During the fourteenth century, the cathedral was a place of popular veneration; it was here that the arch-

bishop, Thomas Becket, was murdered by Henry II's en-
voys (A.D. 1170). In opposing the king's will, the renowned churchman had been a staunch defender of
religious principles; in effect, his death was a case of evident martyrdom. Chaucer's focus on the theme of "pilgrimage" was the result of pure ingenuity. It allowed him
to paint humanity from numerous angles. Medieval pilgrimages were hardly exclusive in their piety. Though
motivated by sincere religious feeling, these voyages were
often a colorful spectacle. Their pageantry necessarily involved a secular dimension; life was lived in the course of
travel. Pilgrimages, moreover, concerned people from every walk of life; after all, they had to do with transcendent
ideals. In **The Canterbury Tales**, therefore, the pilgrimage
becomes a metaphor for life; it offers the opportunity to
treat all individuals on equal terms. In this sense, Chaucer
was an author of the "egalitarian spirit", a spirit which
sincere, gifted artists have always understood, long before
legalistic—and therefore artificial—formulations of "equal
rights" took hold of the modern day political arena. Although Chaucer's work gives the reader an excellent cross-
section of fourteenth-century life, conveying, as no other
work ever has, the mind and spirit of Western man at the
time, in the final analysis, it carries universal meaning as
well: it is fundamentally "a showcase of humanity at
large".

Before addressing details of "The Prologue", it may
be useful to review some underlying philosophical assumptions. Today, man views the universe as "open" and
"changing"; personal development, as a result, involves
the penetration of "the self". The so-called ego prevails
above all else and leads the way in the advancement of
ideas. In short, it is a proud world we live in. In days of
old, on the other hand, it was the "medieval mind" that

stood firmly at the helm; the humble mindset was a wonderful source of comfort and stability. The universe of the Middle Ages was "closed" and "unchanging"; the individual or person was seen against a background of God's law, i.e. social and spiritual guidelines were objective and fixed. Although in Chaucer's day this approach was still dominant, the author's biography, as we have seen, is ready evidence of incipient change; it shows, for example, that the middle class was on the rise and that the role of individual choice in spiritual, economic, and political matters was about to gain unprecedented importance. As Derek Brewer puts it: "The milling social unrest, the turmoil of external social events, were interrelated with deep inner stirrings and confusions, the painful birth of new feelings about the individual and his relation to the world. A developing in the outer world accompanied a developing need for inner experience, as inner and outer became more clearly separated, and the apparently divergent drives towards outer and inner experience needed ordering and reconciliation."*

In modern society, man takes for granted the disparity between political realities and personal aspirations. Understanding Chaucer's world requires that one forget these assumptions; one must imagine a world where there is no such disparity, but faith in a permanent order of the universe. Indeed, as we have already noted, Chaucer's time did see the beginning of modern skepticism—doubts which would ultimately challenge the reality of Christian faith. But, for present purposes, it must be remembered that society at the time was not yet an urbane, heterogeneous entity; most of the world was in the domain of agrarian rule,

---

*Derek Brewer, *Chaucer in His Time* (London: Thomas Nelson and Sons Ltd., 1963).

dominated by a feudal structure. One needs only to recall that the printing press and table fork were not invented until the fifteenth century!!**

The first thing to notice about "The Prologue" is that it is written in heroic couplet. Couplet refers to the fact that the work is written in pairs of lines, each pair being distinguished by an end-rhyme. "Heroic", on the other hand, has two possible meanings; it may refer (1) to the rhythm of iambic pentameter or (2) to the sense of breadth and grandeur imparted by the poetry. There is an anticipation of humor in the fact that there will be no single hero in **The Canterbury Tales** but only a cast of conspicuously normal people. The notation that a work of literature should have a particular hero or heroine comes, in part, from the Christian idea of God or Jesus as central figures in the Old and New Testaments. When the idea of a strictly ordered, objective universe began to break down during the Renaissance, the concept of the "hero" as a primary feature and focal point in literature also began to be questioned. **The Canterbury Tales** is one of the first instances of such a decline.

The opening lines of "The Prologue" establish the time of year as April with its "shoures soote" (sweet showers). April comes after winter and is an appropriate time for people to prepare for a journey; closed in for the preceding months, it is a time when people wish to socialize. In religious terms, April suggests a rebirth. Traditionally, it is the time of Easter, the celebration of the "Resurrection". It is a fitting time to refresh or renew one's spiritual bonds through new efforts of mission and pilgrimage. Finally, Chaucer's choice of April is appropriate because, as he emphasizes it is a very sexual time of year:

**John Gardner, *The Life and Times of Chaucer* (New York: Alfred A. Knopf, 1977), p. 53.

> Whan that Aprille with hise shoures soote
> The droghte of March hath perced to the roote,
> And bathed very veyne in swich licour,
> Of which vertue engendered is the flour;
> Whan Zephirus eek with his swete breeth
> Inspired hath in every holt and heeth
> The tendre croppes, and the yonge sonne
> Hath in the Ram his halfe course y-ronn...

To inspire the tender crops is a detail of the setting presented which emphasizes a sexual element. An important facet of **The Canterbury Tales** is the degree to which they explore the lustier, greedier, more earthy side of human nature. Thus in these opening lines, Chaucer immediately reveals that the processes through which nature goes to seed and fertilizes itself anew will—in human terms—play an important role in this work.

The "knyght" who is described as practicing "Trough and honor, fredom and curteisie" introduces a member of the gentry into the pilgrimage. The implied contrast, however, is that between military values and those required to make him, in the courtly and Christian sense, a "gentil knyght". In the line at the bottom of page 364, for example—"As wel in cristendom as in hethenesse"—Chaucer suggests the difference between Christian and heathen values. The heathen values are, however, underplayed until the lustier side of his son, the Squire, is described. A knight, we know, must practice both.

The knight's son, the Squire, represents the more earthy side of the knight's life which Chaucer did not emphasize in the preceding section. Lines describing the squire's passionate nature such as those at the bottom of page 365—"So hoote he lovede, that by nyghtertale / He sleep no more than dooth a nyghthngale"—were very daring portrayals of life as it was in Chaucer's day. Compared to the more superficial work of his contemporaries, this is radical and direct treatment of a subject.

The nun described on pages 366-7 is distinguished on the one hand for being simple and coy ("That of hire smylyng was ful symple and coy") and on the other is a serious eater ("Wel koude she carie a morsel and wel kepe, / That no drope ne fille up-on hire breste"). The point is that all of Chaucer's characters, just as in real life, are complicated beings sometimes composed of many contradictory elements. In this way, Chaucer shows himself to be a shrewd observer of human nature.

To be a sympathetic observer of people, however, was not enough. Chaucer's use of detail as the primary groundwork upon which he built his narrative is a crucial aspect of the success of **The Canterbury Tales** as a work of literature. Notice, for example, such well-focused touches as the nun's forehead. Indeed, what a focus!

> It was almoost a spanne broad, I trowe
> For hardily she was nat undergrowe

Or, note the squire's dress and manner:

> Embrouded was he, as it were a meede
> Al ful of fresshe floures whyte and reede.
> Syngynge he was, or floytynge, al the day;
> He was as fressh as is the month of May.
> Short was his gowne, with sleves longe and wyde.
> Wel Cowde he sitte on hors, and faire ryde.

Such careful touches of description reveal Chaucer's true talent as a story teller.

In conclusion, we might say that "The Prologue" offers invaluable testimony:

In all literature there is nothing that touches or resembles "The Prologue". It is the concise portrait of an entire nation, high and low, old and young, lay and clerical, learned and ignorant, rogue and righteous, land and sea, town and country, but without extremes. Apart from the stunning clarity, touched with nuance, of the characters presented, the most notable thing about them is their normality. They are the perennial progeny of men and women. Sharply individual, together they make a party.*

The author of these words is Nevill Cognill, a scholar widely respected for his efforts in rendering Chaucer's masterpiece into modern English.

---

*Geoffrey Chaucer, *The Canterbury Tales*, trans. into modern English by Nevill Coghill (Harmondsworth: Penguin Books, 1959), introduction.

VIII
National Spirit

Preface

Poems of national spirit appeal to a dimension of public consciousness. They address subjects which are patriotic and have to do with the life of a nation as a whole. Generally, they are hardly the place for private, introspective considerations. The poetry must express the kind of emotion which is meaningful to all.

Nationalistic sentiments surface especially during periods of turmoil. Throughout history, for example, wartime has provided opportunities to bolster morale, galvanized nations into massive action, and brought about broad visionary perspectives; troubled periods have also been a time for questioning and evaluating the means by which a nation attains its goals. During times of peace and prosperity, on the other hand, different approaches are possible. Nationalism and the deep feelings of satisfaction and contentment associated with it promote more leisurely assessments of the past as well as cautious projections into the future.

Richard Lovelace
(1618–1658)

To Althea From Prison

This famous example of seventeenth-century English court poetry treats concepts of basic importance to the political thinker. It suggests that a constructive attitude towards government hinges on philosophical principles and that any idea of "freedom" is unrealistic unless it is anchored to a definite structure of ruling power. Lovelace had particular reasons for addressing these issues: during his lifetime, England experienced widespread economic, social, political, and religious change which threatened to upset traditional ways. Expansionism had altered the nature of the economy, causing struggles over such issues as tariffs and monopolies. As international trade flourished, bankers and merchants attained unprecedented affluence and came to represent the distinct and influential force we have come to call "middle class society". Unrest in church circles over ideas concerning the Protestant Reformation resulted in the well-known Puritan faction. Finally, revolution during the 1640's culminated in regicide and the takeover by Oliver Cromwell.

In **To Althea From Prison**, Lovelace takes a stand on controversial questions and expresses the point of view of a courtier loyal to the king. His adherence to established norms is first of all evident in an approach to poetic form. The poem is a highly polished work. Its rhetoric and imagery emerge in the context of a structure which reflects a carefully contained sense of order and design. Four Sicilian octaves (eight-line stanzas) come in the pattern rhymed ababcdcd; each stanza, in turn, contains lines of iambic octameter alternating with lines of iambic hexameter. Further organization is evident in the use of similar semantic entities; thus, in the initial three stanzas; the first and fifth lines open with "when" and the final line becomes a kind of refrain: "Know no such liberty." The concluding stanza deviates from this pattern in order to alert the reader to a special message; it is as if the poet breaks loose from bondage. This final stanza has Lovelace's well-known lines: "Stone walls do not a prison make / Nor iron bars a cage."

A calculated approach to structure provides a vehicle for developing the poet's thought. Lovelace wrote this poem while in jail for petitioning to reestablish the king's rule. His ideas at the time, therefore, were centered on a particular understanding of freedom; he wished to show that "freedom" is compatible with the monarchy and does not require Cromwell's drive towards legal representation, religious tolerance, and human rights. To Lovelace, a nobleman and member of the English court, "freedom" is a state of mind accessible in all circumstances—even in the course of life in prison.

Lovelace bases his thought on an underlying assumption about human behavior, namely, that civilization requires a qualified definition of liberty and that outside certain prescribed parameters men fall into a depraved, animal-like state. Moreover, as one of the so-called "Cavalier" poets, Lovelace espouses the principles of courtly life. These mainly concern four areas of sanctioned deportment: (a) love, governed by rules of courtship; (b) honor, maintained by loyalty to the crown; (c) patronage, inspired by an appreciation for the arts; and (d) faith, prescribed by church doctrine. The concept of freedom proposed by the poet is, therefore, shaped by firm adherence to tradition.

In the first stanza, Althea's love, which "tangles" and "fetters" the poet, is set in opposition to "birds that wanton in the air". Lovelace's choice of imagery in this case follows convention: he sees nothing admirable in the unruliness of birds, creatures whose lust and licentiousness are renowned themes recurring throughout poetic lore. To make his point, he contrasts the divine nature of human love to that of animals who are driven solely by instinct and, therefore, "Know no such liberty". Of course, Lovelace does appreciate love "with unconfined wings". But his perception comes only within the confines of "gates" and "grates", i.e. the prison.

A different, somewhat more involved formulation of the same idea occurs in the second stanza. The reader's attention is drawn to a familiar image of heroism—warriors returning home after battle. As a man of military rank, Lovelace includes himself in this valiant group; he speaks in the first person plural. The action being described is that of carefree, unconstrained drunkenness: "when thirsty grief in wine we steep / When healths and draughts go free." Lovelace examines the quality of such activity and contrasts it to that of "fishes that tipple in the deep". Fish, he seems to tell us, have no understanding of what is "freedom"; their drinking is compulsive. Men who serve in battle, on the other hand, have a measure of discrimination. Occasionally, at appropriate times of relaxation after the fight, they can afford to drink with abandon, for their heads are "crowned with roses", i.e. honor. They are loyal servants to the king.

In the third stanza, Lovelace applies his ideas directly to his own predicament. As a loyalist imprisoned for outspoken defense of the monarchy, he assumes a role which is comparable to that of "committed" or caged birds, particularly so-called "linnets" known for an extraordinary quality of song. Emanating from prison, the poet's voice maintains its freedom and becomes a powerful tool for political activism:

> When, like committed linnets, I
>   With shriller throat shall sing
> The mercy, sweetness, majesty
>   And glories of my King...

Following the pattern already established in the first two stanzas, Lovelace makes his point on the basis of a comparison. Antithetical to his own persuasion, is that of the "enlarged winds that curl the flood". At first glance, this image presents something of a problem: what are these winds? What do they stand for? The answer requires a measure of interpretation. One reasonable suggestion might be that the "winds" are the forces inciting revolt; they are the basic cause of insurrection leading towards lawlessness and barbarism. This interpretation would conform to the poet's general view of the political climate in England at the time, a climate which he feels is anarchic and does not attain the measure of true liberty.

Finally, Lovelace addresses the crucial issue: how do order and constraints serve to liberate mankind? In the fourth stanza, he tackles the paradoxical assertion in religio-philosophical terms. The prerequisite, he tells us, is "innocence" and "quiet". The mind that abides by these two criteria is ready to attain lofty heights under any conditions; for example, it will make prison a "hermitage", an opportunity for spiritual retreat and contemplation. It is within the confines of a philosophical approach to external circumstances that the individual comes to the basic realization that a lack of restrictions is degrading, while imposed limitations and control serve to uplift and dignify. In short, there appears to be no solid proof for Lovelace's idea; it is in some sense a circular concept. There remains only the possibility of taking the poet's word "on faith" and relying on his first-hand knowledge of the "angelic" reality. His voice, after all, is the voice of experience. It witnesses in a powerful way.—It comes to us from behind the bars of a prison cell.

Alfred, Lord Tennyson
(1809–1892)

The Charge of the Light Brigade

On one occasion during the Crimean War (1853-56), due to mistaken military orders, a brigade of British cavalry attacked a stronghold of Russian artillery. The doomed attack resulted in the massacre of more than three-quarters of the six-hundred-man armed force. After reading an account of this event in the *London Times*, Tennyson was moved to compose what was to become his famous poem, **The Charge of the Light Brigade**. Although this work has every element of a descriptive record, Tennyson's aim is to go beyond the boundaries of sheer historical fact and to transform tragic wartime headlines into lines of verse that are compelling and universally significant.

Unlike a newspaper reporter, whose approach is intentionally simple and matter-of-fact, Tennyson takes liberty to interpret the meaning of a seemingly irrational tragedy. Sacrificed to the clumsy machination of human error, the soldiers may appear to have been nothing more than victims of circumstance; to the observer of this historical event, the death of these men may seem unnecessary and lacking explanation. Tennyson, therefore, adopts a particu-

lar view: the tragic wartime maneuver must be seen as an
act of heroism.

Tennyson lends meaning to strategic blunder by en-
dowing the soldiers with extraordinary faith in military
command.

> Theirs not to make reply,
> Theirs not to reason why,
> Theirs but to do and die.

These poignant lines in the second stanza bring the point
home; they demonstrate the unquestioning nature of an
army brigade completely devoted to fulfilling the urgent
needs of a national cause. This is the principal virtue and
ultimate achievement of heroes in wartime struggle. At the
same time, the poet stresses the way in which the soldiers
carry out the task. Although it is clear that "Someone had
blundered", the fighters remain undaunted by evident error; on the contrary, their courage stands fast and their execution of orders is perfect: "Boldly they rode and well."

The real justification for such action, however, is
necessarily a religious one. This comes in the form of allusions to sacred imagery. In appealing to the soldiers' un-
swerving faith ("Was there a man dismayed?"), Tennyson
draws on a chivalric understanding of virtue: he finds a religious model for the secular convention of military obedience. The brigade is called "the Light Brigade" not
without reason; the image is that of a common phrase
coined to describe the Deity—"the Light of the World". It
is usually understood that this "Light" shines fearlessly in
a dark and hostile environment. Religious overtones are
further brought to bear in the metaphor of "the valley of
Death", an image originating in the following well-known
passage from Psalm 23:

The Lord is my shepherd, I shall not want;
He makes me lie down in green pastures.
He leads me beside still waters;
He restores my soul.
He leads me in paths of righteousness for his
   name's sake.
Even though I walk through the valley of the
   shadow of death, I fear no evil;
For Thou art with me;
Thy rod and They staff, they comfort me.
Thou preparest a table before me in the
   presence of my enemies;
Thou anointest my head with oil, my cup
   overflows.
Surely goodness and mercy shall follow me all
   the days of my life;
And I shall dwell in the house of the Lord
   forever.

Of course, the reader may question some of the reasoning behind Tennyson's religious model. The model, we might say, has evident limitations. In the first place, the Crimean War was not a "holy" war in the sense of a medieval campaign or crusade; it was only a war between temporal states. Therefore, the soldier bravely dying for his country is not necessarily a saint; he is a martyr of the State who attains glory, honor, and immortality primarily through recognition by fellow citizens. In other words, no religious conception can serve to vindicate the victims of an earthly struggle possibly characterized by immoral, selfish motives. The modern reader will no doubt have a special perspective on this matter; today's view of the military is colored especially by the gruesome realities of World War II, Vietnam, and other tragic conflicts in the course of which obedience to military orders was used many times to excuse measures

of abuse and brutality. The reader may also question the
validity of the Old Testament image of ''the valley''. In
the case of **The Charge of the Light Brigade**, does this
''valley'' really afford the benefits promised by the psalm
(''to dwell in the house of the Lord'')? Or, is the outcome
of riding ''into the valley'' nothing other than sheer
tragedy? Of course, Tennyson's main point is to grant
philosophical meaning to the wartime sacrifice. But then,
the questions remain: what kind of vindication can there be
if the soldiers nevertheless ride ''into the valley of
Death. . .into the jaws of Death. . .into the mouth of
hell. . .shattered and sundered''? Why does Tennyson build
up such a sequence of powerful images? And in the end,
why does he do nothing to dispel the sense of tragedy they
convey?

Elements in this poem also reveal Tennyson's desire to
evoke compassion on the part of the reader. The poet
wishes to speak in a way which is true to life and depicts
the sense of horror experienced by the cavalry. The repetitive nature of the lines thus serves to mirror the basic act
of riding into battle. To convey the headstrong, determined
rhythm of the horserider, Tennyson uses short lines composed chiefly of monosyllables:

> Half a league, half a league
> Half a league onward,
> All in the valley of Death
>   Rode the six hundred.
>
> *or*:
>
> Cannon to right of them,
> Cannon to left of them,
> Cannon in front of them
>   Volleyed and thundered.

The Charge of the Light Brigade is a poem which should be read with a breathless rush. Its particular use of words and phrases contributes to a powerful metaphor for human struggle, a struggle which is governed by forces beyond control. In view of this, an emphasis on heroism seems essential in dispelling a vision of complete helplessness. It suggests that, in the face of all that is frightening and dangerous, courage offers perhaps the only means to transcend the inevitability of approaching death.

IX

Tragedy and Humor

Preface

Dramatic, disastrous events profoundly influence the course of human life. "Youth," said the philosopher Alfred North Whitehead, "is life as yet untouched by tragedy"*—implying that no one escapes the experience. If nothing else, the inevitability of "death" is proof enough that everyone must at one time or another confront the ultimate reality.

The real difficulty, however, lies in the basic understanding that tragedy requires relief. Tragedy is a constant, universal presence. Its drama does not go by unnoticed and is a source of insistent concern for every individual. As a result, it is in the context of "a search for explanation" that man finds refuge in "humor"; the "comic interpretation" offers a uniquely accessible outlet for despair. In general, "meanings" and "solutions" for "the tragic" are not easy to uncover. Moreover, the quest for a moral lesson or conclusion is often exhausting and overwhelming. Throughout the centuries, as a result, "tragedy" and "humor" have become inseparable partners. Nowhere is this better evident than in the world of literature where the real impact of these two seemingly disparate spheres is perceived only in terms of a deeply-rooted sense of intense psychological contrast.

---

*Alfred North Whitehead, *Adventures of Ideas* (New York: The Macmillan Company, 1933), Chapter 20.

William Shakespeare
(1564–1616)

Macbeth (excerpts)

The way to read Shakespeare's plays is to learn, to some
small degree, how Shakespeare's mind works. Shakespeare
utilizes the power of imagination to form links between the
words we use in everyday speech, on one hand, and history, psychology, sociology, and other areas of human experience, on the other. That is to say, it is necessary to
recognize how Shakespeare is using language in his plays
to meditate upon the essential nature of civilization. The
rendering in immediate, tangible terms that which is abstract in our own thought is one of Shakespeare's unique
talents.

In the passages of **Macbeth**, act II, scenes I and II,
quoted in *The World's Best Poetry*, the theme of prosperity
versus destruction manifests itself in many ways and illustrates Shakespeare's multidisciplinary approach. The passage from act II, scene I, opens with the question, "Is this
a dagger which I see before me,/ The handle toward my
hand?", and the reader is drawn into Macbeth's psychological struggle over carrying out the murder of Duncan, King
of Scotland. The idea of murder is both repugnant and
compelling to him. Macbeth is compelled, in part, by the
power he envisions such a murder will afford him: "Come

let me clutch/ thee...", he says to the dagger. However, the act of murder and destruction of life weighs more heavily on him than his desire to rise politically: "It is the bloody business which informs/ Thus to mine eyes./ Now o'er the one half world/ Nature seems dead, and wicked dreams abuse/ the curtain'd sleep".

A similar conflict can be witnessed on another level if one focuses on the dagger, itself, as a tool. On a technological level, the dagger both thrusts civilization forward, protecting man and helping him to flourish, and sets civilization back through indiscriminate killing and destruction. Macbeth's conflict is a specific case of either potential: should he view the dagger as a tool for maximizing the opportunity of getting ahead or is it a weapon for seizing what is not rightfully his and destroying human life in the process? The correlation between the anthropological and the psychological issues revolving around the image of the dagger reveals Shakespeare's sensitivity to the fact that humanity's development throughout history can be witnessed by the type of tools it creates, the uses they are put to, and how those uses reflect upon the psychological state of both the culture and the individual. The soliloquy is certainly about Macbeth's individual ruminations, but the rich imagery suggests additional insights as well.

The theme of prosperity versus destruction develops further in act II, scene II, through the image of sleep. In this scene, in which Lady Macbeth and her husband meet after Macbeth has murdered Duncan, Macbeth says, "Methought I heard a voice cry/ "Sleep no more!/ Macbeth does murder sleep.../ Chief nourisher in life's feast". Sleep is the necessary complement to daytime activity; it renews and strengthens. As the state in which dreams dominate, sleep not only rejuvenates but allows a reformulation of one's past which either enables repressed (and possibly "barbaric") desires to be acted out in a harmless fashion or allows a deeper reorganization of stimuli that is coming into the brain. In this scene, the idea that "Macbeth does murder sleep" implies that Macbeth, and the barbarism which his character leans towards, is somehow involved in the destruction of these built-in mechanisms through which the human race regenerates itself. Shakespeare is portraying the tendency in human nature to sabotage those very resources which are necessary to the evolution of mankind and, again, illustrates the relationship between an issue that seems totally personal and the race as a whole through the image of sleep.

At the end of act II, scene I, Macbeth refers to the "...knell/ That summons thee to heaven, or to hell". The same can be said about the choice of moving toward destruction or toward prosperity facing Macbeth, in particular, and mankind, in general. When a shift in theology occurred around the eighth century B.C., away from the "eye for an Eye, tooth for a tooth," a new line of thought emphasizing mercy offered people an alternative. It is out of the conflict between these two modes of human response, one a primal response, the other a more considered and elevated response, that the central issues in *Macbeth* emerge.

Lewis Carroll
(1832–1898)

Jabberwocky

Although regarded by many as nonsensical, Lewis Carroll's **Jabberwocky** may well be one of the most serious
poems in the English language. It represents a bold experiment probing into dangerous territory. The poem explores
a precarious realm of semantics and raises provocative
questions concerning the nature of words, language, and
communication. This is immediately evident upon first
reading. A sudden encounter with thoroughly unfamiliar
nouns and adjectives conveys the fact that we are to deal
with remote quantities to which there is, at best, only par-
tial cognitive access. "Wabe" at the end of line two, for
example, may suggest "wave". But can one ever really be
sure? For, in view of the context dictated by the presence
of numerous other strange terms, the reader must continue
to leave all options open. We are inevitably left guessing.
Moreover, the question becomes: how does one penetrate
into the meaning of the poem? And, what is Carroll really
trying to tell us? The discovery is somewhat startling: although the poem retains a sense of grammatical logic, its
actual substance is elusive and hardly recognizable.

Language is intrinsically tied to the logic of thought.
As such, it consists of words or "quantities" placed into
orderly "clusters" or sentences. It is precisely this

rudimentary dimension of human communication that Carroll sets out to test. In **Jabberwocky**, the poet does away with the familiar ground of words and therefore leaves the reader "dangling" in a seemingly vacuous skeleton of grammatical syntax. To put it another way, we might say that Carroll "pulls the rug of everyday speech"; he deprives the reader of essential assumptions. He asks us, if only for a moment, to attempt existence without what is normally considered to be the secure nature of word definition.

To say the least, the outcome of Carroll's experiment is exciting. In particular, it suggests new avenues of approach to the world of poetry and to the way in which poets have intuitively implemented the methods of a highly sophisticated art of communication. In leading the reader to recognize how much more there is to language than just words, Carroll underscores the extent to which poetry is indebted to a strictly auditory dimension. Read, for example, the following selection aloud:

> Beware the Jabberwock, my son!
>   The jaws that bite, the claws that catch!
> Beware the Jubjub bird, the shun
>   The frumious Bandersnatch!

When forced to suspend conventional expectations, the reader thus indulges in the unusual experience of perceiving language as pure sound. The experience is much like that of hearing a foreign tongue.

Far from being a fabrication of sheer ridicule, therefore, **Jabberwocky** is a poem which invites careful study and analysis. Evidently, the work offers much of what is interesting and unusual. Among its main objectives is to catapult the reader into a realm of the unknown, and it is not surprising that much of its impact should rest on a somewhat violent-sounding word usage. It is as if to heighten the sense of ''disturbance'' that Carroll selects meaningless words with a characteristically harsh sound.

> The jaws that bite, the claws that catch
> The vorpal blade went snicker-snack!
> He left it dead, and with its head
> He went galumping back.

This kind of usage helps to buttress the poet's essential point. When taken in conjunction with an absence of meaning, it suggests the existence of a frightening surrounding—a territory which is unfamiliar, threatening, and is in fact the domain of an awful monster. Ironically, we might hypothesize that Carroll's attempt to convey a sense of danger is grounded in a thoroughly keen sense of reality. The world we live in is a threatening place and it can be argued that what the poet has done is to mirror a very real aspect of an intellectual and emotional environment which lies outside the sphere of rational comprehension.

Being trained in logic and mathematics, Lewis Carroll had an advanced intuition about the processes of language. In **Jabberwocky**, for example, he makes us smile. But the entertainment is hardly frivolous or trite. For Carroll succeeds in touching a sorely painful wound in our psyche; he makes us confront a world which is all too familiar and hidden deeply within the recesses of our consciousness. This is a disturbing world from which there is no obvious escape. In short, we should conclude, Lewis Carroll is fun to read. But one should never take him too lightly. Though considered a children's poet, he is undoubtedly an equal among the great masters.

Henry Wadsworth Longfellow
(1807–1882)

The Wreck of the Hesperus

Henry Wadsworth Longfellow, both as a poet and as a professor of literature and languages at Harvard during the nineteenth century, was one of the most important influences in his day upon cultural life in America. As America became established as an independent political entity at the end of the eighteenth century, Longfellow, like other Americans, became aware that we lacked the rich cultural heritage which Europeans enjoyed. Writers such as Herman Melville, Walt Whitman, and Emily Dickinson, in the second half of the nineteenth century, would create an independent and uniquely American point of view; however, Longfellow's solution was to study European literature and to incorporate into his work many of the traditional approaches while addressing distinctly American concerns. In his poem, **The Wreck of the Hesperus**, Longfellow calls into question the growing myth of self-reliance in America, derived from the desire to control and shape our lives in the face of natural interference, an orientation which we associate with the writings of Ralph Waldo Emerson as well as the Puritan instinct for survival in the seventeenth century New England wilderness.

The term "myth" has one of two corollary meanings: it is a story or fable which, though literally not true, expresses a people's fears and their attempt to feel secure in an overwhelming world, or it is a story which through a complex of elements evokes the supernatural or suprahuman.* The belief that there are forces beyond our control with which we need to find a means of coping, and the disaster that results from refusing to recognize that we cannot control some things are central issues in the poem.

Longfellow deals with these issues by creating a universe operating on two levels. One level is the world of man where adults live under the illusion of total control. The other level is the world of nature which can seem benign at times but which is really never under man's control. One method by which Longfellow links both worlds and adds new significance to straightforward events is through the use of metaphor, identifying one event with something not ordinarily associated with it. For example, in the second stanza, the daughter's cheeks are "like the dawn of day,/ And her bosom white as the hawthorn buds,/ That ope in the month of May". The imagery suggests gentleness operating in both the world of man and the world of nature. In the first three stanzas of the poem, there is a sense of calm and control. The skipper has "sailed the wintry sea" and is experienced. He has even taken his daughter along with him for company, as if he expects this to be another uneventful expedition.

However, as the poem progresses the sense of tranquility starts to breakdown; there is a tension created between man's world and the world of nature. Though the skipper in stanza five responds to the news of an impending hurri-

---

*Alex Preminger, ed., *Princeton Encyclopedia of Poetry and Poetics* (Princeton: Princeton University Press, 1972), pp. 538-541.

cane with "a scornful laugh", in stanza seven the ship becomes "like a frightened steed" that "leaped her cable's
length". After the skipper gives his "scornful laugh", nature is never described in a solely hospitable way again. In
stanza six when "yeast" is used in a simile, it is not as a
raw material that will help create sustenance but as a part
of "billows froth[ing]". Similarly, in stanza eighteen,
when the ship is drifting on the sea, the waves "looked
soft as carded wool" but rather than providing comfort or
protection, they harbor "cruel rocks [that] gored her side".

Despite all the signs in stanzas six and seven that the
skipper should not try to weather this storm, he does not
heed them but rather asserts that he "can weather the
roughest gale/ That ever wind did blow". At the beginning
of stanza eight when the skipper assures his daughter that
everything is under his control with "Come hither! come
hither...", he is addressing both the "steed/ship" and his
daughter, condensing for the reader his desire to control
both the destiny of his ship against nature's forces and his
daughter's psychological state. However, it is nature and
the "angry sea" that maintains primacy in every area the
skipper wished to control. The skipper becomes a "frozen
corpse" the ship sinks, the daughter and the crew are
thrown into the sea, and the use of "glass" or "icicle"
imagery in stanzas thirteen, seventeen and nineteen suggest
the ultimate frailty of all mortal existence.

translated by William Collins

"Women's Chorus" from Aristophanes' The Thesmophoriazusae

In Aristophanes' comic play, *The Thesphoriazusae*, the women of Athens are gathered in protest of the insulting way their gender had been portrayed in Euripides' tragedies, and are in agreement that the poet should be punished by death. Mnesilochus, Euripides' father-in-law, tries to intercede on behalf of the poet by infiltrating the protest in the guise of a woman. But, the defense he constructs for his son-in-law, by pointing out the many feminine evils Euripides had tactfully excluded, is so inflammatory that during the ensuing pandemonium, Mnesilochus' true identity is found out. As this impudence is being reported to the authorities, the women console their battered egos by coming to their own defense. It is this passage from Aristophanes' play that William Collins has crystalized into the pointed verse entitled **Women's Chorus**. But, even without the knowledge of the poem's context in the play, it is not especially difficult to understand; its humorous twist reads like a paraphase of the old aphorism regarding women (provided it is a man who is speaking): "can't live

with them; can't live without them." A closer examination
of this poem does not contradict this simple explication,
but uncovers how truly clever this work is.

According to the play, the Athenian women are infuri-
ated by the unfair portrayal of them given by Euripides in
his famed tragedies. The fact that these women are using
an art form to redress this issue demonstrates that this
poem is written with a greater sense of self-consciousness
than may have initially been supposed. What appears to be
a flippant verse dealing with a somewhat tired and clichéd
theme is actually a fascinating piece of rhetoric designed as
a "logical proof" of women's superiority to men.

Contributing to the effectiveness of the argument is a
deceptively obvious point—the matter of emphasis. Instead
of answering the accusations made specifically of them,
they place the rationality of the accusors in question. This
makes a stronger case against all slanders (whether true or
false) that are being made at the present time or will be
made at some time in the future. The argument itself is
based on a rhetorical substitution, "plague" for "women,"
which had been suggested by certain men who are referred
to in the poem as "they." "They" seem to have thought
that "as a terrible Plague" is an accurate description of
women in general; and yet, it is apparent that "they" are
just as likely to be attracted to, fall in love with, become
jealous of, feel protective of, and even miss the presence
of the same. Therefore, the women use this insult to expose the logical inconsistence between what men say and
the way in which they behave. Because ancient Greek
thought did not tend to sentimentalize the emotions, reason
was considered to be the apex of the human condition.
Thus, the women, demonstrating the irrationality of men,
show themselves to be much closer to that human ideal.

However, an aspect of the poem which is more interesting than the clever sophistry designed to convince us that one gender is superior to the other, is the psychology behind why men would habitually subject their wives, sisters, mothers and daughters to verbal abuse. The inconsistencies of these men toward women may appear irrational, but not necessarily without explanation. To describe men, as they are described in the poem, as belittling women in general while acting as if women are the most important part of their lives, make men seem foolish. Yet, this contradiction is understandable when reordered to read like this: women have a powerful effect on men that men can neither understand nor control; therefore, men try to compensate for this feeling of helplessness by objectifying and vilifying women. The use of the word "plague," as opposed to some other derogatory word, supports this interpretation. A plague, after all, is experienced as an impersonal and destructive force which men neither can control nor understand. The parallels are too close to be accidental.

In spite of the sober reality suggested by the **Women's Chorus** it remains a comic piece. The poem uses logical inversions which are typically humorous; and because an element of truth that had transcended ancient Athenian society is to be found, we find the poem funnier still, and clever to be sure, but not without a hint of irony.

Bibliography

Secondary Material (by Period).

A. CLASSICAL

Cambridge Ancient History, ed. S.A. Cook et al., 1923-39.; 2 ed. 1961.
Hall, F. W., *A Companion to Classical Texts*, 1913.
Halporn, J. et al., *The Meters of Greek & Latin Poetry*, 1963.
Jones, H. Stuart, *Companion to Roman History*, 1912.
Lindsay, W. M., *Early Latin Verse*, 1922.
Maas, P., *Greek Metre* (tr. H. Lloyd-Jones) 1962.
Oxford Classical Dictionary, 2nd ed. 1970.
Raven, D. S., *Latin Metre*, 1965.
Rose, H. J., *Handbook of Greek Literature from Homer to Age of Lucian*, 1957.
Whibley, L., *A Companion to Greek Studies*, 1931.
Feder, L., *Crowell's Classical Handbook*, 1980.
Graves, R., *The Greek Myths*, 2v. 1960.

B. MEDIAEVAL

Beale, W. H., *Old & Middle English Poetry*, Detroit 1976.
Matthews, W., *Old & Middle English Literature*, NY 1968.
Zesmer, D. M., *Guide to English Literature from Beowulf to Chaucer*, NY 1961.
Ackerman, R. W., *Backgrounds to Medieval English Literature.*, NY 1966.
Bloomfield, M. W., *The Seven Deadly Sins*, E. Lansing 1952.
Gradon, P., *Form & Style in Early English Literature.*, London 1971.

Ker, W. P., *Epic & Romance*, London 1908, 1957.
Paetow, L. J., *Guide to Study of Medieval History*. NY 1917, 1959.
Reynolds, L. D. & N. G. Wilson, *Scribes & Scholars*, Oxford 1968.

C. *RENAISSANCE*

Allen, J. W., *History of Political Thought in the Sixteenth Century*, London 1928.
Bindoff, S. T., *Tudor England*, Harmondsworth 1950.
Byrne, M. S., *Elizabethan Life in Town & Country*, London 1961.
Cassirer, E., *The Individual & the Cosmos in Renaissance Philosophy.*, Oxford 1963.
Dobson, E. J. *English Prounciation 1500-1700*, 2v. Oxford, 1957.
Elton, G. R., *England Under the Tudors*, 1962.
Knights, L. C., *Drama & Society in the Age of Jonson*, London 1937.
Kokeritz, H., *Shakespeare's Pronunciation*, New Haven 1953.
Kristeller, P., *Renaissance Thought*, 2v. NY 1961-65.
Lovejoy, A. O., *The Great Chain of Being*, Cambridge, Massachusetts 1936.
Wilson, J. D., *Life in Shakespeare's England*, London 1911.

D. *SEVENTEENTH CENTURY*

Ashley, M., *Life in Stuart England*, London 1967.
Butterfield, H., *Origins of Modern Science 1300-1800*, rev. London 1957.

Haller, W., *Rise of Puritanism 1570-1642*, NY 1938.

Gardner, H., *The Metaphysical Poets*, Harmondsworth 1957.

Grierson, H., & G. Bullough, *Oxford Book of Seventeenth Century Verse*, Oxford , 1934.

Lewalsker, B. K. & A. J. Sabol, *Major Poets of Earlier Seventeenth Century*, NY 1973.

Muir, K., *Eliz & Jacobean Prose 1550-1620*, Harmondsworth 1956.

Tayler, E. W., *Seventeenth Century Literature Criticism.* NY 1969.

Warnke, F. J., *European Metaphysical Poetry*, NY 1961.

White, H. C. & R. C. Wallerstein, R. B. Quintana, *Seventeenth Century Verse & Prose*, NY 1951.

E. RESTORATION & EIGHTEENTH CENTURY

Allen, B. S., *Tides of English Taste 1619-1800*, 2v. 1937.

Bate, W. J., *The Burden of the Past & the English Poet*, 1970.

Clark, G., *The Later Stuarts 1660-1714*, 1956.

Foucault, M., *Madness & Civilization: History of Insanity in Age of Reason*, 1965.

Fussell, P., *The Rhetorical World of Augustan Humanism*, 1965.

George, M. D., *English Social Life in the Eighteenth Century*, 1923.

Hart, J., *Political Writers of the Eighteenth Century*, NY 1964.

Johnson, S., *The Works of the English Poets*, 68v. London 1779-81.

Peake, C., *Poetry of the Landscape & the Night*, London, 1967.

Pinto, V. de s., *Poetry of Restoration 1653-1700,* NY 1966.

Quintana, R. & A. Whitley, *English Poetry of Mid & Late Eighteenth Century,* NY 1964.

F. ROMANTIC

Beach, J. W., *The Concept of Nature in Nineteenth Century English Poetry,* 1936.

Briggs, A., *The Making of Modern England: 1783-1867,* 1959.

Frye, N. (ed)., *Romanticism Reconsidered,* 1963.

Halevy, E., *The Liberal Awakening,* 1815-30, rev. 1949.

Williams, R., *Culture & Society 1780-1950,* 1960.

Bernbaum, E., *Anthology of Romanticism* 5v. rev. 1948-9.

Milford, H. S., *Oxford Book of English Romantic Verse,* Oxford 1934.

Bowra, C. M., *The Romantic Imagination,* London 1950.

Bloom, H., *The Visionary Company,* rev. 1971.

Lucas, F. L., *Decline & Fall of Romantic Ideal,* Cambridge 1936.

G. AMERICAN LITERATURE

Spiller, Robert E., et al., eds. *Literary History of the United States.* 4th ed. 2 vols. New York, 1974.

Miller, Perry. *The New England Mind: From Colony to Province.* Cambridge, Mass., 1953.

Matthiessen, F. O. *American Renaissance.* New York. 1941.

Krapp, G. P. *The English Language in America.* 2 vols. New York, 1925.

Pearce, R. H. *The Continuity of American Poetry.* Princeton, 1961.

Waggoner, H. H. *American Poets from the Puritans to the Present Day.* Boston, 1968.

Gelpi, A. *The Tenth Muse: The Psyche of the American Poet.* Cambridge, Mass., 1975.

Jones, Howard Mumford. *The Theory of American Literature.* 2nd ed. Itahca, 1965.

H. BRITISH VICTORIAN & EDWARDIAN

Altick, R. D., *Eng. Common Reader 1800-1900,* Chicago 1957.

Cockshut, A. O., *The Unbelievers: English Agnostic Thought 1840-90, 1964.*

Irvine, W., *Apes, Angels, & Victorians,* London 1955.

Strachey, L., *Eminent Victorians,* London 1918.

Evans, M. R., *Anthology of Victorian Verse,* London 1949.

Hayward, J., *Nineteenth Century Poetry,* London 1932.

Miles, A. H., *Poets & Poetry of Nineteenth Century,* 12v. London 1905-7.

Miller, G. M., *English Literature: Victorian Period,* NY 1930.

Quiller-Couch, A. T., *Oxford Book of Victorian Verse.,* Oxford 1912.

Biographical Data
On Poets

Biographical Data On Poets Included in the Foundation Volumes and in Supplements I and II

Abercrombie, Lascelles (1881-1938) English poet, critic, and scholar.

Exponent of Georgian movement in poetry. Included in the Oxford Poets Series in his lifetime.

Adam, Jean (1710-1765) Scottish schoolmistress.

Works include: "There's nae luck about the house."

Adams, Charles Follen (1842-1918) American poet.

Descendant of revolutionary patriot Samuel Adams. Produced many poems in German dialect. Works include: "Hans and Fritz"; "Der Oak und der Vine."

Adams, John Quincy (1767-1848) American President.

Defended Washington's policy of neutrality under the signature "Marcellus." Appointed Minister to the Hague by Washington. Works include: "The Lip and the Heart"; "To Sally."

Adams, Leonie (b. 1899) American poet.

Received the Bollinger Prize in 1955. Combines the metaphysical and the romantic in her poetry. Works include: "Bell Tower"; "Home Coming."

Adams, Sara Flower (1805-1849) English hymn writer and poet.

Works include: "Vivia Perpetua" (1841); "Nearer My God to Thee."

Addison, Joseph (1672-1790) English essayist.

Wrote humorous character sketches in the satirical publication *The Spectator.* Works include: "A Letter From Italy"; "Cato"; "The Campaign."

A.E. (see Russell, George William)

Aeschylus (525-456 B.C.) Greek tragic poet.

Works include: *The Trilogy Orestes; Prometheus Bound; Agamemnon.*

Agathias (about 536-581 B.C) Greek poet and historian.

Works include: *Cycle; Epigrams; History Years* (553-558).

Aiken, Conrad (1889-1973) American poet.

Won the Pulitzer Prize in 1929 for *Selected Poems*. Works include: *Earth Triumphant; The Jig of Froslin; The Charnel Rose; The House of Dust.*

Ainslee, Hew (1792-1878) Scottish songwriter and poet.

Emigrated to America. Remembered for *Pilgrimage to the Land of Burns.*

Akenside, Mark (1721-1770) English doctor.

Studied originally for the Presbyterian ministry. Published several medical essays. Works include: "The Pleasures of Imagination"; "Against Suspicion."

Akerman, Lucy Evelina (1816-1874) American poet.

Works include: "Nothing but Leaves."

Akers, Elizabeth ["Florence Percy"] (1832-1911) American poet.

Works include: *Forest Birds*; "Rock Me to Sleep"; "Mothers."

Aldrich, James (1810-1856) American poet.

Gained attention through Poe's comments on his poem, "A Death Bed."

Aldrich, Thomas Bailey (1836-1907) American author, editor, and essayist.

Edited *Every Saturday* and *The Atlantic Monthly*. Works include: *Marjorie Daw; Other People.*

Alexander, Cecil Frances (1818-1895) Irish poet.

Wrote sacred poetry. Works include: "The Burial of Moses"; "There Is a Green Hill Far Away."

Alger, William Rounseville (1822-1905) American Unitarian clergyman and writer.

Principal works include: *A History of the Doctrine of a Future Life; Genius of Solitude; Friendships of Women.*

Allingham, William (1824-1889) Irish poet and editor.

Edited *Fraser's Magazine* in 1874. Noted for descriptions of Irish life and scenery. Works include: "Lawrence Bloomfield in Ireland"; "Day and Night Songs"; "Wild Rose."

Allston, Washington (1779-1843) American painter and poet.

Works include: "Monaldi"; *The Sylph of Seasons and Other Poems; Lectures on Art and Poems.*

Altenburg, Michael (1583-1640) German poet. Works include:

"Battle-Song of Gustavus Adolphus" (translation).

Ames, Mary Clemmer (see Hudson, Mary Clemmer Ames)

Anacreon (1562?-1477 B.C) Greek poet.

Composed odes in praise of wine and women under the patronage of Samos.

Anderson, Alexander ["Surfaceman"] (1845-1904) Scottish librarian.

Works include: "Cuddle Doon"; "Nottman."

Anster, John (1793-1867) Irish poet and professor of civil law.

Remembered for his translation of *Faust.*

Aristophanes (448-380 B.C.) Greek comic writer and poet.

Only eleven of his forty four plays still exist. Works include: *The Frogs; The Birds; The Clouds.*

Arndt, Ernest Moritz (1769-1860) German poet.

Kindled patriotic enthusiasm through his works "What Is the German Fatherland" and *Spirit of the Times.*

Arnold, Sir Edwin (1832-1904) English poet and journalist.

Inspired by Oriental themes and legends. Works include: "The Light of Asia"; "A Poetic Presentation of the Life and Teaching of Gautama" (1876).

Arnold, George (1834-1865) American poet and humorist.

Wrote for *New York Magazine.* Works include: *A Seashore Idyl and Others; Poems Grave and Gay.*

Arnold, Matthew (1822-1888) English poet, critic, and essayist.

A poet with classical roots. Works include: "Merope"; *New Poems; The Strayed Reveler.*

Attar, Farid-Uddin (1119-1230) Persian dervish and mystic.

Works include: *The Welcome; Biography of the Saints.*

Auden, Wystan Hugh (1907-1973) English poet.

Greatly influenced younger poets and artists. Lived a great portion of his later life in the United States. Received the Pulitzer Prize in 1948 for "The Age of Anxiety." Other works include: "Journal of an Airman"; "Paid on Both Sides"; "Look Stranger!"

Auslander, Joseph (b. 1897) American poet.

Pioneered a new kind of travel book which followed a poet's

pilgrimage through the world of literature. Works include: *Sunrise Trumpets Cyclop's Eyes; Hell in Harness; Letters to Women.*

Austin, Alfred (1835-1913) English editor and poet.

Edited the *National Review* (1883-93). Appointed Poet Laureate of England (1896). Works include: "The Tower of Babel"; "Savonarola"; "Veronica's Garden."

Austin, Sara Taylor (1793-1867) English poet.

Translated "The Passage" (German of Uhland).

Averill, Anna Boynton (n.d.) American poet.

Wrote "The Birch Stream."

Ayton (or Aytoun), Sir Robert (1570-1638) Scottish editor and writer.

Works include: "Woman's Inconsistencies"; "I Loved Thee Once."

Aytoun, William Edmonstoune (1813-1865) Scottish poet and writer.

Contributed to *Blackwood's Magazine* and published *The Life and Times of Richard I.* Most popular work: "Lays of the Scottish Cavaliers."

Bacon, Francis, Baron Verulam (1561-1626) English statesman, philosopher, and Viscount St. Albans.

Espoused a philosophy based on the observation of nature. Affected a profound change in the manner of education. Works include: *Essays* or *Sermones Fideles.*

Bacon, Leonard (1802-1881) American clergyman, professor, and abolitionist.

Taught didactic theology at Yale. Published reviews, pamphlets, and theological and historical pieces. Works include: "Night Laughter"; "The Day of Slaves."

Bailey, Philip James (1816-1902) English poet and barrister.

Wrote a dramatic poem based on Faust entitled "Festus." Works include: "The Angel World"; "The Mystic"; "The Age."

Baillie, Joanna (1762-1851) Scottish poet.

A friend of Sir Walter Scott who greatly admired her writing. Best known work: *Plays on the Passions.*

Baker, George Augustus (b. 1849) American lawyer and writer.

Wrote verse and stories. Works include: *Point Lace and Diamonds; Bad Habits of Good Society.*

Ballantine, James (1808-1877) Scottish artist and poet.

Studied drawing under Sir William Allen. Revived the art of glass painting. Works include: "Castles in the Air"; "Creep Afore Ye Gang."

Banin, John (1798-1842) Irish novelist, dramatist, and poet.

Famous for the *O'Hara Tales.* Major novels: *The Nowlans; Boyne Water; The Croppy.*

Banks, George Linnaeus (1821-1881) English journalist.

Works include: "What I Live For"; "My Aim."

Barbauld, Anna (1743-1825) English poet and essayist.

A friend of Sir Walter Scott and William Wordsworth. Wrote a fifty volume edition of the best English novels. Works include: "The Doll's House"; "Ode to Spring."

Barbier, August (1805-1882) French poet and satirist.

Works include: *The Iambles.*

Barclay, Alexander (1475-1552) Scottish Roman Catholic priest.

Translated Brandt's *Ship of Fools.*

Barham, Richard Harris (1788-1845) English humorist.

Wrote for periodical edited by Dickens. Achieved huge success with *Ingoldsby Legends.*

Baring-Gould, Sabine (1834-1924) English novelist.

Wrote prolifically on religion, history, romance, and archaeology. Works include: *The Book of the Werewolves; Curious Myths of the Middle Ages; Lives of the Saints.*

Barker, Edward (n.d.) American poet.

Works include: "Go to Sleep, Ma Honey."

Barker, George (b. 1913) English romantic poet.

Works include: "Epistle I"; "The Leaping Laughters"; "Sonnet to My Mother."

Barlow, George (1847-1913) English poet.

Works include: "The Old Maid"; "The Soul."

Barlow, Jane (1857-1917) Irish poet.

Works include: *Irish Idylls; Bogland Studies; Kerrigan's Quality.*

Barnard, Lady Anne (1750-1825) Scottish poet.

Known for "Auld Robin Gray" (1772).

Barnes, William (1800-1886) English poet and philologist.

Wrote books on philology and poems on English rural life.

Barr, Amelia Edith (1831-1919) British/American novelist.

Works include: *Romance and Reality* (1872); *Jan Vedder's Wife* (1885); *A Sister of Esau* (1891).

Barry, Michael Joseph (1817-1889) Irish editor.

Works include: "The Place Where Man Should Die"; "The Sword."

Barton, Bernard (1784-1849) English poet.

Known as "The Quaker Poet." A friend of Charles Lamb. Works include: "Bruce and the Spider"; "Caractacus"; "The Sea."

Bates, Arlo (1850-1918) American author and professor of English literature.

Works include: "The Pagans"; "A Lad's Love"; "The Wheel of Fire"; "The Philistines."

Bates, Charlotte Fiske ["Mme. Roge"] (1838-1916) American poet.

Assisted Longfellow in compiling *Poems of Places*. Works include: "The Living Book"; "Andre."

Bax, Clifford (1886-1962) English author and playwright.

Wrote frequently on historical themes. Works include: *Some I Knew Well; Evening in Albany; Ideas and People.*

Bayly, Thomas Haynes (1797-1839) English novelist and songwriter.

Achieved success as a ballad writer. Works include: *The Aylmers; Perfection.*

Beattie, James (1734-1803) Scottish professor of moral philosophy.

Wrote metaphysical essays and poems. Chief work: "The Minstrel."

Beatty, Pakenham Thomas (b. 1855) English poet.

Works include: "When Will Love Come?"

Beaumont, Francis (1584-1616) English dramatist.

A contemporary of Shakespeare. Collaborated with John Fletcher. Works include: "In Westminster Abbey"; "The Indifferent."

Beddoes, Thomas Lowell (1803-1849) English physiologist and politician.

Lived in Germany and Switzerland. Works include: *The Bride's Tragedy; Death's Jest Book.*

Beers, Ethelinda Elliott ["Ethel Lynn"] (1827-1879) American poet.

Works include: *All Quiet Along the Potomac and Other Poems* (1879).

Beers, Henry Augustin (1847-1926) American professor.

Taught English literature at Yale. Works include: *A Century of American Literature; A History of English Romanticism; Poems.*

Belloc, Hilaire (1870-1953) English author.

Catholic advocate and writer of essays, satire, poetry, and historical pieces. Works include: *A History of England; The Battleground; The Bad Child's Book of Beasts; Verses and Sonnets.*

Benet, Stephen Vincent (1898-1943) American poet.

Won the Pulitzer Prize in 1929 for "John Brown's Body." Works include: *Five Men and Pompey; Heavens and Earth; Tiger Joy.*

Benet, William Rose (1886-1950) American poet.

Older brother of Stephen Vincent Benet. Helped establish *Literary Review* of the *New York Evening Post,* which became the *Saturday Review of Literature* in 1924.

Benjamin, Park (1809-1864) American journalist, poet, and lecturer.

Works include: *The Contemplation of Nature; Poetry and Infatuation.*

Bennett, G. (n.d.)

Works include: "The Time for Prayer."

Bennett, Henry Holcomb (1863-1924) American magazine writer.

Works include: "The Flag Goes By."

Bennett, Lucy Ann (1850-1927) English poet.

Works include: "Asleep, Asleep."

Bennett, William Cox (1820-1895) English poet and songwriter.

Works include: "The Trial for Salamis"; "Soup for Sailors"; "Sea Songs."

Benton, Joel (1832-1911) American journalist, poet, and author.

Works include: "Another Washington"; "The Scarlet Tanager."

Benton, Myron B. (1834-1902) American farmer and writer.

Works include: "Midsummer Invitation"; "The Mowers."

Beranger, Pierre Jean de (1780-1857) French national poet.

Wrote satires. Works included: "The Daughter of the People"; "Falling Stars."

Berkeley, George (1684-1753) Irish clergyman, author, and philosopher.

Wrote numerous philosophical, religious, and politico-economical pieces. Works include: *Treatise on the Principles of Human Knowledge; Three Dialogues Between Hylas and Philonous; Alciphron, or the Minute Philosopher.*

Bernard of Cluny ["Bernard de Morlaix"] (1122-1156) French Benedictine monk and poet.

Noted for "On Contempt of the World."

Berryman, John (1914-1972) American poet.

Received the Guggenheim Fellowship (1952) and the Pulitzer Prize (1965) for *Seventy Seven Dreams.* Works include: "Canto Amor"; "The Spinning Heart"; *His Toy, His Dream, His Rest.*

Bethune, George Washington (1805-1862) American orator.

Works include: *British Female Poets; Lays of Love and Faith.*

Betjeman, John (1906-1984) English poet.

Modeled himself after 19th century poets. Respected by critics and other poets for his skill.

Binyon, Laurence (1869-1943) English poet.

Deputy Keeper of Oriental prints in the British Museum. Won the Newdigate Prize in 1890. Works include: *Primavera.*

Bishop, Elizabeth (1911-1979) American poet.

Acquired a devoted following of readers, poets, and critics. Works are characterized by precise poetic descriptions. Works include: "A Cold Spring"; "From the Country to the City."

Bishop, John Peale (1892-1944) American poet.

Close friends with Pound, Hemingway, and Fitzgerald. Highly regarded by critics and writers. Works include: *Now With His Love; Act of Darkness; Minute Particulars.*

Bjornson, Bjornstjerne (1832-1910) Norwegian novelist, dramatist, and poet.

Established his reputation with "Synnove" (1857) and "Arne"

(1858). Works include: *Poems and Songs* (1870).

Blackie, John Stuart (1809-1895) Scottish author, poet, and professor of Greek.

Taught at Edinburgh University, promoted educational reform, championed Scottish nationality. Works include: *Lays of the Highlands and Islands; Wisdom of Goethe; Life of Burns.*

Blackmore, Richard Dodridge (1825-1900) English novelist.

Published a version of Virgil's *Georgics.* Achieved success with *Lorna Doone.*

Blackmur, Richard Palmer (1904-1965) American poet and critic.

Works include: *From Jordan's Delight; The Second World; The Good European and Other Poems.*

Blake, William (1757-1827) English artist and poet.

Was attracted equally by painting and poetry. Invented and published his own method of printing. Works include: *Songs of Innocence; The Marriage of Heaven and Hell.*

Blamire, Susanna (1747-1794) English poet.

Works include: "The Siller Crown"; "What Ails This Heart O' Mine."

Blanchard, Lamon (1804-1845) English journalist and humorist.

Works include: "The Mother's Hope"; "The Ode to the Human Heart."

Bland, Robert (1766-1823) English clergyman.

Works include: "Home" (Greek of Leonidas); "Memory and Oblivion" (Greek of Macedonius); "Time's Revenge" (Greek of Agathias).

Blind, Mathilde (1847-1896) German critic and poet.

Works include: *The Prophesy of St. Oran and Other Poems; Life of George Eliot; Madame Roland.*

Blood, Henry Ames (1838-1900) American poet.

Works include: "Song of the Savoyards."

Blunden, Edmund (1896-1974) English poet.

World War I poet influenced by Thomas Hardy. Wrote books and articles on English history and literature.

Blunt, Wilfred Scawen (1840-1922) English poet.

Works include: *Sonnets and Songs by Proteus; Ideas about India.*

Bodenheim, Maxwell (1893-1954) American writer.

Works include: *Lights in the Valley; Selected Poems; My Life and Loves in Greenwich Village* (autobiography).

Bodenstedt, Friedrich Martin Von (1819-1892) German journalist and poet.

Works include: *Poetic Ukraine; The People of the Caucasus and Their Struggle for Freedom Against the Russians; From the Atlantic to the Pacific.*

Bogan, Louise (1897-1970) American poet.

Contributed book reviews and criticism to the New Republic. Works include: *Body of This Death; Dark Summer.*

Boker, George Henry (1823-1890) American poet and dramatist.

Minister to Turkey (1871) and Russia (1875). Plays include: *Calaynos; Anne Boleyn; Francesca di Rimini.* Poems include: *Poems of the War; The Book of the Dead; Sonnets.*

Bolton, Sara Knowles (1841-1916) American editor and writer.

Works include: *Her Creed; The Inevitable* and *Other Poems.*

Bolton, Sara Tittle (1815-1893) American author.

Organized various reforms, notably property rights for women. Works include: "Paddle Your Own Canoe"; "Songs of a Lifetime"; *Left on the Battlefield.*

Bonar, Horatius (1808-1889) Scottish hymnist.

Member of the Free Church. Wrote more than twenty volumes on religion. Works include: *Hymns of Faith and Hope.*

Boner, John Henry (1845-1903) American editor.

Works include: *Whispering Pines; Sparrow in the Snow.*

Bottomley, Gordon (1874-1948) British dramatist and poet.

Won the Femina-Vie Heureuse Prize (1923). Works include: *Gruach.*

Bouricault, Dion (1822-1890) Irish dramatist and actor.

Works include: *Love in a Maze; Used Up, After Dark; Rescued; Wearing of the Green.*

Bourdillon, Francis William (1852-1921) English educator.

Works include: "The Night Has a Thousand Eyes"; *Nephele; Among the Flowers and Other Poems.*

Bowen, Sir Charles (1835-1894) English writer.

Works include: "The Fall of Troy" (Latin of Virgil).

Bowen, John Eliot (1858-1890) American editor.

Works include: "Fodder-Time" (German of Carmen Sylvia).

Bowles, Caroline Anne (1787-1854) English poet.

Works include: "The Greenwood Shrift"; "The Young Gray Head"; "The Cuckoo Clock."

Bowles, William Lisle (1762-1850) English poet.

Influenced Wordsworth and Coleridge with his 1789 Sonnet Series. Works include: "The Grave of Howard"; "Coombe Ellen"; "The Battle of the Nile"; "The Spirit of Discovery."

Bowring, Sir John (1792-1872) English linguist, author, and diplomat.

Edited the Westminister Review (1825). Works include: anthologies of Polish, Serbian, Cheskian, and Magyar poetry and writings on travel, politics, and religion.

Brainard, John Gardiner Calkins (1796-1828) American journalist and poet.

Graduated from Yale University. Edited and wrote for Connecticut Mirror. Works include: "Niagra"; "Connecticut River."

Branch, Anna Hempstead (1875-1937) American journalist and poet.

Established the International Poetry Society. Wrote a series of brief plays for children.

Branch, Mary Lydia Bolles (1840-1922) American author.

Works include: "The Petrified Fern."

Brandt, Sebastian (1828-1857) Irish journalist.

Works include: "Come to Me Dearest."

Breton, Nicholas (1545-1626) English poet.

Wrote satires, romances, lyrical, pastoral, and religious poetry.

Bridges, Madeline (See Devere, Mary Ainge)

Bridges, Robert ["Droch"] (1858-1941) American poet and editor.

Works include "For a Novel of Hall Caine's"; "The Unilluminated Verge"; "Overheard in Arcady."

Bridges, Robert Seymour (1844-1930) English physician and poet laureate.

Poems written as poet laureate appear in *October and Other Poems* (1913). Works include:

"Asian Birds"; "The Sea Poppy"; "So Sweet Love Seemed."

Brooke, Rupert (1887-1915) English poet.

Celebrated patriot-soldier-poet, killed in action in France during World War I. Works include: "The Busy Heart"; "The Great Lover"; "1914."

Brooks, Charles Timothy (1813-1883) American Unitarian minister, translator, and poet.

Gained renown as translator of German verse.

Brooks, Maria Gowen ["Maria Del Occidente"] (1795-1845) American poet.

Wrote an autobiography from "Idomen," or the "Vale of Yumuri," but is known for "Zophiel," or the "Bride of Seven."

Brooks, Phillips (1835-1893) American Episcopal Bishop of Massachusetts.

Published many volumes of sermons and lectures, notably *Letters of Travel; Lectures on Preaching; Essays and Addresses.*

Brown, Joseph Brownlee (1824-1888) American journalist.

Works include: "Thalatta! Thalatta!"

Brown, Sterling A. (b. 1901) American author.

Son of a former slave. His writings reflect his Black-American heritage. Works include: *The Negro in American Fiction; Negro Poetry and Drama.*

Brown, William Goldsmith (b. 1812) American editor and educator.

Works include: "The Hills Were Made for Freedom."

Browne, Frances (1818-1879) Irish poet.

Works include: "O, the Pleasant Days of Old."

Browne, William (1591-1643) English poet.

Noted for descriptions of English scenery. Works include: *Britannias Pastorals.*

Brownell, Henry Howard (1820-1872) American lawyer, poet, and historian.

Known for his war poems, written while in battle. Works include: "The River Fight"; "Bury Them."

Browning, Elizabeth Barrett (1809-1861) English poet.

Wife of Robert Browning. Their lives were celebrated in novels and plays. Works include: *Sonnets from the Portuguese.*

Browning, Robert (1773-1820)
English poet.

Influenced by Keats, Byron and
Shelley. Works include: "Rabbi
Ben Ezra"; "My Last Duch-
ess"; "Andrea Del Sarto."

Bryant, John Howard (1807-
1902) American farmer.

Works include: "The Little
Cloud"; "The Valley Brook";
"The Winter."

Bryant, William Cullen (1794-
1878) American lawyer, editor,
and poet.

Founded the *New York Review*
and edited the *Evening Post*
newspaper. Produced a translation of *The Iliad* and *The
Odyssey.*

Brydges, Sir Samuel Egerton
(1762-1837) English poet.

Works include: "Echo and
Silence."

Buchanan, Robert (1841-1901)
English dramatist, poet, and
novelist.

Works include: "The Ballad of
Judas Iscariot"; "Fra Gia-
como"; "The Little Milliner."

**Bulwer-Lytton, Edward George,
1st Baron Lytton** (1803-1873)
English novelist, dramatist, and
parliamentarian. Wrote prolifically, frequently on the occult.
Works include: *Last Days of*

*Pompeii; Last of the Barons;
Kenelm Chillingly.*

**Bulwer-Lytton, Edward Robert,
1st Earl of Lytton ["Meredith,
Owen"]** (1831-1891) English
diplomat and poet.

Viceroy of India and later ambassador to France. Works include: "Lucille"; "The Wan-
derers"; "Fables in Song";
"Glenaveril"; "King Poppy."

Bunyan, John (1628-1688) English preacher and author.

Imprisoned for dissent from the
established church. Works include: *The Pilgrim's Progress*
(1678).

Burdette, Robert Jones (1844-
1914) American lecturer and humorist.

Famous for humorous newspa-
per skits. Works include: "The
Rise and Fall of a Mustache";
"Chimes from a Jester's Bells."

Burger, Gottfried August (1747-
1794) German poet.

Established his reputation with
"Lenore" (1773). Works include: "The Parson's Daughters"; "The Wild Huntsmen";
"The Song of the Brave Man."

Burgess, Frank Gelett (1866-
1951) American humorist and
illustrator.

Famous for writing and illustrating nonsense rhymes. Works include: "The Bohemians of Boston"; "The Purple Cow."

Burleigh, William Henry (1812-1871) American journalist and lecturer on anti-slavery.

Wrote frequently on solitude. A friend of John Greenleaf Whittier. Works include: *Poems; The Rum Friend and Other Poems.*

Burns, Robert (1759-1796) Scottish national poet.

Known for writing in his native Scottish dialect. Works include: "Halloween"; "The Cotter's Saturday Night"; "To a Mouse"; "The Jolly Beggars."

Burroughs, John (1837-1921) American naturalist, journalist, and essayist.

Wrote frequently on rural themes. Works include: *Wake Robin; Winter Sunshine and Fresh Fields; Whitman, A Study; The Light of Day.*

Burton, Richard (1861-1940) American educator and author.

Works include: "Dumb in June"; "The Polar Quest"; "Memorial Day."

Busch, Wilhelm (1832-1908) German poet.

Wrote for a comic journal. Works include: "The Pious Helen"; "Max and Moritz."

Butler, Samuel (1612-1680) English secretary and satirist.

Studied music and painting. Gained instant success with "Hudibras" Part I (1663). "Hudibras" Parts II and III appeared in 1664 and 1678, respectively.

Butler, William Allen (1825-1902) American lawyer.

Famous for his humorous *Nothing to Wear*. Wrote legal books and biographies. Works include: *Martin Van Buren: Lawyer, Statesman, and Man.*

Butts, Mary Frances Barber (1836-1902) American poet.

Works include: "The Happy Hour."

Byers, Samuel Hawkins Marshall (1838-1933) American soldier, author, and consul.

Served in Union army and taken prisoner. Works include: *Switzerland; Military History of Iowa.*

Byron, George Noel Gordon, 6th Baron (1788-1824) English poet.

Established his reputation with "Childe Harold." Works include: "Don Juan"; "Manfred."

Calderon, Pedro de la Barca (1600-1681) Spanish dramatist.

Known for his heroic comedies. Works include: "Life Is a Dream"; "El Magico Prodigioso."

Call, Walthen Marks Wilkes (1817-1890) English reformer and writer.

Works include: "Summer Days"; "The People Petition."

Callimachus (3rd c. B.C.) Greek poet.

Wrote epics, tragedies, comedies, elegies, and hymns. Works include: "Hecale and Galatea"; "Timon's Epitaph."

Calverley, Charles Stuart (1831-1884) English poet and humorist.

Known for his verses and translations. Works include: "First Love"; "The Auld Wife"; "Idylls."

Camoens, Luis de (1524-1579) Portuguese soldier, poet, and adventurer.

Celebrated the glories of the Portuguese conquests in India with "Lusiad." Wrote sonnets, songs, epigrams, and dramas.

Campbell, Roy (1901-1957) South African lyric poet.

Became a controversial but popular figure with "The Flaming Terrapin." Works include: "African Moonrise"; "Rounding the Cape."

Campbell, Thomas (1777-1844) Scottish poet.

Achieved the height of fame with "Pleasures of Hope." Works include: "Ye Mariners of England"; "Hokenlinden"; "The Exile of Erin."

Campion, Thomas (1575-1619) English physician.

Known for the songs contained in the *Four Books of Airs*. Works include: "Come, Cheerful Day!"; "First Love."

Canning, George (1770-1827) English parliamentarian and orator.

Supported abolition of the slave-trade. Works include: "The Elderly Gentleman"; "The Soldier's Friend."

Canton, William (b. 1845) Irish journalist.

Works include: "Laus Infantium."

Carbery, Ethna (See MacManus, Anna Johnson).

Carducci, Giosue (1835-1907) Italian philologist and poet.

Works include: "The Decenniels"; "Serious Trifles."

Carew, Thomas (1598-1639) English poet.

A friend of Ben Jonson, Sir John Suckling, and Sir Kenneth

Digby. Wrote mostly songs and odes. Famous for *Caelum Britannacum*, which had Charles I in the cast.

Cary, Henry (1696-1743) English playwright and author.

Works include: "Sally in Our Alley"; "Namby Pamby"; *Hanging and Marriage*.

Carleton, Will (18459-1912) American poet.

Known for ballads on home life. Works include: *Poems; Farm Legends; City Ballads and City Legends*; "Over the Hill to the Poorhouse."

Carlyle, Thomas (1795-1881) Scottish biographer and historian.

Wrote biographies and articles for the Edinburgh Encyclopedia. Famous for Sartot. Works include: *The History of Frederick the Great; Shooting Niagra and After*.

Carman, Bliss (1861-1929) Canadian editor and poet.

Relative of Ralph Waldo Emerson. Founded the "open road" school of poetry. Works include: *Echoes of Vagabondia, Behind the Arras,* "An April Morning"; "Ballad of John Camplejohn."

Carnegie, Sir James, Earl of (1827-1905) Scottish poet.

Works include: "Kate Temple's Song"; "November's Cadence."

Carroll, Lewis [pseudonym] (see Dodgson, Charles Lutwidge)

Cary, Alice (1820-1871) American poet.

Works include: *Clover Nook or Recollections of Our Neighborhood in the West; Hagar; A Story of Today; Snow Berries*.

Cary, Henry Francis (1772-1844) English poet and translator.

Known for his translation of Dante's *Divine Comedy*.

Cary, Phoebe (1824-1871) American poet and hymn writer.

Sister of Alice, chiefly remembered for "Nearer Home." Works include: *Poems* (1849); *Poems and Parodies* (1854).

Casimer the Great (1309-1370) Polish king and patron of the arts.

Founded the University of Cracow (1364).

Works include: "It Kindles All My Soul."

Caswell, Edward (1814-1878) English poet and translator.

Works include: "My God, I Love Thee" (Latin of St. Francis Xavier); "Come Wandering Sheep"; "Sleep Holy Babe."

Catullus, Caius Valerius (84-54 B.C.) Roman lyric poet.

Friend of Cicero, Cinna, Plancus and Ovid. Works include: "Attis"; "Ave Atque Vale"; "Hymn to Diana."

Cawein, Julius Madison (1865-1814) American author.

Works include: *Blooms of the Berry* (1887); *The Triumph of Music* (1888); *Lyrics and Idyls* (1890).

Celano, Thomasa ["Tommaso da"] (fl. 1250) Italian writer.

Purported author of the Latin hymn "Dies Irae." Devoted to St. Francis of Assisi and wrote his biography.

Chadwick, John White (1840-1904) American clergyman and writer.

Attracted attention with his radical sermons. Works include: *A Book of Poems; Origin and Destiny; The Faith of Reason.*

Chalkhill, John [pseudonym] It is uncertain whether this name represents a friend of Izaak Walton or Walton himself.

Poems written under this name include: "The Angler"; "Oh the Brave Fisher's Life."

Chambers, Robert William (1865-1933) American artist.

Works include: *Common Law; The Sire Phillippa; War Paint and Rouge.*

Channing, William Ellery (1780-1842) American preacher and writer.

Attracted attention with a review of Milton's Treatise of Christian Doctrine and Life of Napolean. Other writings include sermons, reviews and tracts on war, temperance, education, and slavery.

Chapman, George (1558-1634) English poet, dramatist, and translator.

A classical scholar, translated Homer's Iliad and Odyssey. A friend of Spenser, Marlowe, Shakespeare. The subject of Keats' famous ode, "On First Looking into Chapman's Homer." Works include: "The Pilot"; "Praise of Homer."

Chateaubriand, Francois Auguste ["Viconte de"] (1769-1848) French statesman, novelist and historical writer. Works include: "Rene"; "The Natchez"; *A Journey from Paris to Jerusalem*; "Maid and Flower."

Chatterton, Thomas (1752-1770) English poet.

Works include: "Aella"; "The Death of Nicov"; "Goddwyn."

Chaucer, Geoffrey (1340-1400) English poet.

One of the greatest English poets, particularly for his masterpiece, *The Canterbury Tales*. Works include: *The Book of the Dutchess; Parlement of Foules*.

Cheney, John Vance (1848-1922) American librarian, poet, and essayist.

Works include: *Wood Blooms and Poems; The Happiest Heart; The Golden Guess*.

Cherry, Andrew (1762-1812) English poet.

Works include: "The Bay of Biscay"; "The Shamrock."

Chesterton, Gilbert Keith (1874-1936) English author.

A profilic writer and active Catholic, he co-founded New Witness magazine to speak against corrupt politics. Works include: the popular *Father Brown* detective stories, *The Man Who Was Thursday; Short History of England ; biographies of Robert Browning, Charles Dickens, and Chaucer*.

Chroley, Henry Fothergill (1808-1872) English writer and critic.

Works include: *Conti; The Prodigy; The Lion*.

Clare, John (1793-1864) English poet.

Works include: "The Shepherd's Calendar"; "Early

Nightingale"; "I Am"; "The Returned Soldier."

Clark, Willis Gaylord (1810-1873) American journalist and humorist.

Editor of *Knickerboker Magazine*; made it the leading literary magazine. Works include: "A Remembrance."

Clarke, Ednah Proctor (b. 1870) American poet.

Works include: "A Good-Bye"; "The Mockingbird"; "A Salem Witch."

Clark, James Freeman (1810-1888) American clergyman and author.

Known for *Ten Great Religions*. Prepared the memoirs of Margaret Fuller.

Claudius, Matthias (1740-1815) German poet and writer.

Chief work is *Complete Works of the Wandsbeck Messanger* (1775). Works include: "At My Father's Grave"; "The Most Acceptable Gift."

Cleanther (331-232 B.C) Greek Stoic philosopher.

Disciple and successor of Zeno. Best known for "Hymn to Zeus."

Cleland, William (d. 1689) English poet.

Works include: "Hallo, My Fancy."

Clemmer, Mary (see Hudson, Mary Clemmer Ames)

Clephane, Elizabeth Cecilia (1830-1869) Scottish poet.

Works include: "The Lost Sheep"; "The Ninety and Nine."

Cleveland, John (1613-1659) English poet.

Works include: "To The Memory of Ben Jonson"; "Mark Antony."

Clough, Arthur Hugh (1819-1861) English poet.

Works include: *Bothie of Toberna-Vuolich; Armours de Voyage; The Tragedy of Dipsychus.*

Coatsworth, Elizabeth J. (b. 1893) American poet.

Works include: "Fox Footprints"; "Atlas and Beyond"; "Compass Rose."

Coleridge, Hartley (1796-1849) English poet and critic.

Son of Samuel Taylor Coleridge. Works include: "From Country to Town"; "On Wordsworth"; "She Was a Queen."

Coleridge, Mary Elizabeth (1861-1907) English novelist and poet.

Works include: *Fancy's Following*; "Broken Friendship"; "Street Lanterns."

Coleridge, Samuel Taylor (1772-1834) English critic and poet.

An influencial and controversial figure, he was a major literary figure of his time. His best known work is "The Rime of the Ancient Mariner." Works include: "Christabel"; "Kubla Khan"; "Dejection: an Ode"; "Fears in Solitude"; "Zapolya."

Coles, Abraham (1813-1891) American physician.

Published thirteen original translations of "Dies Irae." Works include: "The Microcosm"; "The Light of the World."

Collins, Mortimer (1827-1876) English novelist.

Works include: *Idyls and Rhymes; Summer Songs; The British Birds and Other Works.*

Collins, William (1721-1759) English poet.

Works include: "The Passion"; "Ode to Everything"; "Dirge in Cymbeline"; "Ode to the Death of Thompson."

Colman, George ["The Younger"] (1762-1836) English dramatist and humorous poet.

Works include: *The Heir-at-Law; Broad Grins and Poetic Vagaries; John Bull.*

Cone, Helen Gray (1859-1934) American poet and educator.

Works include: *Oberon and Puck* (1885); *The Ride to the Lady and Other Poems.*

Conford, Frances ["Darwin"] (1886-1960) American poet.

Granddaughter of Charles Darwin. Works include: "The Old Witch in the Corpse"; "Autumn Morning at Cambridge."

Conkling, Grace Hazard (b.1878) Professor of English at Smith College.

Works include: "The Different Day"; "Modern Sonnet"; "This Is Not Loneliness."

Cook, Elizabeth (1818-1889) English poet.

Works include: *Melaia and Other Poems; The Old Armchair; The Home in the Heart.*

Cooke, Phillip Pendleton (1816-1850) American lawyer.

Works include: "Life in the Autumn Woods"; "The Power of the Bards."

Cooke, Rose Terry (1827-1892) American author and poet.

Wrote about English rural life. Works include: *The Gentian; The Two Villages.*

Coolbrith, Ina Donna (1842-1928) American poet and librarian.

Works include: "The Mariposa Lily"; *The Perfect Day and Other Poems; Songs of the Golden Gate.*

Coolidge, Susan (see Woolsey, Sara Chauncey)

Cooper, James Fenimore (1789-1851) American novelist and historian.

Works include: *The Last of the Mohicans; Leather Stocking Tales; Pathfinder; The Pilot.*

Corneille, Pierre (1606-1684) French dramatist.

Known as the father of French tragedy and classic comedy. Wrote elegies, sonnets, epistles, and essays. Works include: *El Cid; Horace; Cinna.*

Cornall, Barry (see Proctor, Bryan Waller)

Cornwall, Henry Sylvester (1831-1886) American physician.

Works include: *The Land of Dreams and Other Poems.*

Cory, William (n.d.) English poet and translator.

Works include: "The Dead Poet-Friend" (the Greek of Callimachus); "The Two Captains"; "Anteros."

Costello, Louise Stuart (1815-1870) Irish artist, writer, and translator.

Works include: "To Mary Stuart" (French of De Tonsard); "On the Death of Francis I" (French of Marguerite); "Sonnet" (French of Labe); "To Diane De Poiters" (French of Marot).

Courthope, William John (1842-1917) English man of letters.

Works include: "The Trail of the Bird"; "The Paradise of Birds."

Cowley, Abraham (1618-1667) English essayist and poet.

Helped establish the Royal Academy. Works include: "The Mistress"; "Davideis"; *Miscellancies and Essays.*

Cowley, Malcom (b. 1898) American author.

Popularized the "lost generation" of American writers he knew in Europe after the First World War in *Exile's Return* (1934). Edited several popular anthologies, including *The Portable Faulkner, The Portable Hemingway,* and *The Portable Hawthorne.* Works include: *Blue Juniata; The Dry Season; Blue Juniata: Collected Poems.*

Cowper, William (1731-1800) English hymnwriter and poet.

Works include: *Olney Hymns;* "The Task."

Coxe, Arthur Cleveland (1818-1896) American poet and Episcopal Bishop of New York.

Works include: *Christian Ballads; The Pascal.*

Cozzens, Frederick Swartwout (1818-1869) American humorist.

Works include: *Prismatics; Richard Haywarde; Sparrow-Grass Papers.*

Crabbe, George (1754-1832) English clergyman and poet.

Practiced medicine for some time. Built a literary reputation with "The Library" (1781) and "The Village" (1783).

Craik, Dinah Maria Mulock (1826-1887) English author.

Works include: *John Halifax, Gentleman;* "Autumn's Processional"; "Now and Afterwards."

Cranch, Christopher Pearse (1813-1892) American artist.

Works include: *Ariel and Caliban; Last of the Huggermuggers; Poems.*

Crane, Hart ["Harold"] (1899-1932) American poet.

A tragic figure tormented by personal problems culminating in suicide. Crane established himself during his brief life as one of the most original poets of the time. Works include: *White Buildings* (1926); *The Bridge* (1930).

Cranstoun, James (1837-1901) Scottish poet.

Works include: "The Immortality of Genius" (Latin of Propertius).

Crashaw, Richard (1613-1650) English clergyman and poet.

One of the metaphysical poets. A convert to Catholicism; best known for his religious poems. Works include: *Steps to the Temple; Other Delights of the Muses.*

Crawford, Isabella Valancey (1857-1887) Irish poet.

Works include: "The Axe"; "Malcom's Katie."

Crawford, John Martin (1845-1916) American physician.

Works include: "Poem to the Kalevala" (from the Finnish).

Crawford, Julia ["Macartney, Louise"] (1808-1885) Irish poet.

Author of the song, "Kathleen Mavourneen."

Cross, Mary Ann Evans Lewes ["George Eliot"] (1820-1880) English novelist.

One of the major writers of her time. Works include: *Adam Bede; The Mill on the Floss; Silas Marner; Romola; Middlemarch.*

Crowquill, Alfred ["Forrester, Alfred"] (1806-1872) English poet.

Works include: "To My Nose."

Cullen, Countee (1903-1946) American poet.

One of the premiere black American poets. Works include: "Color"; *Caroling Dusk.*

Cummings, Edmund Estlin (1894-1962) American poet.

Won the Dial award in 1925 for distinguished service to American Literature. Wrote lyrics and satirical verses. Works include: *95 poems* (1958); *Tulips and Chimneys* (1923); "Life Is More True"; "The Cambridge Ladies."

Cunningham, Allan (1784-1842) Scottish poet.

Works include: "Poet's Bridal-Day Song"; "Thou Hast Sworn by Thy God, My Jeanie"; "A Wet Sheet and a Flowing Sea."

Cunningham, John (1729-1773) Irish poet.

Works include: "Morning."

Currier, Ellen Barlett (n.d.) Works include: "O Oberlin, Silent Baby."

Dana, Richard Henry (1787-1879) American critic and poet.

Wrote for and edited the *North American Review*. Works include: "The Change of Home"; "The Dying Raven"; "The Buccaneers."

Daniel, Samuel (1562-1619) English poet and historian.

Wrote sonnets and lyrics. Works include: *A History of England; Delia.*

Dante Alighieri (1265-1321) Italian poet and statesman.

One of the major figues of Italian literature. Banished from his native Florence for political reasons, his masterpiece *The Divine Comedy* was written in exile. His love for Beatrice Portinari inspired "La Vita Nuova."

Darley, George (1795-1846) Irish poet, critic, and mathematician.

Known for his critical studies. Works include: "Sylvia, or the May Queen."

Davenant, Sir William (1606-1668) English playwright and poet.

Succeeded Ben Jonson as poet laureate. Works include: *The Cruel Brother; Gondibert.*

Davidson, John (1857-1909) Scottish dramatist and teacher.

Works include: "A Runnable Stag"; *Fleet Street; Ecologues; Ballads and Songs.*

Davies, Sir John (1569-1626) English poet and judge.

Works include: "Know Thyself"; "The Orchestra."

Davies, William Henry (1871-1940) Welsh poet.

Much of his poetry reflects the hardships of his early life. Works include: "The Heap of Rags"; "Dreams of the Sea"; "Days too Short."

Davis, Thomas Osborne (1814-1845) Irish poet.

Wrote on patriotic themes. Works include: "Celts and Saxons"; "The Girl I Left Behind Me"; "My Land."

Day, Thomas Fleming (1861-1927) English editor.

Works include: "The Coasters"; "The Clipper"; "Making Land."

Day Lewis, Cecil (1904-1972) English author.

One of the dominant English poets, with Auden and Spender, in the period between world wars. Poet laureate (1968-72). Works include: "From Feathers to Iron"; "You That Love England."

de la Mare, Walter John (1873-1956) English author.

Famous for his books for children; he also wrote novels, plays, essays, anthologies, and more than 20 volumes of verse. Works include: "Come Hither"; *Songs of Childhood*; "All That's Past"; "The Burning Glass."

Dekker, Thomas (1570-1641) English poet and dramatist.

Literary antagonist of Ben Jonson. Works include: *The Shoemaker's Holiday; Old Fortunatus; Entertainment to James.*

Deland, Margaretta Wade (1857-1945) American author and poet.

Works include: *The Old Garden and Other Verses.*

Demarest, Mary Lee (n.d.) Scottish poet.

Works include: "My Ain Countree."

Derzhavin, Gavril Romanovich (1743-1816) Russian poet.

A favorite of Czarina Catherine II, he was poet laureate and later minister of justice. Works include: "Ode to God"; "O, Thou Eternal One!."

de Vere, Mary Ainge ["Madeline Bridges"] (b. 1840) American poet.

Works include: "Friends and Lovers"; "The Spinners."

de Vere, Sir Stephen Edward (1812-1904) Irish poet.

Works include: "Country Gentleman"; "To Thalcarchus" (Latin of Horace).

de Vere, Thomas Aubrey (1814-1902) Irish poet and political essayist.

Works include: *The Irish Odes; Legends of St. Patrick; Religious Poems.*

Dibdin, Charles (1745-1814) English actor and dramatist.

Works include: "The Quaker"; "Sea Songs"; *Blindman's Buff; The Pirates.*

Dickens, Charles (1812-1870) English novelist and satirist.

One of the great English novelists. Wrote the masterpieces *Oliver Twist, The Old Curiosity Shop, Pickwick Papers.*

Dickinson, Charles Monroe (b. 1842) American poet.

Works include: "The Children."

Dickinson, Emily (1830-1886) American poet.

One of America's greatest poets, Dickinson lived most of her life as a recluse. Wrote prolifically in forms peculiar to herself but published very little. Most of her verse was published posthumously. Works include: "A Narrow Fellow in the Grass"; "I Never Saw a Moor"; "This World Is Not Conclusion."

Dickinson, Mary Lowe (1839-1914) American educator.

Works include: "If We Had but a Day."

Dimond, William (1800-1836) English theatrical manager.

Works include: "The Mariner's Dream."

Dix, John Adams (1798-1879) American statesman and soldier.

Secretary of the Treasury in 1861; Govenor of New York in 1874. Works include: "Dies Irac" (Latin of Celano).

Dobell, Sydney Thompson ["Sidney Yendys"] (1824-1874) English merchant.

His interest in Italian freedom inspired "The Roman." Works include: *America; Balder.*

Dobson, Austin (1840-1921) English author.

Wrote biographies of Hogarth, Fielding, Steele and Goldsmith. Works include: *Old Work Idyls; Eighteenth Century Vignettes.*

Doddridge, Philip (1702-1751) English author, Nonconformist clergyman, and hymn writer.

Achieved international fame through translations. Works include: "Awake My Soul"; "Hear Us, in This Thy House."

Dodge, Mary Elizabeth Mapes (1838-1905) American editor, author, and poet.

Edited New York's *St. Nicholas Magazine.* Best known for *Hans Brinker* or the *Silver Skates.* Works include: "Once Before"; "Snowflakes."

Dodgson, Charles Lutwidge ["Lewis Carroll"] (1832-1898) Lectured on mathematics at Oxford.

Wrote *Alice in Wonderland* (1865) for a young friend. Works include: *The Hunting of the Smark* (1876); *Sylvie and Bruna* (1889-93).

Dole, Nathan Haskell (1852-1935) American editor.

Noted for his edition of "The Rubaiyat" of Omar Khayyam. Works include: "Not Angels Quite"; "On The Point"; "A Summer Idyl"; "Flowers from Foreign Gardens."

Dolliver, Clara G. (n.d.) American poet.

Works include: "No Baby in the House."

Domett, Alfred (1811-1887) English colonial official and poet.

Works can be found in the volumes *Ranolf and Amohia, and Flotsam and Jetsam: Rhymes Old and New.*

Donne, John (1573-1631) English poet and clergyman.

Greatest of the "metaphysical poets," he is known for his religious verse, satires, love poetry, and essays. Works include: *Songs and Sonnets; Holy Sonnets; Devotions* (1624).

Doolittle, Hilda ["H.D."] (1886-1961) American poet.

First woman to receive the Award of Merit Medal for poetry from the American Academy of Arts and Letters. Works include: "Sea Garden"; "Priapus"; "Hermes of the Ways"; "Moonrise."

Dorr, Julia Caroline Ripley (1825-1913) American poet and novelist.

Works include: *Daybreak; Easter Poem; Afternoon Songs; Poems.*

Dorset, Charles Sackville, 6th Earl of (1637-1706) English poet.

Works include: "The Mirror for Magistrates"; "Dorinda."

Douglas, Keith Castellaine (1920-1944) English poet.

Published first poem at age sixteen. Works include: "Desert Flower"; "The Sea Bird"; "Remember Me."

Dowden, Edward (1843-1913) Irish critic.

Remembered for his lecture series at Princeton University (1898). Works include: Southey; *Studies In Literature; Robert Browning; Introduction to Shakespeare.*

Dowling, Bartholomew (1823-1863) Irish journalist.

Works include: "The Brigade at Fontenoy"; "The Revel."

Downing, Ellen Mary Patrick (1828-1869) Irish poet.

Works include: "Were I but His Own Wife"; "The Old Church at Lismore."

Doyle, Sir Arthur Conan (1859-1930) Scottish novelist.

Served as a physician in the Boer War. Works include: *The Adventures of Sherlock Holmes; The Hound of the Baskervilles; History of Spiritualism.*

Doyle, Sir Francis Hastings (1810-1888) English professor.

Taught poetry at Oxford. Works include: *The Return of the Guards and Other Poems* (1866).

Drake, Joseph Rodman (1795-1820) American poet.

Popular for his collaboration with Fitz-Greene Halleck in "The Croakers," a series of humorous poems published in the *New York Evening Post*. Works include: "The Culprit Fay"; "The American Flag"; "Abelard to Heloise."

Drayton, Michael (1563-1631) English poet laureate (1626-1631) Writing pastorals, he began his career late with "Ides, the Shepherd's Garland." Wrote an immense work, *Polyolbion*, of 10,000 lines which he left unfinished.

Drinkwater, John (1882-1937) English poet and dramatist.

Published *Poems* and *The Death of Leander* by the age of twenty five. Works include: *Collected Poems* (1923); *The Pilgrim of Eternity* (1925); *All About Me* (1928); *American Vignettes* (1930).

"Droch" (see Bridges, Robert)

Drummond, William, of Hawthornden (1585-1649) Scottish author.

Remembered for the purity of his English imitations of Spencer and the Italian sonneteers. Works include: *Tears on the Death of Moeliades; Poems; History of the Reigns of the Five Jameses.*

Dryden, John (1631-1700) English poet, critic, and dramatist.

Poet laureate and convert to Roman Catholicism. Works include: *The Hind and the Panther; Absalom and Achitophel; Mac Flecknoe.*

Dschellaleddin Pumi ["Jallal-addin Rumi"] (1207-1273) Persian poet.

Wrote many spiritual and mystical odes. Teaching and doctrines are still followed by the Maulawi sect of dervishes.

Dufferin, Lady Helen Selinda Sheridan ["Lady Gifford"] (1807-1867) Irish poet.

Works include: "The Irish Emigrant"; "Katy's Letter."

Dunbar, Paul Lawrence (1872-1906) American librarian, poet, author, and journalist.

One of the first black American writers to utilize black themes and dialects. Lectured and gave public readings. Works include: "Oak and Ivy"; "Lyrics of Lowly Live."

Dunbar, William (1465-1530) Scottish diplomat, poet, and Fransican friar.

Works include: "The Thistle and the Rose" (1503); "The Golden Targe" (1508); "Visitation of St. Francis."

Dunlop, John (1755-1820) Scottish songwriter.

Works include: "Oh, Dinna Ask Me Gin I Lo'e Ye."

Durbin, Harriet Whitney (n.d.) American poet.

Works include: "A Little Dutch Garden."

Durivage, Francis Alexander (1814-1881) American journalist and author.

Wrote verse and novelettes. Translated *Lamartines' History of the Revolution of 1848.*

Durrell, Lawrence (b. 1912) English poet and novelist.

Writes short lyrics, meditations, comedies, and metaphysical poems and portraits of artists. Works include: *The Alexander Quartet*; "Eight Aspects of Melissa."

Dwight, John Sullivan (1813-1893) American music critic and editor.

Best known for his poem "God Save the State."

Dwight, Timothy (1752-1817) American clergyman and educator.

President of Yale University; a leading member of the "Connecticut Wits." Wrote theological works, epics, pastorals, and satires. Works include: "The Conquest of Canaan," "Greenfield Hill"; "The Triumph of Infidelity."

Dyer, Sir Edward (1540-1607) English courtier and elegiac poet.

Works include: "My Mind to Me a Kingdom Is"; *The Shepherd's Conceit of Prometheus and Other Poems.*

Eastman, Charles Gamage (1816-1861) American journalist and poet.

Wrote frequently on rural life in New England. Popular contributor to periodicals. Works include: "A Picture"; "A Snow Storm."

Eastman, Elaine Goodale (b. 1863) American educator and poet.

Works include: "Ashes of Roses"; "Goldenrod"; "Apple Blossoms"; "Verse from Sky Farm."

Eaton, Arthur Wentworth Hamilton (b. 1849) Canadian Episcopal minister.

Works include: "The Heart of the Creeds"; "Arcadian Legends and Lyrics."

Eberhart, Richard (b. 1904) American poet.

A basic theme is man's fallen state and his subsequent search for unity. Works include: "Brotherhood of Men"; "If This Be Love"; "At Lake Geneva."

Edwards, Amelia Blandford
(1831-1892) English Egyp-
tologist.

Works include: "My Brother's
Wife"; "In the Days of My
Youth"; "A Thousand Miles
Up the Nile."

Eliot, George (see Cross,
Maryann Evans Lewes)

Eliot, Samuel Atkins (1821-1898)
American writer, translator, and
mayor of Boston.

Works include: "Labor Done";
"The Liberty of Rome"; *Stories from the Arabian Nights.*

Eliot, Thomas Stearns (1888-
1965) English poet and editor.

Born in America; became a
British subject in 1927. A prin-
cipal literary figure of the cen-
tury. Influenced by French sym-
bolist poets. Works include:
"The Wasteland"; "Homage to
John Dryden"; *An Essay of
Poetic Drama.*

**Elizabeth, Queen of Roumania
["Carmen, Sylvia"]** (1843-
1916) German poet.

Began writing with an elegy on
her child's death. Works include: "Storms and Thoughts of
a Queen."

Elliott, Lady Charlotte (b. 1830)
English songwriter.

Wrote popular sacred songs.

Works include: "Just As I
Am."

Elliott, Ebenezer (1781-1849)
English reform poet.

Works include: "Spring";
"Corn Law Rhymes."

Emerson, Ralph Waldo (1803-
1882) American poet, philosopher, and writer.

A founder of the New England
literary movement, "Transcen-
dentalism." Works include:
"Brahma"; "Each and All";
"Friendship"; *Self-Reliance;
American Scholar.*

Empson, William (1906-1984)
English poet.

Concerned with philosophical
and metaphysical matters.
Works include: *Seven Types of
Ambiguity.*

English, Thomas Dunn (1819-
1902) American physician and
legislator.

Works include: "Ben Bolt."

**Erskine, Francis Robert St.
Clair, Earl of Rosslyn** (1833-
1890) English poet.

Works include: "Bedtime."

Erskine, Ralph (1685-1752) English poet.

Works include: "Smoking
Spiritualized."

Euripides (480-406 B.C.) Greek tragic poet.

Published his first play in 455 B.C. Composed ninety two tragedies. Works include: *Alcestis; Media; Electra; Ipihgenia; Among the Tauri; The Peliades.*

Eytinge, Margaret (n.d.) American writer.

Works include: "Baby Louise."

Faber, Frederick William (1814-1863) English clergyman.

Best known for the hymns: "O Paradise! O Paradise!"; "Pilgrims of the Night"; "Land Beyond the Sea."

Fairfax, Edward (d. 1635) English poet.

Works include: *a metrical translation of Godrey of Boulogne*; "Jerusalem Delivered"; "Erminia and the Wounded Tancred."

Falconer, William (1732-1769) Scottish seaman and poet.

Came from a family of deaf mutes. Wrote odes and satires. Works include: "The Shipwreck"; *The Universal Dictionary of the Marine.*

Fanshawe, Catherine Maria (1765-1834) English poet.

Rarely consented to publication. Works include: "A Riddle"; "A Letter for You."

Fearing, Kenneth (1902-1961) American writer.

Interested in urban problems, specifically the loss of love and meaning in industrial society. Works include: "Angel Arms"; "Dead Reckoning"; *Afternoon of a Pawnbroker* and *Other Poems.*

Fenner, Cornelius George (1822-1847) American poet.

Works include: "Gulf Weed."

Ferguson, Sir Samuel (1810-1886) Irish barrister.

Works include: "The Forging of the Anchor"; "Lays of the Western Gael."

Ficke, Arthur Davison (1883-1945) American poet.

Wrote sonnets and lyrics. Works include: "Among Shadows"; "Fathers and Sons"; "The Oracle."

Field, Eugene (1850-1895) American humorist and journalist.

Started as a regional writer but soon gained attention nationally. Popular for his poems for children. Works include: "Love Song of Childhood"; *A Little Book of Western Verse; The Holy Cross and Other Tales.*

"Field, Michael" [pseudonym of two English poets, Bradley, Katherine** (1848-1914) **and**

Cooper, Edith (1862-1913)]
Works include: "The Burial of
Robert Browning"; "The
Dancers."

Fielding, Henry (1707-1754)
English novelist and dramatist.

Author of one of the great English novels, *Tom Jones* (1749).
Works include: *Tom Thumb*
(1730); *Amelia* (1752).

Fields, James Thomas (1816-
1881) American publisher.

Edited the *Atlantic Monthly*.
Works include: *Poems* (1849);
Yesterdays with Authors.

Finch, Francis Miles (b. 1827)
American poet and judge.

Works include: "Nathan Hale";
"The Blue and the Gray."

Fitzgerald, Edward (1809-1883)
English scholar and poet.

Formed friendships with Thackeray, Tennyson, and Carlyle.
Masterpiece is his translation of
Omar Khayyam's "Rubaiyat."

Fitzgerald, Robert (b. 1910)
American poet and educator.

Known for his translations of
the *Iliad; Odyssey; Aeneid*.
Works include: *Poems* (1935);
A Wreath for the Sun (1943).

Fitzgibbon, H. Macaulay (b.
1887) English poet.

Works include: "Advise" (from
the early English of Dunbar).

Flagg, Wilson (1805-1884)
American naturalist and political
writer.

Works include: *Studies in the
Field and Forest; Halcyon
Days; A Year Among the Trees*.

Flecker, James Elroy (1884-
1915) English poet.

Though not prolific, he exerted
an important influence on English literature. Works include:
"Brumana"; "November
Eves"; "Stillness."

Fleming, Paul (1609-1640) German diplomat.

Gained success with *German
Poems* (1642).

Fletcher, John (1579-1625) English dramatist and poet.

Collaborated with the dramatist
Francis Beaumont. Works include: "Hence, All the Vain
delights"; "Take, O, Take
Those Lips Away."

Fletcher, John Gould (1886-
1950) American critic, translator, and author.

Works include: "The Attitude
of Youth"; "Autumnal
Clouds"; "Evening Sky."

Follen, Elizabeth Lee Cabot
(1787-1860) American writer.

Works include: *Poems* (1839);
Twilight Stories (1858); *Home
Dramas* (1859).

Forrester, Alfred (see Crowquill, Alfred)

Forrester, Fanny (see Judson, Emily Chubbuck)

Fosdick, William Whiteman (1825-1862) American poet.

Works include: "Tecumseh."

Foss, Sam Walter (1858-1911) American librarian and poet.

Works include: "He'd Had No Show"; "The House by the Road."

Foster, Stephen Collins (1826-1864) American songwriter.

Wrote dialect songs for minstrel group. Many of his early songs were published anonymously. Works include: "Old Black Joe"; "My Old Kentucky Home"; "Swanee River"; "Oh, Susannah."

Fox, William Johnson (1786-1864) English Unitarian clergyman.

Works include: "The Martyr's Hymn" (German of Luther).

Francis Xavier, Saint (1506-1552) French Roman Catholic missionary.

Canonized in 1619. Works include: "My God, I Love Thee" (Caswell's translation).

Franklin, Benjamin (1706-1790)

American philosopher and statesman.

Influenced national and colonial politics with his writing. Made outstanding scientific discoveries. Active in defeating The Stamp Act and promoting the abolition of slavery. Works include: "The Mother Country"; "Here Skugg lies snug"; "The Downfall of Piracy."

Freiligrath, Ferdinand (1810-1876) German poet.

Gained popularity with *Gedichte*. Published *Poems* in 1838. Works include: "The Lion's Ride."

Freneau, Philip (1752-1832) American poet and journalist.

America's first major poet; remembered for his lyrical, descriptive, and reflective poetry. A propagandist for the American Revolution, his poem "The British Prison Ship," decribing the treatment of American prisoners-of-war, created a furor. Works include: "The American Soldier"; "The Royal Adventurer."

Frost, Robert (1874-1963) American poet.

Received the Pulitzer Prize for poetry in 1924. Established an international reputation with *A Boy's Will* (1913) and *North of Boston* (1914). Works include: *New Hampshire* (1923); *A Wit-*

ness Tree (1942); *Steeple Bush* (1947).

Fuller, Roy (b. 1912) English poet.

Paved the way for a school of English poetry which rejected experimentation and called for technically proficient verse. Works include: "The Emotion of Fiction"; "Defending the Harbour."

Gale, Norman (b. 1862) English poet.

Works include: "The Country Faith."

Gallagher, William Davis (1808-1894) American journalist and agricultural writer.

Works include: "The Laborer"; "The Wreck of the Hornet"; "Miami Woods."

Gannett, William Channing (1840-1923) American Unitarian clergyman.

Works include: *Memoir of E. S. Gannett; A Year of Miracles.*

Garnett, Richard (1835-1906) English librarian and editor.

Edited works of Shelley, Peacock, and others. Works include: biographies of Carlyle, Emerson, Milton; *Poems from the German; Twilight of the Gods and Other Tales.*

Garrison, William Floyd (1805-1879) American editor and abolitionist.

Founded the *Liberator* (1831), the first abolitionist journal. Works include: *Sonnets* (1843); *Selections* (1852).

Gascoyne, David (b. 1916) English poet.

Wrote surrealistic poetry. Works include: *Poems* (1937-1942) ; "The Gravel-Pit Field"; "The Uncertain Battle."

Gassaway, Frank Harrison (n.d.) American poet.

Works include: "Bay Billy."

Gay, John (1685-1732) English poet and playwright.

Best known for *The Beggar's Opera* (1728) satirizing society. Works include: *The Shepherd's Week; Trivis; Of the Art of Walking the Streets of London; The Captives.*

Geoghegan, Arthur Gerald (1810-1889) Irish revenue collector. Works include: "The Mountain Fern."

Gerock, Carl (1815-1890) German religious poet.

Established his reputation with "Palm Leaves." Works include: "In Lonely Ways"; "Flowers and Stars."

Gibbons, James Sloane (d.1892) American journalist.

Works include: "Three Hundred Thousand More."

Gibson, Wilfred Wilson (1878-1962) English poet.

Prolific poet, who took his subjects from common life and his characters from humble people. Works include: "Fires"; "Battle"; "Home"; "Kestral Edge."

Gilbert, Sir William Schwenk (1836-1911) English playwright, poet, and barrister.

Collaborated with Sir Arthur Sullivan on a series of popular light operas, such as Pinafore, Pirates of Penzance, The Mikado, Iothanthe. Works include: *Bad Ballads*; "The Captain and the Mermaids."

Gilder, Richard Watson (1844-1909) American educator, poet, and editor.

Edited *Scribner's Monthly* (1870). Works included: "The Cello"; "Dawn"; "Life-Mask of Lincoln."

Gillfillen, Robert (1798-1850) Scottish poet.

Works include: *Original Songs*; "The Exile Song."

Gilman, Charlotte Perkins Stetson (1860-1935) American Socialist lecturer.

Works include: "Rock and the Sea"; "A Conservative."

Gilmore, James Roberts ["Edmund Kirke"] (b. 1822) American author.

Works include: "Among the Pines"; "Adrift in Dixie"; "Patriot Bays."

Gladden, Washington (1836-1918) American author and clergyman.

Writings emphasize social reforms. Works include: "The Ideal City"; "O Happy Soul."

Gluck, Willibald Christoph (1714-1787) German composer.

Collaborated with poet Ranieri di Calzabigi on *Helen and Paris.*

Goethe, Johann Wolfgang von (1749-1832) German writer, scientist, and philosopher.

A genius in many fields, he used the German language with an unprecedented ease and freedom. Most of his writings have been translated into English. Works include: *The Earl-King; The Fisher; Faust.*

Golau, Solomon von (see Logau, Friederick von)

Goldsmith, Oliver (1728-1774) Anglo-Irish novelist and dramatist.

Gained immediate popularity

with *The Vicar of Wakefield* (1766). Works include: *The Deserted Village* (1770); *She Stoops to Conquer* (1773).

Goodale, Dora Read (b.1866) American poet.

Works include: "A Twilight Fancy"; "Sister"; "The Flight of the Heart."

Goodale, Elaine (see Eastman, Elaine Goodale)

Gorman, Herbert (1839-1954) American writer and traveler.

Lived in France, England, and Mexico. Wrote three historical novels set in Mexico. Works include: "The Fountain"; "A Tarter Horse."

Goose, Sir Edmund William (1849-1928) English poet, essayist, and critic.

Works include: *Madrigals, Songs and Sonnets; "The Unknown Lover"; Northern Studies.*

Gould, Hannah Flagg (1789-1865) American poet.

Best known for "The Snowflake" and "The Frost." Works include: "The Wild Violet"; "A Name in the Sand."

Gould, Sabine Baring (see Baring-Gould, Sabine)

Graham of Gartmore, Robert (1750-1797) Scottish poet.

Works include: "If Doughty Deeds My Lady Please"; "To His Lady."

Graham, William Sydney (b.1918) Scottish poet.

Gained critical and popular acclaim with *Malcolm Mooney's Land* (1970). Four recurrent themes: the difficulty of human communication, the crisis of identity, the nature of aethetic experience, the celebration of life.

Graham, James (see Montrose, Marquess of)

Grahame, James (1785-1838) Scottish lawyer and minister.

Works include: *The Sabbath*; "The Wild Duck and Her Brood."

Grant, Sir Robert (1785-1838) British poet.

Member of the parliament and Governor of Bombay. Works include: "When Gathering Clouds Around I View"; "Faith and Hope."

Graves, Alfred Perceval (1846-1931) Irish school inspector, editor, and poet.

Works include: "The Little Red Lark"; "The Irish Spinning-Wheel."

Graves, Robert (1895-1986) English poet, scholar, and critic.

Works include: *Good-bye To All That* (1929); *I, Claudius* (1934); *Greek Myths* (1955).

Gray, David (1838-1861) Scottish poet.

Works include: "The Cross of Gold"; "I Die, Being Young"; "In the Shadows."

Gray, Thomas (1716-1771) English scholar and poet.

Rejected position of poet laureate in favor of a professorship of history at Cambridge University. Immortal for "Elegy Written in a Country Churchyard."

Greene, Albert Gorton (1802-1868) American lawyer and poet.

Famous for "Old Grimes" and "Baron's Last Banquet."

Greene, Robert (1560-1592) English dramatist.

Educated at Cambridge University. His "The Triumph of Time" supplied Shakespeare with hints for the plot of *The Winter's Tale*. Works include: "The Farewell to Folly"; "Francesco's Fortune"; "Pandosto."

Greene, Sarah Pratt McLean (1858-1935) American novelist.

Works include: "De Massa ob de Sheepfol"; "The Lamp."

Greenwood, Grace (see Lippincott, Sara Jane)

Gregory, Horace (1898-1982) American critic, biographer, and editor.

Named Guggenheim fellow (1951) and awarded the Bollinger Prize for *Collected Poems* in 1965. Works include: "Chelsea Rooming House" (1930); "No Retreat" (1933); "Chorus for Survival" (1935); "Medusa in Grammercy Park" (1961).

Gregory I, Saint [Saint Gregory the Great] (544-604) Italian, pope (590-604).

Embraced monastic life in a society he founded. Works include: *Pastoral Care*; "Darkness Is Thinning"; "Morning Hymn."

Grieve, Christopher Murray ["Hugh MacDiarmid"] (1891-1978) Scottish poet.

A Communist and Scottish nationalist, he progressed from writing in English to a pure Scottish dialect. Works include: "The Glen of Silence"; "A Herd of Does."

Griffin, Bartholomew (fl. 1596) English poet.

Works include: "Fidessa, More Chaste Than Kind."

Griffin, Gerald Joseph (1803-1840) Irish journalist.

Gained success with *Holland Tide*, or *Munster Popular Tales*. Works include: "Tales of My Neighborhood"; "Eileen Aroon."

Griffith, George Bancroft (b. 1841) American poet.

Works include: "Our Fallen Heros"; "Before It Is Too Late."

Grimald, Nicholas (1519-1562) English poet.

Works include: "The Friend" (On Friendship); "A True Love"; "Description of Virtue."

Grissom, Arthur (1869-1901) American editor.

Works include: "The Artist"; "Ballade of Forgotten Loves."

Guiney, Louise Imogen (1861-1920) American essayist, poet, and editor.

Works include: *Songs at the Start; A Roadside Harp; Goose-Quill Papers; Brownies and Bogles; Monsieur Henri.*

Habington, William (1605-1654) English poet.

Works include: "To Roses in the Bosom of Castara"; Love's Anniverary to the Sun"; "Castara."

Haliburton, Hugh (see Robertson, James Logie)

Hall, Christopher Newman (1816-1902) English religious writer and clergyman.

Works include: "Come to Jesus"; "My Times Are in Thy Hands."

Hall, Gertrude Brownell (b. 1863) American author.

Works include: "Far from Today"; "Allegretto"; "Blind-Man's Bluff."

Hall, Joseph (1576-1656) English, Bishop of Exeter and Norwich.

Works include: "Hollow Hospitality"; "Virgidemiarum."

Halleck, Fitzgreene (1790-1867) American accountant and poet.

Collaborated with Joseph Rodman Drake in "The Croaker" series of satiric newspaper verse. Profilic, popular, and well regarded poet of the time. Works include: "Young America and Fanny"; "Marco Bozzaris"; "Fanny."

Hamilton, Elizabeth (1758-1816) Scottish author and poet.

Works include: *Memoirs of Modern Philosophers; Letters on Education; Life of Agrippina.*

Hardinge, William M. (n.d.) English writer and translator.

Works include: "Generous Air" (Greek of Palladas); "Grave of

Sophocles'' (Greek of Simmias); "The Wreath" (Greek of Meleager).

Hardy, Thomas (1840-1928) English novelist and poet.

One of the great English novelists of the 19th century, he wrote only poetry after 1898. Works include: *Tess of the D'Ubervilles; The Mayor of Casterbridge; The Return of the Native; Jude the Obscure.*

Harpur, Charles (1817-1868) Welsh civil servant.

Works include: "A Midsummer's Noon in the Australian Forest"; "A Similitude."

Harington, Sir John (1561-1612) English soldier, courtier, and scholar.

Translated Ariosto's "Orlando Furioso." Works include: "Fair, Rich, and Young"; "Of a Precise Tailor."

Harrison, Susan Frances ["Seranus"] (1859-1935) Canadian poet.

Works include: "Chateau Papineau"; "Down the River."

Harte, [Francis] Bret[t] (1839-1902) American writer.

Famous for combining his characters and scenes with local Western color. Works include: "The Luck of Roaring Camp"; "Mrs. Skagg's Husband."

Harte, Walter (1700-1774) Welsh poet.

Works include: "A Soliloquy."

Havergal, Francis Ridley (1836-1879) English religious poet.

Works include: "God's Faithful"; "Increase Our Faith"; "Thy Presence."

Hawker, Robert Stephen (1804-1875) English clergyman.

Works include: "Song of the Western Men"; "The Southern Cross."

Hawtrey, Edward Craven (1789-1862) English poet and translator.

Works include: "Hector to His Wife" (Greek of Homer).

Hay, John (1838-1905) American statesman and writer.

Worked on the New York Tribune. Works include: *Life of Abraham Lincoln; Pike County Ballads; Castitian Days.*

Hayes, Ednah Proctor Clarke (b. 1870) American poet.

Works include: "Hawaiian Islands Live"; "An Opal."

Hayne, Paul Hamilton (1830-1886) American lawyer and writer.

Works include: *Legends and Lyrics; The Mountain of Lovers; The Wife of Brittany.*

Hayne, William Hamilton (1865-1929) American author.

Works include: "An Autumn Breeze"; "Moonlight Song of the Mockingbird"; "Night Mists."

Hazewell, Edward Wentworth (b. 1853) American poet.

Works include: "Veteran and Recruit."

Heath, Leonard (n.d.) American poet.

Works include: "Grave of Bonaparte."

Heber, Reginald (1783-1826) English, Bishop of Calcutta.

Works include: "From Greenland's Icy Mountains"; "Breed of the World."

Hedge, Frederick Henry (1805-1890) American Unitarian clergyman.

Works include: "A Mighty Fortress is our God" (translated from Luther's German); "Questionings."

Heine, Heinrich (1799-1856) German poet.

Leading figure in the literary movement "Young Germany" and advocate of social reforms. Most of his work has been translated into English. Works include: *Deutschland*; "The Lorelei"; "Dear Maiden."

Hellman, George Sidney (b. 1878) American journalist.

Works include: "The Hudson."

Hemans, Felicia Dorothea (1793-1835) English poet.

Works include: *Lays of Many Lands*; "Casabianca"; *Hymns for Childhood*.

Henley, William Ernest (1849-1903) English journalist and poet.

Gained fame for "Invictus." Works include: *Book of Verses; Lyrics and Poems*.

Herbert, George (1593-1632) English clergyman and poet.

"Metaphysical poet" famous for devotional poems. Works include: *The Temple* (1631); *Jacula Prudentum* (1640).

Herbert, W. (n.d.) English poet.

Works include: "Thor Recovers His Hammer" (Icelandic of Saemund).

Herford, Oliver (1863-1935) American journalist and comic writer.

Works include: "A Belated Violet"; "Elf and the Dormouse"; "First Rose of Summer."

Hermes, Paul (see Thayey, William Roscoe)

Herrick, Robert (1591-1674) English clergyman.

Leading Cavalier poet, famous for his secular and pious lyric poems, many of which have been set to music. Works include: "Gather Ye Rosebuds"; "Corinna's Going A-Maying."

Hervey, Thomas Kibble (1799-1859) Scottish editor.

Works include: "Love."

Herwegh, Georg (1817-1875) German poet.

Abandoned theological studies for poetry. Works include: "The Trooper Death"; "The Lyrics of a Live Man."

Heywood, Thomas (1575-1650) English dramatist.

Famous for *A Woman Killed with Kindness*. Works include: "The Golden Age"; "A Challenge for Beauty."

Hickey, Emily Henrietta (1845-1924) Irish author and poet.

Works include: "A Sea Story"; "Beloved, It Is Morn."

Higgins, John (n.d.) English poet.

Works include: "Time of Elizabeth"; "Books."

Higginson, Thomas Wentworth (1823-1911) American clergyman and soldier.

Active in the anti-slavery cause. Publications include: *Woman and Her Wishes; Sympathy of Re-Religious; Cheerful Yesterdays.*

Hildegarde, Saint (1098-1179) German visionary.

Noted for *Scivia.*

Hinkson, Katherine Tynan (1861-1931) Irish novelist and poet.

Works include: "Sheep and Lambs"; "Turn O' the Year."

Hobart, Mrs. Charles (n.d.) English poet.

Works include: "The Changed Cross."

Hodgson, Ralph (1871-1962) English poet.

Works include: "The Bull"; *Eve and Other Poems;* "The Song of Honor."

Hoffman, Charles Fenno (1806-1884) American novelist and songwriter.

Founded the *Knickerbocker Magazine*. Works include: "Sparkling and Bright"; "The Myrtle and Steel."

Hoffman, Heinrich (1809-1894) German physician and poet.

Works include: "Cruel Frederick" (Struwwelpeter); "Johnny Head-in-Air" (Struwwelpeter).

Hogg, James (1770-1835) Scottish poet.

Established his career with "Queen's Wake." Published a volume of ballads titled *The Mountain Bard*. Works include: "A Boy's Song"; "The Lark."

Holland, Josiah Gilbert (1819-1881) American physician and editor.

Works include: "Bitter Street"; "Kathrina"; "The Mistress of the Manse."

Holmes, Oliver Wendell (1809-1894) American physician, author, and educator.

Father of the great jurist, Oliver Wendell Holmes, Jr. Wrote voluminously in prose and verse. Works include: "The Autocrat of the Breakfast Table"; "The Ballad of the Oysterman"; "Old Ironsides."

Holtz, Ludwig Heinrich Christoph (1748-1776) German poet.

Works include: "Harvest Song" (Brooks' Translation); "Winter Song" (Brooks' Translation).

Homer (700-1000 B.C.) Greek poet.

Most important ancient Greek author whose two epic poems, the *Iliad* and the *Odyysey*, are among the great works in European literature.

Homer, Greene (b. 1853) American writer and lawyer.

Works include: "The Blind Brother"; "A Story of the Pennsylvania Coal Mines."

Hood, Thomas (1798-1845) English poet and humorist.

Concerned with the poor and under-privileged of society. Edited several magazines, and founded *Hood's Magazine*. Works include: "The Song of a Shirt"; "The Bridge of Sighs"; "The Lay of a Laborer."

Hooper, Ellen Sturgis (n.d.) American poet.

Works include: "Duty"; "The Straight Road."

Hooper, Lucy Hamilton Jones (1835-1893) American journalist and novelist.

Works include: *Poems* (1864-71); *The Tzar's Window.*

Hoppin, William James (1813-1895) American poet.

Works include: "Charlie Machree."

Horace ["Quintus Horatius Flaccus"] (65-8 B.C.) Latin lyric poet, satirist, and critic.

Well educated son of a freed slave. Noted work: "Ars Poetica."

Horne, Richard Henry Hengist (1803-1884) English critic and poet.

Was an adventurer prior to his literary career. Works include: *The Poems of Geoffrey Chaucer Modernized; The Dreamer and the Worker; Prometheus the Fire Bringer.*

Houghton, Richard Monckton Milnes, Lord (1809-1885) English critic and statesman.

Works include: *Poems of Many Years; Palm Leaves.*

Housman, A[lfred] E[dward] (1859-1936) English poet and classicist.

Wrote frequently on themes of love, beauty, and mortality. Known best for *A Shropshire Lad* (1896).

Hovey, Richard (1864-1900) American journalist and poet.

Abandoned the Episcopal ministry for a life in Europe as an actor and dramatist. Works include: "Launcelot and Guenevere"; "The Laurel"; *Songs from the Vagabondia.*

How, William Walsham (1823-1897) English, Bishop of Wakefield.

Works include: "The Word"; "For All the Saints."

Howarth, Ellen Clementine Doran (1827-1899) American poet.

Works include: "'Tis but a Little Faded Flower"; "Thou Wilt Never Grow Old."

Howe, Julia Ward (1819-1910) American editor, lecturer, and suffragette.

Edited the anti-slavery journal *Boston Commonwealth.* Works include: "Battle-Hymn of the Republic."

Howells, William Dean (1837-1920) American novelist and critic.

Influential critic; associated with both the *Atlantic Monthly* and *Harper's Magazine.* Works include: *A Modern Instance; The Rise of Silas Lapham.*

Howitt, Mary (1799-1888) English storywriter and poet.

Works include: "The Fairies of the Caldon Low"; "The Spider and the Fly"; "The Use of Flowers."

Howitt, William (1792-1879) English poet and historian.

Wrote in an easily accessible style. Works include: *Woodburn Grange; The Student Life of Germany.*

Howland, Mary Woolsey (1832-1864) English poet.

Works include: "Rest"; "First Spring Flowers."

Hoyt, Ralph (1806-1878) American Episcopal clergyman.

Works include: "Old"; "Snow -A Winter Sketch."

Huckel, Oliver (1864-1940) American Congregational clergyman.

Works include: "Easy to Drift"; "My Quaker Grandmothers"; "Prayer and Answer."

Hudson, Mary Clemmer Ames ["Mary Clemmer"] (1839-1884) American journalist.

Washington correspondent for the *New York Independent.* Wrote *Ten Years in Washington* from her experiences. Works include: *A Woman's Right; His Two Wives; Victoire.*

Hughes, [James] Langston (1902-1967) American poet.

A leading black poet of the 20th century; received many prizes for his poetry, which have been widely translated. Works include: "Jazz Band in a Parisian Cabaret"; "Saturday Night"; "African Dance."

Hugo, Victor Marie (1802-1885) French poet and novelist.

Leading literary figure of his time. Exiled in 1851 because of opposition to Napoleon II, he returned to Paris in 1870 where his popularity was enormous. Works include: *Les Miserables* (1862) and *The Hunchback of Notre Dame* (1831).

Hume, Alexander (1560-1609) Scottish minister.

Works include: "The Story of a Summer Day."

Hunt, [James Henry] Leigh (1784-1859) English critic and essayist.

Personal friend of Byron, Shelley, and Coleridge. Imprisoned for an alleged libel against the Prince Regent and refused to retract or stop writing as before. Works include: "The Story of Rimini"; "Jenny Kissed Me."

Ingalls, John James (1833-1900) American journalist and U.S. Senator.

Works include: "Opportunity."

Ingelow, Jean (1830-1897) English novelist and poet.

Won fame with *Round of Days.* Works include: "Divided"; "Like a Laverock in the Lift."

Ingoldsby, Thomas (See Barham, Richard Harris)

Irwin, Wallace (b. 1876) American author.

Works include: *Seed of the Sun; The Golden Bed; Mated; The Days of Her Life.*

Jackson, Helen Fiske Hunt ["H.H."] (1831-1885) American poet and novelist.

Concerned with the treatment of American Indians. Works include: *Verses; The Story of*

Boon; A Century of Dishonor; Romona.

Jackson, Henry R. (1820-1898) American lawyer and soldier.

Works include: "My Wife and Child."

Jacoby, Russell Power (1862-1899) American journalist.

Works include: "My Love."

Jacopone, Fra ["Jacopone da Todi"] (1230-1306) Italian poet, satirist, and monk.

Involved in politics. "Stabat Mater" is attributed to him, although authorship is disputed. Works include: "The Little Angels."

Jallal-Ad-Din (see Dschellaleddin Rumi)

Janvier, Margaret Thompson ["Margaret Vandergrift"] (1845-1913) American juvenile writer.

Works include: "The Dead Doll"; "Little Helpers."

Japp, Alexander Hay (1839-1905) Scottish journalist and critic.

Works include: "Shelley."

Jarrell, Randall (1914-1965) American poet, critic, and educator.

Wrote on the loss of innocence and the pain of loneliness in the adult world. Works include: "The Black Swan"; "A Country Life"; "A Sick Child."

Jeffers, Robinson (1887-1962) American poet.

Works include: "Flagons and Apples"; "Californians"; "Tamar"; "Cawdor"; "Flight of Swans."

Jenks, Edward (b. 1835) American poet.

Works include: "Going and Coming."

Jenks, Tudor (1857-1922) American editor.

Works include: "Small and Early."

Jenner, Edward (1749-1832) English physician and poet.

Discovered vaccine for smallpox. Works include: "Signs of Rains."

Johnson, James Weldon (1871-1938) American author and lawyer.

A founder of the National Association for the Advancement of Colored People. Works include: *The Autobiography of an Ex-Colored Man; The Book of American Negro Poetry.*

Johnson, Robert Underwood (1853-1937) American editor and United States ambassador to Italy.

Worked toward internationalizing copyright laws. Best known for "Ode on St. Gardens."

Johnson, Samuel (1709-1784) English lexicographer and critic.

Created the first English language dictionary. Associated with Goldsmith, Burke, Garrick, and Sir Joshua Reynolds. Works include: "Rasselas, Prince of Abyssinia"; "The Vanity of Human Wishes."

Johnson, Anna (see MacManus, Anna Johnson)

Jones, Ebenezer (1820-1860) English political agitator and writer.

Works include: "To Death"; "When the World Is Burning."

Jones, Ernest Charles (1819-1868) English barrister and novelist.

Works include: "The Song of the Lower Classes"; "The Lass and the Lady"; "Lord Lindsay."

Jones, Sir William (1746-1794) English judge and orientalist.

Most celebrated linguist of his time. Translated from Sanskrit, Hindu, and Persic. Works include: "To an Infant Newly Born"; "The State."

Jonson, Ben (1574-1637) English dramatist and poet.

Satirist and moralist, he was very influential. His patron, James I, appointed him poet laureate. Works include: *Volpone*; "Epicoene"; *The Alchemist*.

Joyce, James (1882-1941) Irish novelist.

One of the major 20th century English language writers. Renowned for such novels as *Ulysses* and *Finnegan's Wake*. Works include: "A Flower Given to My Daughter"; "She Weeps Over Rahoon."

Judson, Emily Chubbuck (see Forester, Fanny)

Juvenal [Decimus Junius Juvenalis] (60-140 A.D.) Roman satirist and poet.

Most famous work: "The Satires."

Kalidasa (b. 6 A.D.) Indian writer.

A court poet of King Vikramaditza. Works include: *Sakuntala*.

Keats, John (1795-1821) English poet.

One of the greatest English poets. Works include: "Endymion"; "Hyperion"; "Ode to a Nightingale"; "Ode to a Grecian Urn."

Keble, John (1792-1866) English public examiner and professor of poetry.

Best known for the hymns in *The Christian Year*.

Kemble, Francis Anne (1809-1893) English actress and writer.

Wrote *Francis I* in which she played a part. Works include: "Dream Land"; "Faith"; "Woman's Heart."

Kennedy, Crammond O. (1842-1918) American lawyer.

Born in Scotland. Served as a chaplain in the American Civil War. Works include: "Greenwood Cemetery;" 'The Nation's Prayer."

Keppel, Lady Caroline (n.d.) Scottish poet.

Works include: "Robin Adair."

Key, Francis Scott (1780-1843) American poet and lawyer.

Composed the lyrics for "The Star Spangled Banner." Works include: "With Glowing Heart I'd Praise Thee."

Keyes, Sidney (1922-1943) English poet.

Killed in action in Tunisia during World War II, his poetry was published posthumously. Works include: "The Promised Landscape"; "A Hope for Those Separated by War."

Khayyam, Omar (see Omar Khayyam)

King, Henry (1591-1669) English, Bishop of Chichester.

Works include: "Sic Vita"; "Even Such Is Man"; "The Double Life."

King, Henry (n.d.) Scottish poet and translator.

Works include: "A Transformation" (Latin of Ovid).

Kingsley, Charles (1819-1875) English clergyman and novelist.

A pupil of Samuel Coleridge; involved in a religious controversy with John Henry Newman. Works include: *The Water Babies*; "A Farewell"; "The Old, Old Song"; *Westward Ho!*

Kinney, Coates (1826-1904) American lawyer and journalist.

Edited the *Cincinnati Times* and *Ohio State Journal*. Best known for "Rain on the Roof."

Kipling, Rudyard (1865-1936) English short-story writer, novelist, and poet.

Born in Bombay, India.

Awarded the Nobel Prize for Literature in 1907. Important works include: *Captains Courageous; The Light That Failed*; "Kim."

Kirks, Edmund ["Gilmore, James Roberts"] (1823-1903) American author and journalist.

Works include: "Among the Kines"; "Adrift in Dixie."

Klopstock, Friedrich Gottlieb (1724-1803) German poet.

Works include: "Messiah."

Knowles, James Sheridan (1784-1862) Irish preacher, actor, and dramatist.

Works include: "William Tell"; "The Hunchback."

Knox, William (1789-1825) Scottish poet.

Works include: "Mortality"; "Oh, Why Should the Spirit of Mortal be Proud?"

Korner, Karl Theodore (1791-1813) German poet and dramatist for the Vienna Theater.

Works include: "Good Night"; "Men and Boys"; "Sword Song."

Kreymborg, Alfred (1893-1966) American poet, lecturer, and puppeteer.

Edited avante garde literary magazines. Works include:

Mushrooms; Plays for Merry Andrews; Troubadour.

Krummacher, Friedrich Adolph (1767-1845) German preacher.

Best known for his parables. Works include: "Alpine Nights"; "The Moss Rose."

Labe, Louise (1526-1566) French poet.

Wrote sonnets and lyrics, influenced by Petrarch. Works include: "As Soon as I Ever Begin to Overtake"; "Time Makes an Ending of the Pyramids."

La Conte, Maria (n.d.) American poet.

Works include: "Somebody's Darling."

La Fontaine, Jean de (1621-1695) French poet.

Achieved international recognition for his suberbly rendered fables. Works include: *Selected Fables* (1668-94); *Tales and Novels in Verse* (1664-74); "The Cat and the Fox."

Laing, Alexander (1787-1857) Scottish poet.

Works include: "The Happy Mother"; "My Ain Wife."

Lamb, Charles ["Elia"] (1775-1834) English essayist.

Works include: *Rosamund Gray*

(1798); "In My Own Album";
"A Farewell to Tobacco."

Lamb, Mary (1765-1847) English
author.

With her brother Charles, she
wrote *Tales from the Plays of
Shakespeare for Youthful
Readers*. Works include:
"Aspiraton"; "Choosing a
Name."

Lampman, Archibald (1861-
1899) Canadian poet.

Wrote frequently about his love
for nature. Works include: "After Rain"; "The Song
Sparrow."

Landon, Letitia Elizabeth (1801-
1838) English poet.

Works include: "Death and the
Youth"; "The Wind"; "The
Factory."

Landor, Walter Savage (1775-
1864) English poet and essayist.

Works include: *Hellenics;
Poems and Inscriptions; Last
Fruit of an Old Tree.*

Lang, Andrew (1844-1912) Scottish critic and poet.

Wrote very popular series of
stories for children. Works in-
clude: *The Blue Fairy Book;
Ballads and Lyrics of Old
France; Customs and Myths;
Letters to Dead Authors.*

Lanier, Sidney (1842-1881)
American poet and musician.

Works include: *Corn, Clover
and the Bee; Song of the Chat-
tahoochee; Sunrise Song.*

Lanigan, George Thomas (1845-
1886) Canadian journalist.

Founded *Freelance*, a journal of
satire and humor. Works include: "A Threnody"; "The
Amateur Orlando."

Larcom, Lucy (1826-1893)
American editor and poet.

Works include: *Ships in the
Mist; Roadside Poems; Hillside
and Seaside in Poetry.*

Lascelles, Sir Frank Cavendish
(b. 1841) English diplomat.

Works include: "Hackon's
Defiance" (Danish of Oeh-
lenschlages).

Lazarus, Emma (1849-1887)
American poet.

Devoted her writing largely to
Jewish themes. Her sonnet
celebrating the Statue of Liberty, "The New Colossus," is a
part of the monument. Works
include: "Mater Amabilis";
"The World's Justice."

Lear, Edward (1812-1888) English humorist and artist.

His limericks and nonsense
verse are still widely read.

Works include: *Sketches of Rome and Its Environs* (1842); *Illustrated Excursions in Italy; Journal in Greece and Albania.*

Lecky, Rt. Hon. William Edward Hartpole (1839-1903) Irish historian.

Published *The Leader of Public Opinion* anonymously. Works include: *History of the Rise and Influence of the Spirit of Rationalism in Europe; History of England in the 18th Century.*

Lee, Laurie (b. 1914) English writer.

Published plays, memoirs, and travel books. Works include: *The Sun My Monument; The Bloom of Candles; Pocket Poems.*

Lee-Hamilton, Eugene (1845-1907) English diplomat.

Works include: "Mimma Bella"; "Sea Shell Murmurs"; "Wood Song."

Le Gallienne, Richard (1866-1947) English writer.

Works include: George Meredith; *The Religion of a Literary Man; The Quest of the Golden Girl.*

Leggett, William (1801-1839) American journalist.

Worked for the New York Evening Post . Works include: *Lei-*

sure Hours at Sea; Naval Stories; Tales of a Country Schoolmaster.

Leland, Charles Godfrey (1824-1903) American scholar and editor.

Published four valuable works on the language and customs of the gypsies. Works include: *Pennsylvania Dutch; The Hans Brinker Ballads.*

Leonard, William Ellery (1876-1944) American poet.

Works include: *Sonnets and Poems; The Vaunt of Man; This Midland City.*

Leonardo da Vinci (1452-1519) Italian artist, engineer, and writer.

One of the greatest geniuses of all time. Works include: *Treatise on Painting and Perserverance.*

Leonidas (59-102 B.C.) Greek poet and King of Sparta.

His style influenced the later Greek epigram. Works include: "Home"; "On the Picture of an Infant."

Le Roux, Guirade (12th c.) French poet.

Works include: "Fidelity in Danbt" (Preston's Translation).

L'estrange, Sir Roger (1616-1704) English poet.

Works include: "In Prison"; "Loyalty Confin'd."

Lever, Charles James (1806-1872) Irish novelist.

Edited the *Dublin University Magazine*. Works include: "Charles O'Malley"; "Tom Burke"; "Jack Hinton."

Lewes, Mary Ann (see Cross, Mary Ann Evans Lewes)

Lewis, Alun (1915-1944) Welsh poet.

Killed while on duty as a soldier during World War II. A frequent theme is the loneliness and alienation of a soldier at war. His best work is *Raider's Dawn.*

Lewis, Cecil Day (see Day Lewis, Cecil)

Lewis, Matthew Gregory ["Monk"] (1775-1818) English poet and dramatist.

Works include: *The Monk; Feudal Tyrants; The Castle Spectre.*

Leyden, John (1775-1811) English author and orientalist.

Admired for his Scottish ballads. Works include: "Scenes of Infancy"; "Lords of the Wilderness."

Lighthall, W.D. (see Schuyler-Lighthall, W.D.)

Lindsay, Caroline Blanche Elizabeth Fitzroy, Lady (1844-1912) English painter.

Works include: "My Heart is Lute"; "Sonnet."

Lindsay, [Nicholas] Vachel (1879-1931) American poet.

Works include: "The Congo"; "General William Booth Enters Into Heaven"; "Every Soul Is a Circus."

Linton, William James (1812-1898) English wood engraver and author.

Works include: *The Plain of Freedom; Claribel and Other Poems.*

Lippincott, Sara Jane Clarke ["Grace Greenwood"] (1823-1904) American editor and author.

Noted for writing "Ariadne." Works include: *Greenwood Leaves; Recollections of My Childhood.*

Little, Lizzie Mary (n.d.) English poet.

Works include: "Life."

Littledale, Richard Frederick (1833-1890) Irish clergyman.

Works include: *The Catholic Ritual in the Church of England; Pharisaic Proselytism; A Short History of the Council of Trent.*

Locker-Lampson, Frederick (1821-1895) English poet.

Wrote for the Admiralty Office. Works include: *London Lyrics; Lyra Elegantiarum; Patchwork.*

Lockhart, John Gibson (1794-1854) Scottish biographer and critic.

Edited the Quarterly Review. Wrote the definitive biography of his father-in-law, Sir Walter Scott. Works include: "Beyond"; "The Moor Calaynos."

Lodge, Thomas (1557-1625) English dramatist and poet.

Wrote *Rosalynde* while on a sea expedition; it served as a source for Shakespeare's *As You Like It.* Works include: "Accurst Be Love"; "A Blith and Bonny Country Lass."

Logan, John (1748-1788) Scottish minister and poet.

Works include: "To the Cuckoo"; "The Braes Were Bonny."

Logau, Frederick von ["Salomon von Golau"] (1604-1655) German epigrammatist.

Works include: "Retribution" (Longfellow's translation).

Longfellow, Henry Wadsworth (1807-1882) American poet.

Professor at Harvard University. Famous works include: "The Song of Hiawatha"; "The Courtship of Miles Standish"; "Keramos"; "Tales of a Wayside Inn."

Longfellow, Samuel (1819-1892) American clergyman, poet, and novelist.

Brother of Henry Wadsworth. Won acclaim for his hymns. Works include: *Hymns of the Spirit; Life of Henry Wadsworth Longfellow; A Few Verses of Many Years.*

Lovelace, Richard (1618-1658) English poet and dramatist.

One of the Cavalier poets, he was imprisoned by Cromwell for royalist sentiments. Works include: "To Althea from Prison"; "To Lucasta on Going to the Wars."

Lover, Samuel (1797-1866) Irish novelist.

Famous for *Legends and Tales* Illustrative of Irish character. Works include: "Rory O More"; "Handy Andy"; "Treasure Trove."

Loveridge, Richard (18th c.)
English poet.

Works include: stanzas added to
"The Roast Beef of Old
England."

Lowell, Amy (1874-1925) American poet and critic.

Turned away from traditional
verse forms in 1913, becoming
a leader of the Imagists in England. Works include: "Anticipation"; "The Dinner Party";
"Shooting the Sun."

Lowell, James Russell (1819-
1891) American man of letters,
diplomat, abolitionist, and
critic.

His literary reputation was inter-
national. Works include: "The
Cathedral"; *Among My Books;
My Study Windows*; "Centennial
Ode"; *Conversations on Some
of the Old Poets.*

Lowell, Maria White (1821-
1853) American poet.

Wife of James Russell Lowell.
Works include: "The Alpine
Shepherd"; "The Morning
Glory."

Lowell, Robert (1917-1977)
American poet.

His career was marked by constant experimentation. Works
include: "The Quaker Grave-
yard in Nantucket"; "The Exile's Return."

Lowell, Robert Trail Spence
(1816-1891) American
clergyman.

Best known for *The New Priest
in Conception Bay*. Works include: *Fresh Hearts and Other
Poems; Anthony Brade.*

Lunt, George (1803-1888)
American lawyer, editor, and
poet.

Edited the Boston Courier.
Works include: *The Age of
Gold; Lyric Poems; The Union.*

Luther, Martin (1483-1546) German reformer.

Excommunicated from the Catholic church (1520) because of
his writings. Instituted a total
reform of the Church which led
to the founding of Protestantism. Works include: "A
Mighty Fortress Is Our God."

Lyall, Sir Alfred Comyns (1835-
1911) English civil servant.

Works include: *Asiatic Studies;
Religious and Social; English
Men of Action.*

Lyly, John (1554-1606) English
dramatist and member of
Parliament.

Famous for his attempts to use
words as musical notes, subor-
dinating content to sound.
Works include: "Alexander and
Campaspe"; "Endymion."

Lynn, Ethel (see Beers, Ethelinda Elliott)

Lyte, Henry Francis (1793-1847) Scottish clergyman and hymn writer.

Remembered for his hymns, although he also wrote secular poetry. Works include: "Abide With Me."

Lytle, William Haines (1826-1863) American soldier-general and poet.

Works include: "Antony to Cleopatra"; "Jacaqueline."

Lyttelton, George, Baron (1709-1773) English poet.

Works include: "Tell Me, My Heart, If This Be Love."

Lytton, Edward George (see Bulwer-Lytton, Edward, 1st Baron Lytton)

Lytton, Edward Robert Bulwer, Earle ["Owen Meredith"] (see Bulwer-Lytton, Robert, 1st Earl Lytton)

MacAndrew, Barbara Miller (n.d.) Scottish poet.

Works include: "Coming."

Macaulay, Thomas Babington, Macaulay, 1st Baron (1800-1859) English historian, essayist, parliamentarian, and poet.

Works include: *The History of England.*

MacCarthy, Denis Florence (1817-1882) Irish lawyer and poet.

Won admiration for his lyrics on Irish history and legend. Works include: "Spring Flowers from Ireland"; "Waiting for the May."

MacDiarmid, Hugh (see Grieve, Christopher Murray)

MacDonald, Elizabeth Roberts (1864-1922) Canadian poet.

Works include: "A Song of Seasons."

MacDonald, George (1824-1905) Scottish novelist and poet.

Works include: "David Elginbrod"; "Robert Falconer"; "Lilith."

Mackail, John William (1859-1945) English poet.

Works include: "An Entruscan Ring."

MacKay, Charles (1814-1889) Scottish journalist and songwriter.

Nearly all of his verse was set to music and became popular. Also wrote biographies and books on history and travel. Works include: "'Climbing to the Light"; "Small Beginnings."

McKay, Claude (1889-1948) Jamaican poet.

Wrote verse in his native dialect. First black to receive the medal of the Institute of Arts and Sciences for *Songs of Jamaica and Constabulatory Ballads.* Works include: "After the Winter"; "The Barrier."

MacLeish, Archibald (1892-1982) American poet.

Awarded Pulitzer Prizes for his verse-drama, *J.B.* (1958) and *Collected Poems* (1952). Served as librarian of Congress (1939-1944). Works include: "Exploration by Air"; "The Jungle."

MacManus, Anna Johnston ["Ethna Carbery] (1866-1902) Irish poet.

Works include: "Hills O' My Heart"; "Mea Culpa!"; "The Other."

McCreery, John Luckey (1835-1906) American poet.

Works include: "There Is No death."

Mclellan, Isaac (1806-1899) American lawyer and poet.

Wrote poems about sports themes. Works include: "The Death of Napoleon"; "New England's Dead."

McMaster, Guy Humphreys (1829-1887) American jurist and poet.

Works include: *A Dream of Thanksgiving Eve; The Commanders.*

MacNeice, Louis (1907-1963) Irish poet.

Concerned with political ideas and social protest. Works include: *Blind Fireworks; Eulogue for Christmas; Holes in the Sky: Poems.*

Mace, Frances Laughton (1836-1899) American poet.

Works include: "The Angelus"; *Only Waiting.*

Macedonius (n.d.) Greek poet and heretic.

Works include: *Memory and Oblivion* (Bland's translation).

Maginn, William (1793-1842) Irish journalist, editor, and poet.

Works include: *The City of Demons; Bob Burke's Duel with Ensign Brady.*

Mahony, Francis Silvester ["Father Prout"] (1804-1866) Irish clergyman, poet, and journalist.

Works include: "The Bells of Shandon"; "The Flight into Egypt."

Mangan, James Clarence (1803-1849) Irish poet.

Demonstrated a great command of language. Works include: *Romances and Ballads of Ireland; German Anthology; Poets and Poetry of Munster.*

Marguerite de Valois ["Queen of Navarre"] (1492-1549) French poet.

Cultivated literature and art at her court. Works include: *The Heptameron.*

Markham, Edwin (1852-1940) American educator, reformer, and poet.

Famous for *The Man with the Hoe.*

Marlowe, Christopher (1564-1593) English poet and dramatist.

A contemporary of Shakespeare. Works include: *Tamburlaine; Doctor Faustus; Tragedy of Edward II.*

Marot, Clement (1495-1544) French poet.

Leading French poet of his age. Works include: "Ballade of a Friar"; "A Love-Lesson."

Marston, Philip Bourke (1850-1887) English poet.

Works include: "After"; "Garden Fairies."

Martial [Marcus Valerius Martialis] (40 A.D.) Roman poet.

Works include: "Country Pleasures"; "The Bean."

Martin, Edward Sanford (1856-1906) American journalist.

Works include: *Courtship of a Careful Man; Girl of Pompeii; Windfalls of Observation.*

Martin, Sir Theodore (1816-1909) Scottish biographer and poet.

Translator of classics. Works include: *Book of Ballads*; "Love Is All"; "Gazelles."

Martley, John (1844-1882) Irish lawyer and writer.

Works include: "A Budget of Paradoxes."

Marvell, Andrew (1621-1678) English satirist, poet, and political writer.

A leading wit of his time and a member of Pariament, he is best remembered for his lyric poetry. Works include: "To His Coy Mistress"; "The Fair Singer"; "The Garden."

Mary, Queen of Hungary (1505-1558)

Works include: "Prayer."

Marzials, Theophilus Julius Henry (1850-1920) English composer and poet.

Of French heritage. Works include: *Gallery of Pigeons and*

Other Poems; "Twinckenham Ferry."

Mason, Caroline Atherton Briggs (1823-1890) American poet.

Works include: "The Voyage."

Massey, Gerald (1828-1907) English poet and editor.

Founded and edited the *Spirit of Freedom.* A firm believer in spiritualism. Works include: "War Waits"; *My Lyrical Life.*

Massinger, Philip (1584-1639) English dramatist.

Few of his works have survived. Works include: *New Way to Pay Old Debts; The City Madam; The Roman Actor.*

Meleager (ca. 50 B.C.) Greek poet.

Works include: "Eros Is Missing"; "Spring"; "The Wreath."

Mellen, Grenville (1799-1841) American lawyer.

Works include: "The Lonely Bugle Grieves."

Mercer, Margaret (1791-1847) American educator.

Works include: "Exhortation to Prayer."

Meredith, George (1828-1909) English novelist and poet.

Educated in Germany. Works include: *Diana of the Crossways; The Ordeal of Richard*; "Modern Love"; "Faith on Trial."

Meredith, Owen (see Bulwer-Lytton, Edward Robert, 1st Earl Lytton)

Messinger, Robert Hinckley (1811-1874) American magazine writer.

Works include: "A Winter Wish."

Metastasio, Pietro (1698-1782) Italian court poet.

Created the modern Italian opera. Composed twenty operas and eight sacred dramas.

Meynell, Alice Thompson (1875-1898) English essayist and poet.

Spent her childhood in Italy. Works include: *Preludes; Rhythm of Life.*

Michaelangelo Buonarroti (1475-1564) Italian sculptor, architect, painter, and poet.

Poems include: "The Might of One Fair Face"; "Beauty and the Artist"; "Love's Entreaty."

Mickle, William Julius (1735-1788) Scottish poet.

Translated the *Lusiads* into English. Works include: "Alamada Hill."

Millay, Edna St. Vincent (1892-1950) American poet.

Received the Pulitzer Prize for poetry in 1923 for "The Harp Weaver." Works include: "Renascence"; "Bluebeard"; "Lethe."

Miller, Cincinnatus Heine ["Joaquin Miller"] (1841-1913) American poet, lawyer, judge, and journalist. Popular as a frontier poet celebrating the West. Works include: *Collected Poems; Songs of the Soul; Life of Christ.*

Miller, William (1810-1872) Scottish poet, engraver, and writer.

Works include: "Willie Winkie."

Milman, Henry Hart (1791-1869) English writer and historian.

Made the first attempt to apply secular historical methods to the sacred history with *History of the Jews.* Works include: "For Palm Sunday"; "The Holy Field."

Milnes, Richard Monkton, 1st Baron Houghton (1809-1885) English poet, critic and statesman.

Conservative member of Parliament, later joined the Liberals under Lord John Russell. Works include: *Memorials of a Town in*

Greece; Memorials of a Residence on the Continent; Historical Poems.

Milton, John (1608-1674) English poet.

Generally considered the greatest English poet after Shakespeare. Frequently wrote in blank verse. Composed much of his verse while blind. Most famous works: *Paradise Lost* (1660-1674); *Paradise Regained* (1671); *Samson Agonistes* (1671); "Lycidas" (1638).

Mistral, Frederick (1830-1914) French poet.

Received the poet's prize of the French Academy and the Cross of the Legion of Honor for *Mireio.* Works include: "The Leaf Picking."

Mitchell, Agnes E. (n.d.) American poet.

Works include: "When the Cows Come Home."

Mitchell, Silas Weir (1829-1914) American physician, poet, and novelist.

Works include: "Hugh Wayne"; *Adventures of Francois; Autobiography of a Quack.*

Mitchell, Walter (1826-1908) American clergyman and author.

Notable works: *Bryan Maurice;*

"Tackling Off Shore"; "The Mocking-Bird."

Mitford, Mary Russell (1787-1855) English writer.

Best known works: *Our Village; Recollections of a Literary Life; Julian.*

Moir, David Macbeth (1798-1851) Scottish physician and poet.

Wrote the first volume of *Outlines of the Ancient History of Medicine.*

Monro, Harold (1879-1932) English poet.

Helpful to aspiring poets. Works include: "Bird at Dawn"; "The Natural History"; "Strange Meetings."

Montgomery, James (1771-1854) Scottish editor and poet.

Works include: "The Pelican Island"; "The West Indies"; "The Common Lot."

Montreuil, Mathieu de (1611-1691) French poet.

Works include: "To Madam de Sevigne."

Montrose, James Graham, 1st Marquess of (1612-1650) Scottish poet and noble under Charles I.

Hanged for rebellion in Edinburgh. Works include: "Epitaph on King Charles I"; "My Dear and Only Love"; "Heroic Love."

Moody, William Vaughn (1869-1910) American poet.

Wrote primarily in blank verse. Works include: "The Fire-Bringer"; "The Death of Eve"; "Gloucester Moors."

Moore, Clement Clarke (1779-1863) American educational writer.

Compiled the first Hebrew and Greek lexicon published in America. Remembered for: "A Visit from St. Nicholas."

Moore, Marianne (1887-1972) American poet.

Satiric and intellectual poet. Works include: "A Carriage from Sweden"; "The Paper Nautilus"; "Dock Rats."

Moore, Thomas (1779-1852) Irish poet and translator.

Works include: "A Temple to Friendship"; "Tis the Last Rose of Summer"; "The Harp That Once Through Tara's Halls."

Moore, Thomas Sturge (1870-1944) English poet.

Works include: "Days and Nights"; "The Deed."

Morike, Eduard (1804-1875) German novelist and poet.

Considered the greatest German lyrist after Goethe. Best works include: *Poems; Idylls from the Lake of Constancy.*

Morlaix, Bernard de (ca. 1122-1156) French Benedictine Monk.

Works include: "Praise of the Celestial Country" (Neale's Translation).

Morris, George Pope (1801-1864) American journalist and song writer.

Founded *The Home Journal.* Works include: "Woodman, Spare that Tree."

Morris, William (1834-1896) English poet and designer.

Leader of the Socialist movement in Great Britain. Works include: "Jason"; "The Earthy Paradise"; "Love Is Enough."

Moss, Thomas (1740-1808) English clergyman and poet.

Works include: "The Beggar."

Motherwell, William (1797-1835) Scottish journalist.

Edited a collection of songs called *The Harp of Renfrewshire,* and an important collection of ballads entitled *Minstrelsy: Ancient and Modern.* Works include: "The Cavalier's Song"; "Sing on, Blith Bird."

Moulton, Louise Chandler (1835-1908) American journalist and writer.

A prominent literary figure in Boston. Works include: *This, That, and the Other; Stories, Essays and Poems.*

Moultrie, John (1799-1874) English clergyman.

The Rector of Rugby in 1828. Works include: *My Brother's Grave and Other Poems; The Dream of Life and Other Poems.*

Mueller, Wilhelm (1794-1827) German teacher, librarian, and lyric poet.

Some of his songs were set to music by Schubert. Works include: *Poems from the Posthumous Papers of a Traveling Bugler; Songs of the Greeks.*

Muhlenberg, William Augustus (1796-1877) American clergyman.

Worked to improve the condition of the poor. Works include: *Christ and the Bible; I Would Not Live Always.*

Munby, Arthur Joseph (1828-1910) English poet and barrister.

Primarily wrote pastoral idylls. Works include: *Verses, Old and New*; "Dorothy and Susan"; "Steps Backward."

Myers, Frederick William Henry (1843-1901) English poet and critic.

Classics lecturer at Cambridge University. Works include: "St. Paul"; *Renewal of Youth and Other Poems.*

Nairne, Carolina Oliphant, Baroness (1766-1845) Scottish poet.

Scottish nationalist. Works include: "The Land of the Leal"; "The Auld House"; "Will Ye No Come Back Again?"

Nash, Thomas (1567-1601) English dramatist, novelist, and satirist.

Expelled from Cambridge University for satirizing the authorities. Collaborated with Christopher Marlowe. Works include: *Summers Last Will and Testament.*

Naso, Publius Ovidius (see Ovid).

Navarre, Queen of (see Marguerite de Valois).

Neale, John Mason (1818-1866) English church historian and poet.

Gained prominence with his translations of Latin and Greek hymns. Works include: "Art Thou Weary"; "Jerusalem the Golden."

Neele, Henry (1798-1828) English barrister.

Edited an edition of Shakespeare's plays. Works include: *Dramatic Scenes; Odes and Other Poems.*

Neihardt, John G. (1881-1973) American poet.

Appointed poet laureate of Nebraska by an act of the legislature. Works include: "April Theology"; "The Song of Three Friends"; "When I Am Dead."

Newell, Robert Henry ["Orpheus C. Kerr"] (1836-1901) American journalist, humorist, and editor.

Works include: *A Palace Beautiful and Other Poems*; "The Cloven Foot."

Newman, John Henry (1801-1890) English churchman, Roman Catholic cardinal.

Established and proliferated the Oxford movement (the "Catholic character" of the English Church). Works include: *Apologia pro vita sua; History of Arionism*; "Lead Kindly Light."

Nichols, Rebecca S. (1819-1903) American poet.

Works include: "The Philosopher Toad."

Nicholson, Norman (b. 1914) English poet.

Wrote frequently on landscape, the commonplace, and his

Christian faith. Works include: "The Prayer"; "Rockferns"; "The Blackberry."

Nicoll, Robert (1814-1837) Scottish poet.

Gained large success with his first book of poems. Works include: "Bonnie Bessie Lee"; "The Hero."

Noel, Thomas (1799-1861) English poet.

Works include: *Rhymes and Rondelayes.*

Nokes, W.F. (n.d.) English poet.

Works include: "Paulina's Appeal" (French of Corneille).

North, Christopher (see Wilson, John)

Norton, Caroline Elizabeth Sheridan [afterwards Lady Stirling-Maxwell] (1807-1877) English novelist and poet.

Works include: "The Undying One"; *A Voice from the Factories; Aunt Carrys Ballads.*

Norton, Charles Eliot (1827-1908) American author and professor.

Taught history of art at Harvard University. Works include: *The New Life of Dante; Notes of Travel and Study in Italy.*

Noyes, Alfred (1880-1958) English poet and critic.

A visiting professor of English at Princeton University. Best known for "The Highwayman." Works include: "The Loom of Years"; "The Flower of Old Japan"; "The Forest of Wile Thyme."

O'Brien, Fitz-James (1828-1862) Irish magazine writer and soldier.

Works include: "The Lost Steamship"; "The Second Mate"; *The Diamond Lens and Other Stories.*

O'Brien, William Smith (1803-1864) Irish patriot and member of Parliament.

Works include: "Never Despair."

Occidente, Maria del (see Brooks, Maria Gowen)

O'Connor, Joseph (1841-1908) American journalist.

Works include: "The General's Death"; "What Was My Dream."

O'Donnell, John Francis (1837-1874) Irish journalist.

Works include: "A Spinning Song."

Oehlenschlager, Adam Gottlob (1777-1850) Danish dramatic poet.

Works include: "The Death of Balder"; "The Gods of the

North"; "Aladdin Starkadder"; "Axel and Balborg"; "The Admiral Fordens Kjold."

Ogden, Eva L. (n.d.) Works include: "The Sea."

O'Hara, Theodore (1820-1867) American lawyer and soldier.

Works include: "Bivouac of the Dead."

O'Keeffe, John (1747-1833) Irish dramatist.

Works include: "Merry Sherwood"; "I Love a Lass."

Oldys, William (1696-1761) English biographer.

His annotated copy of Langbaine's *Account of the Early Dramatick Poets* is in The British Museum.

Oliphant, Thomas (1799-1873) English poet.

Works include: "Where are the Men" (Welsh of Taliessin); "National Air: Wales."

O'Mahony, Francis Sylvester (see Mahony, F.S.).

Omar Khayyam (1050?-1123) Persian mathematician, astronomer, and poet.

Helped reform the calendar. Famous for the *Rubaiyat.*

O'Reilly, John Boyle (1844-1890) Irish writer and journalist.

Works include: "Songs of the Southern Seas"; "Moondyne"; "In Bohemia."

Orleans, Charles, Duc de Orleans (1391-1467) French poet.

Member of the French royal family. Works include: "The Fairest Thing in Mortal Eyes" (Cary's translation); "The Summer's Harbingers Are Here."

Ormeby, John (n.d.)

Works include: "Battle Scene" (from the Spanish).

Orr, James (1770-1816) Irish poet.

Works include: "The Irishman."

Osgood, Frances Sargent Locke (1811-1850) American poet.

Works include: "Wreath of Wild Flowers"; Poetry of Flowers."

Osgood, Kate Putnam (b. 1841) American poet.

Works include: "Driving Home the Cows."

O'Shaughnessy, Arthur William Edgar (1844-1881) Irish poet.

Follower of the French Romantic school.

Ovid [Publius Ovidius Naso] (43 B.C.-18 A.D.) Roman poet.

Friend of Horace and Propertius. Works include: "The Loves"; "The Art of Loving"; "The Fasti"; "The Tristia"; *The Metamorphoses.*

Oxford, Earl of (see Vere, Edward de)

Pagan, Isabel (1740-1821) Scottish poet.

Works include: "Ca the Yowes to the Knowes"; "The Answer."

Page, H.A. (see Japp, Alexander Hay).

Paine, Thomas (1737-1809) English publicist and political writer.

Works include: *Common Sense; The Rights of Man; Age of Reason.*

Palgrave, Francis Turner (1824-1897) English anthologist and poet.

Famous for his enduring anthology, *The Golden Treasury of the Best Songs and Lyrical Poems in the English Language* (1861). Works include: *The Passionate Pilgrim; The Visions of England.*

Palladas (fl. ca. 400 A.D.) Greek poet.

Works include: "The Generous Air" (Hardinge's Translation); "All the World's a Stage."

Palmer, John Williamson (1825-1906) American physician and editor.

Gained popularity with his Civil War ballads. Associated with Century Dictionary. Works include: *Golden Dragon,* or *Up and Down the Irrawaddi;* "Stonewall Jackson's Way."

Palmer, Ray (1808-1887) American clergyman and hymn writer.

Works include: "My Faith Looks Up to Thee" (translated into twenty languages).

Palmer, William Pitt (1805-1884) American poet.

Works include: "Ode to the Light"; "Orpheus and Eurydice."

Park, Andrew (1807-1863) Scottish poet.

Wrote "Egypt and the East" after an Oriental tour. Works include: "Silent Love"; "The Auld Folks"; "Veritas."

Parker, Dorothy (1893-1967) American writer and humorist.

A member of the "Algonquian Circle," a group of influential New York intellectuals who met informally. Works include: *Enough Rope* (1926); "Big Blond" (1930).

Parker, Sir Gilbert (1862-1932) Canadian journalist and novelist.

Knighted in 1902; became a baron in 1915. Works include: *Pierre and His People; Tales of the Far North; The Seals of the Mighty; The Right of Way.*

Parker, Theodore (1810-1860) American Unitarian clergyman and abolitionist.

Works include: *Sermons for the Times; The Transient and Permanent in Christianity; Discourse on Matters Pertaining To Religion.*

Parnell, Francis Isabel (1854-1882) Irish poet.

Works include: "After Death."

Parnell, Thomas (1679-1717) Irish poet.

Associated with Addison, Congreve, Steele, and other Whigs, but joined Tory wits such as Swift, Pope, Gay, and Arbuthnot. Works include: "The Hermit"; "A Night-Piece on Death."

Parsons, Thomas William (1819-1892) American poet.

Works include: *The Old House at Sudbury; The Magnolia; Ghetto Di Roma.*

Patchen, Kenneth (1911-1972) American poet.

His poetry ranged from the realism of the thirties to the free forms of the "beat poets" of the

fifties. Works include: "At the New Year"; "The Fox"; *Before the brave.*

Patmore, Coventry (1823-1896) English poet.

Works include: *The Angel in the House; The Unknown Eros and Other Odes; Children's Garland.*

Paul, John ["Charles Henry Webb"] (1834-1905) American journalist and humorist.

Works include: *John Paul's Book; Prose and Verse; Vagrom Verse.*

Payne, John Howard (1791-1852) American actor, dramatist, and translator.

Works include: "Home Sweet Home."

Peale, Rembrandt (1778-1860) American artist.

Painted famous portrait of Washington. Works include: *Faith and Hope.*

Peck, Samuel Minturn (1854-1905) American poet and farmer.

Works include: *Cap and Bells; Rings and Love Knots; Alabama Sketches.*

Percival, James Gates (1795-1856) American poet, scientist, and West Point professor.

Considered a leading poet by his contemporaries. Works include: *Prometheus; Clio; Dream of a Day.*

Percy, Thomas (1728-1811) English poet.

Works include: *Reliques of Ancient English Poetry.*

Perry, Nora (1832-1896) American journalist and poet.

Works include: "Cressid"; "In June."

Pettee, G.W. (n.d.) Canadian poet.

Works include: "Sleigh Song."

Pfeffel, Gottlieb Conrad (1736-1809) German poet and fabulist.

Works include: *Nobleman and the Pensioner; The Tobacco Pipe; Dramatic Plays for Children.*

Phelps, Charles Henry (b. 1853) American lawyer and poet.

Works include: *Californian Verses; Henry Ward Beecher.*

Phillips, Ambrose (1675-1749) English politician, poet, and dramatist.

Works include: *The Distressed Mother; The Briton; Humphrey, Duke of Gloucester.*

Philostratus (170-190 A.D.) Greek rhetorician and Sophist.

Works include: *Images; Heroican; The Epistles*; "Lives of the Sophists."

Piatt, John James (1835-1919) American editor and poet.

Works include: *Poems by Two Friends; The Nests at Washington.*

Piatt, Sarah Morgan [Bryan] (1836-1919) American poet.

Works include: "A Woman's Poem"; *A Voyage to the Fortunate Isles; An Enchanted Castle.*

Pierpoint, John (1785-1866) American poet and clergyman.

His abolitionist views forced him to resign his Boston ministry. Works include: *Airs of Palestine and Other Poems*; "Warren's Address at the Battle of Bunker Hill."

Pike, Albert (1809-1891) American lawyer and journalist.

Works include: *Prose Sketches; Poems.*

Pindar, Peter (see Wolcott, John)

Pinkney, Edward Coate (1802-1828) American poet.

Virtually unknown during his short life, his talent was not recognized until Poe, among others, later praised his poetry. Works include: *Poems* (1925).

Piozzi, Hester Thrale (see Thrale, Hester Lynch)

Pitt, William (b. 1840) English poet and shipbuilder.

Works include: "Sailor's Consolation."

Pitter, Ruth (b. 1897) English poet.

Out of the mainstream of contemporary verse, she prefers religious and metaphysical themes. Works include: "The Bat"; "The Eternal Image."

Poe, Edgar Allan (1809-1849) American poet and writer.

Known for perfection of form and language. Works include: "Annabel Lee"; "Ulalume"; *The Fall of the House of Usher; The Raven and Other Poems* .

Pollen, John (1848-1923)

Works include: "The Last Leaf."

Pollok, Robert (1798-1827) Scottish poet.

Works include: *Tales of the Convenanter; The Course of Time.*

Pope, Alexander (1688-1744) English poet.

The leading 18th century English poet, and master verse satirist. Works include: *Essay on Criticism; The Rape of the Lock;* *Essay on Man;* "Eloise to Abelard."

Pound, Ezra (1885-1972) American poet.

Controversial and innovative, he influenced many other important writers, such as T.S. Eliot and James Joyce. Works include: *Cantos;* "Historian"; "The Golden Sestina."

Praed, Winthrop Mackworth (1802-1839) English poet and lawyer.

Member of the Parliament. Wrote light verse. Works include: "Camp-Bell"; "Charade."

Pratt, Anna Maria (1806-1893) English teacher and nature writer.

Works include: "Early News"; "A Little Mistake."

Prentice, George Denison (1802-1870) American poet and editor.

Works include: *Prenticeman; Life on Henry Clay.*

Preston, Annie A. (n.d.)

Works include: *The Green Grass under the Snow.*

Preston, Harriet Waters (1843-1911) American poet and essayist.

Works include: *Ballad of Guibour.*

Preston, Margaret Junkin (1820-1897) American poet.

Writings deal with Civil War period. Works include: *Silverwood; Aunt Dorothy.*

Priest, Nancy Amelia Woodbury (1827-1870) American poet.

Works include: *Heaven; Over the River.*

Prince, F[rank] T[empleton] (b. 1912) South African poet.

Noted for exquisite sense of language and carefully polished stanzas. Works include: "At a Parade"; "Chaka."

Pringle, Thomas (1789-1834) Scottish poet and reformer.

Works show considerable mastery of diction. Works include: *Afar in the Desert.*

Procter, Adelaide Anne (1825-1864) English poet.

Works include: *Legends and Lyrics.*

Proctor, Bryan Waller ["Cornwall, Barry"] (1787-1874) English barrister and man of letters.

Works include: *Dramatic Scenes; The Flood of Thessaly; English Songs.*

Proctor, Edna Dean (b. 1838) American poet.

Works include: *A Russian Journey; Songs of America.*

Propertius, Aurelius Sextur (50 B.C.-15 A.D.) Roman poet.

Works include: *Beauty Unadorned; Immortality of Genius.*

Father Prout (see Mahony, Frances Sylvester).

Pushkin, Aleksandr Sergeyevich (1799-1837) Russian poet and prose writer.

Considered Russia's greatest poet and master of prose. Works include: "Ruslan and Ludmilla"; *Eugene Onegin; Boris Gudonov.*

Quarles, Francis (1592-1644) English poet and civil servant.

Works include: *Emblems; Divine Poems; Divine Fancies.*

Quennell, Peter (b. 1905) English author.

Works include: "The Divers"; "The Flight into Egypt."

Quevedo y Villegas, Francisco de (1580-1645) Spanish satirist and poet.

Works include: *Dreams; Don Pablo of Segovia.*

Quiller-Couch, Arthur (1863-1944) English man of letters and anthologist.

Professor of English literature at

Cambridge University; edited the first edition of *The Oxford Book of English Verse* (1900). Works include: "Dead Man's Rock"; "The Ship of Stars"; completion of Robert Louis Stevenson's unfinished "St. Ives."

Raine, Kathleen (b. 1908) English poet.

Rejecting contemporary verse, she utilizes traditional forms to express eternal truths. Works include: *Blake and Tradition* (1968); *Stone and Flower: Poems 1935-43.*

Raleigh, Sir Walter (1552-1618) English author, admiral, and colonist.

A favorite of Queen Elizabeth I, he led expeditions to America; introduced tobacco to England. Works include: "Dulcina"; "His Own Epitaph."

Ramsay, Allan (1686-1758) Scottish pastoral poet.

Works include: *The Table Miscellany.*

Randall, James Ryder (1839-1908) American journalist and composer.

Aided the Confederacy in the Civil War. Works include: "Maryland, My Maryland."

Randolph, Anson Davies Fitz (1820-1896) American poet and publisher.

Works include: "Hopefully Waiting."

Randolph, Thomas (1605-1634) English poet and dramatist.

Works include: *The Conceited Peddlar; The Jealous Lovers; Hey for Honesty.*

Rands, William Brighty (1823-1882) English journalist and children's writer.

Works include: "The Child's World"; "Gypsy Jane."

Rankin, Jeremiah Eames (b. 1828) American clergyman.

Wrote national hymns. Works include: *For God and Home and Native Land; Keep Your Colors Flying.*

Ransom, John Crowe (1888-1974) American critic and poet.

Founder of the *Kenyon Review,* an influential literary journal. Works include: "Armageddon"; "Blackberry Winter"; "Autumn Love"; *The New Criticism.*

Ravenel, Beatrice (1870-1956) American poet and short story writer.

Works include: *The Arrow of Lightning.*

Raymond, Grace (see Stillman, Annie Raymond).

Raymond, Rossiter Worthington (1840-1911) American poet and lawyer.

Works include: "Cavalry Song"; "The Trooper's Death."

Read, Sir Herbert (1893-1968) English poet and art critic.

Wrote and lectured extensively on literature and art; published ten volumes of verse. Works include: "The Analysis of Love"; "The Falcon and the Dove."

Read, Thomas Buchanan (1822-1872) American portrait painter and poet.

Works include: *Lays and Ballads; Sheridan's Ride; Drifting.*

Realf, Richard (1834-1878) English soldier and poet.

Works include: *Guesses at the Beautiful.*

Reed, Henry (b. 1914) English journalist, poet, and radio dramatist.

Works include: "Chard Withlow" (a parody of T.S. Eliot); *Lessons of the War.*

Requier, Augustus Julian (1825-1887) American poet.

Works include: "Baby Zulma's Christmas Carol"; "Ashes of Glory."

Rice, Edward H. (b. 1900) American poet.

Wrote the famous hymn "Rock of Ages."

Richardson, Charles Francis (1815-1913) American editor and professor of English literature.

Works include: *A Hundred Noble Wishes.*

Riding, Laura (b. 1901) American poet and novelist.

Works include: "After So Much Loss"; "Auspice of Jewels."

Ridler, Anne (b. 1912) English poet and playwright.

An editor at Faber and Faber where she was associated with T.S. Eliot; she revised Michael Roberts' standard poetry anthology. Works include: "Before Sleep"; "Christmas and Common Birth."

Riley, James Whitcomb (1853-1916) American poet.

Writer of popular verse, he was affectionately known as the "Hoosier Poet." Works include: "Old Swimmin Hole"; "An Old Sweetheart of Mine"; *Rhymes of Childhood.*

Ritter, Mary Louise (b. 1837) American poet.

Works include: "Why?"; "Perished."

Robert II, King of France (996-1031) Works include: *Veni, Sancte Spiritus.*

Roberts, Sir Charles George (1860-1943) Canadian poet.

Works include: *Orion and Other Poems; In the Heart of the Ancient Wood.*

Roberts, Sarah (n.d.) American poet.

Works include: *Voice of the Grass.*

Robertson, James Logie ["Hugh Haliburton"] (1846-1922) English poet.

Works include: "The True Philosophy of Life" (Early English of Dunbar); "An Ochil Farmer."

Robertson, T.H. (n.d.)

Works include: *Story of the Gate.*

Robinson, Annie Douglas Green ["Marian Douglas"] (b. 1842) American poet.

Works include: "Two Pictures"; "Little Sorrow"; "The White Kitten."

Robinson, Edwin Arlington (1869-1935) American poet.

The most important American poet at the turn of the 20th century. Often wrote about men who have failed. Works include: "Miniver Cheevy"; "Richard Cory"; "Mr. Flood's Party."

Roche, James Jeffrey (1847-1908) Irish/American editor.

Works include: *Songs and Satires; Ballads of Blue Water.*

Rodger, Alexander (1784-1846) Scottish poet.

Works include: *Scotch Poetry; Songs; Odes.*

Roethke, Theodore (1908-1963) American poet.

Won the Pulitzer Prize, National Book Award, and the Bollingen Prize. Works include: "The Waking"; "Words for the Wind"; "The Far Field."

Rogers, Robert Cameron (1862-1912) American poet.

Works include: "The Shadow Rose"; "Doubt."

Rogers, Samuel (1763-1855) English banker and poet.

Works include: "Pleasures of Memory."

Rolfe, Edwin (1909-1954) American poet.

Wrote about the Spanish Civil War, in which he served as a volunteer. Works include: *The Lincoln Brigade; To My Contemporaries; First Love and Other Poems.*

Ronsard, Pierre de (1524-1585) French poet.

Leader of the movement to establish French rather than Latin as the country's literary language. Works include: "Adieu"; "Deadly Kisses"; "Celestial Dream."

Rooney, John Jerome (1866-1934) American poet.

Works include: "The Men Behind the Guns."

Rossetti, Christina Georgina (1830-1894) English poet.

A religious recluse; sister of Dante Gabriel Rossetti. Works include: "Goblin Market"; "The Prince's Progress"; "At Home"; "If Only."

Rossetti, Dante Gabriel (1828-1882) English painter and poet.

Co-founded the Pre-Raphaelite art movement. Works include: "Autumn Song"; "The Blessed Damozel"; "Love Lily."

Rosslyn, Earl of (see Erskine, Francis Robert St. Clair).

Rouget de Lisle, Claude Joseph (1760-1836) French soldier and poet.

Works include: "The Marseillaise."

Royden, Matthew (fl. 1580-1622) English poet.

Works include: "On Sir Philip Sidney."

Rufinus (6th c.) Greek poet.

Works include: "Golden Eyes"; "Love, the Archer"; "To Melite."

Rukeyser, Muriel (1913-1980) American poet and playwright.

A political activist, she was in the forefront of many protest movements, including civil rights and anti-war. Works include: "The Antagonist"; "Easter Eve"; "Holy Family."

Russell, George William ["A.E."] (1867-1935) Irish poet, philosopher, painter, essayist, politician, and economist.

Works include: "Aphrodite"; "Babylon"; "A Call."

Russell, Irwin (1853-1879) American poet.

Pioneer of the black experience in poetry. Works include: "De First Banjo"; "Nebuchadnezzar."

Ryan, Abram Joseph (1839-1886) American clergyman and poet.

Works include: "The Conquered Banner."

Ryan, Richard (1796-1849) English poet.

Works include: "O, Saw Ye the Lass."

Sackville-West, Victoria Mary (1892-1962) English writer.

A member of the Bloomsbury Group; wife of Sir Harold Nicolson. Her life, friendships, and marriage have been the subject of numerous stories and accounts. She is best known for her novels. Works include: *The Edwardians*; "Bee-Master"; "The Bull"; "King's Daughter."

Saemund, Sigfusson (1056-1133) Icelandic scholar and priest.

Works include: "Thor Recovers His Hammer."

Salis, Johann Gauden von (1762-1834) German scholar, soldier, and poet.

Works include: "Song of the Silent Land."

Sandburg, Carl (1878-1967) American poet and biographer.

Celebratory of America and its common people in his verse, he was awarded the Pulitzer Prize for his biography of Abraham Lincoln. Works include: *The People, Yes*; "Chicago"; *Good Morning America*.

Sangster, Margaret Elizabeth ["Munson"] (1838-1912) Canadian poet and editor.

Works include: *Our Own; The Sin of Omission; Are the Children at Home?*

Santayana, George (1863-1952) American philosopher.

Born in Spain, an emigrant to the United States at an early age, he taught at Harvard University for over twenty years. In addition to philosophical works, he published one novel and poetry. Works include: *Sonnets; Odes; Winds of Doctrine.*

Sappho (600 B.C.) Greek lyric poet.

Works include: "Hymn to Aphrodite"; "Ode to a Beautiful Girl."

Sargent, Epes (1813-1880) American editor and dramatist.

Works include: "Change Makes Change"; "The Priestless"; "Wealth and Work."

Savage-Armstrong, George Francis (1845-1906) Irish professor and poet.

Works include: *Poems: Lyrical and Dramatic*; "My Guide."

Saxe, John Godfrey (1816-1887) American editor, humorist, and poet.

Works include: "Rhyme of the Rail"; "The Proud Miss McBride."

Schiller, Johann Christoph Friedrich von (1759-1805) German dramatist, poet, and physician.

After Goethe, the greatest German literary figure. Works include: "Mary Stuart"; "William Tell"; *Joan of Arc.*

Schneckenburger, Max (1819-1849) German poet and manufacturer.

Wrote the words to *"Watch on the Rhine,"* the national song.

Schuyler, Montgomery (b.1843-1914) American journalist.

Works include: "Carlyle and Emerson."

Schwartz, Delmore (1913-1966) American poet.

Youngest poet to receive the Bollingen Prize. Works include: *The Repetitive Heart; Shenandoah; Summer Knowledge.*

Scollard, Clinton (1860-1932) American poet and editor.

Works include: "Ad Patriam"; "The Book Lover"; "Marathon."

Scott, Clement William (1841-1904) Canadian poet.

Works include: "The Magic House."

Scott, Frederick George (1861-1944) Canadian poet.

Works include: *The Soul's Quest; My Lattice and Other Poems; The Unnamed Lake and Other Poems.*

Scott, Sir Walter (1771-1832) Scottish poet and novelist.

A vivid and enthralling storyteller, in prose and verse, he gained enormous popularity. Works include: "The Lay of the Minstrel"; "Battle of Waterloo"; "Rob Roy."

Scovell, E[dith] J[oy] (b. 1906) English poet.

Known for her delicate and mystical verse. Works include: "Shadows of Chrysanthemum"; "The Midsummer Meadow"; *The River Steamer.*

Scudder, Elizabeth (1821-1896) American poet.

Works include: "The Love of God"; "Vesper Hymn."

Sears, Edmund Hamilton (1810-1876) American clergyman and poet.

Works include: "The Angel's Song."

Sedley, Sir Charles (1635-1701) English dramatist and poet.

Works include: "Phyllis"; *The Mulberry Garden.*

Sewall, Frank (1837-1915) American clergyman and poet.

Works include: "The Hem of His Garment"; "The New Ethics"; "Angels and Ariel."

Sewall, Harriet Winslow (1819-1889) American poet.

Works include: "Why Thus Longing?"; *Poems.*

Shakespeare, William (1564-1616) English dramatist and poet.

The greatest figure of English literature, he is unrivaled for his extraordinary knowledge of human nature and poetic skill. Works include: "Venus and Adonis"; "The Rape of Lucrece"; *Romeo and Juliet; Hamlet.*

Shanks, Edward (1892-1953) English poet, novelist and critic.

First winner of the Hawthornden Prize for "Queen of China" (1919). Works include: "Garden Reverie"; "A Night Piece."

Shanley, Charles Dawson (1811-1875) Irish journalist.

Works include: "The Brier-Wood Pipe"; "Civil War"; "Kitty of Coleraine."

Shapiro, Karl (b. 1913) American poet.

Won the Pulitzer Prize in 1945. Works include: "Nostalgia"; "The Southerner"; "The Waitress."

Sharp, Elizabeth Amelia (1856-1932) English editor.

Edited *Lyra Celtica.*

Sharp, William ["Fiona Macleod"] (1856-1905) English poet, author, and critic.

Works include: *Romantic Ballads; Lyrical Poems; Earth's Voices*; "The Dominion of Dreams"; "Pharais."

Sharpe, R.S. (1759-1835) English poet.

Works include: "The Minute-Gun."

Shelley, Percy Bysshe (1792-1822) English poet.

Recognized as one of the greatest lyric poets. Works include: "Prometheus Unbound"; "Hellas"; "To a Skylark."

Shenstone, William (1714-1765) English poet.

Best known for "The School-Mistress" and "The Pastoral Ballad."

Sheridan, Caroline Elizabeth (see Norton, Caroline Elizabeth).

Sherman, Frank Dempster (1860-1916) American poet and professor of architecture.

Works include: *Madrigals and Catches; Lyrics for a Lute; Lyrics of Joy.*

Shirley, James (1596-1666) English dramatist.

Wrote mostly tragic-comedies. Works include: *The Maid's Revenge; The Traitor; Love Tricks.*

Sidney, Sir Philip (1554-1586) English poet and diplomat.

A member of Queen Elizabeth I's court, he was influential in government and the arts. Works include: "Arcadia"; "Astrophel and Stella"; *The Defense of Poesy*.

Sigerson, George (1839-1925) Irish writer and translator.

Wrote on medical, scientific and political topics. Works include: "Far-Away"; "Lay of Norse-Irish Sea-Kings"; "The Black Bird's Song."

Sigourney, Lydia Huntley (1791-1865) American author.

Works include: *Pleasant Memories of Pleasant Lands*; "The Alpine Flowers"; *A Plea for Temperance; Letter of Life*.

Sill, Edward Rowland (1841-1887) American poet and professor of English literature.

Works include: "Opportunity"; "The Fool's Prayer."

Sillery, Charles Doyne (b. 1897) Irish poet.

Works include: "She Died in Beauty."

Simmias (B.C) Greek poet.

Works include: "The Grave of Sophocles" (Hardinge's Translation); "A Decoy Partridge."

Simmons, Bartholomew (1804-1850) Irish poet.

Works include: "To the Memory of Thomas Hood."

Simms, William Gilmore (1806-1870) American author.

One of the first great men of Southern letters. Works include: "Atlantis: A Tale of the Sea"; *The Maroon and Other Tales; War Poetry of the South*.

Sitwell, Dame Edith (1887-1964) English poet.

With her brothers Osbert and Sacheverell, the Sitwells were a prominent literary family. Her poetry was influenced by the French Symbolists. Works include: "The Sleeping Beauty"; *Rustic Elegies*; "Facade."

Smith, Belle E. (n.d.) American librarian.

Works include: "If I Should Die Tonight."

Smith, F. Burge (1826-1900) American poet.

Works include: "Little Goldenhair."

Smith, Goldwin (1823-1910) English writer and translator.

Frequent contributor to newspapers and magazines. Works include: *Lectures on Modern History; Speeches and Letters on the Rebellion; Essays on Questions of the Day*.

Smith, Horace (1779-1849) English novelist and poet.

Works include: *Rejected Addresses*; "Ode to an Egyptian Mummy"; "A Tale of Drury Lane."

Smith, May Riley (1842-1927) American poet.

Works include: *A Gift of Gentians and Other Verses*; "Sometime"; "Tired Mothers."

Smith, Samuel Francis (1808-1895) American clergyman.

Wrote numerous hymns. Works include: "America"; "Precious Lives."

Smith, Seba ["Major Jack Downing"] (1792-1868) American political satirist and journalist.

Works include: "The Mother's Sacrifice"; *The Life and Writing of Major Jack Downing*.

Smith, Sidney (1771-1845) English clergyman.

Became a Canon of St. Pauls in London. Works include: *Life of Dalton; History of the Atomic Theory Up to His Time; Science in Early Manchester*.

Smith, [Florence Margaret] "Stevie" (1902-1971) English poet and novelist.

Won the Queen's Gold Medal for Poetry. Works include: *A Good Time Was Had by All; Novel on Yellow Paper*.

Smith, Walter Chalmers (1824-1876) Scottish novelist.

Works include: "Olrig Grange"; *Hilda among the Broken Gods; Life Splinters and a Heretic*.

Smits, Dirk (1702-1752) Dutch poet.

Works include: "On the Death of an Infant" (Van Dyke's Translation).

Sophocles (495-405 B.C.) Greek tragic poet.

Works include: *Antigone; Oedipus at Colonus; Oedipus Rex*.

Southesk, Sir James Carnegie, Earl of (1827-1905) Scottish poet.

Works include: "Herminius"; "Meda Maiden"; "Snomiria."

Southey, Caroline Anne Bowles (see Bowles, Caroline Anne).

Southey, Robert (1774-1843) English poet.

Poet laureate. Works include: "Thalaba"; "Madoc"; "The Curse of Kahama."

Spencer, Caroline S. (b. 1850) American poet.

Works include: "Living Waters."

Spencer, William Robert (1770-1834) English poet and translator.

Works include: "Urbania; or,
The Illumine"; "The Year of
Sorrow."

Spender, Stephen (b. 1909) English writer.

A leading literary figure, associated with Auden, Isherwood,
and MacNeice, he has produced
poetry, plays, criticism, and lectures. Awarded the Queen's
Gold Medal for poetry. Works
include: "Call to Action";
"The Fates"; "Mask."

Spenser, Edmund (1552-1599)
English poet.

Regarded as one of the greatest
English poets. Works include:
"The Faerie Queene";
"Amoretti"; "The Shepheardes
Calender."

Spofford, Harriet Elizabeth
(1835-1921) American author.

Gained recognition with *In a
Cellar*. Works include: *Sir Ro-
han's Ghost; The Amber Gods;
New England Legends*.

Sprague, Charles (1791-1875)
American poet and author.

Works include: "The Winged
Worshippers"; "Curiosity";
Poetical and Prose Writings.

**Squire, Sir John Collings
["Solomon Eagle"]** (1884-
1958) English poet and politician and anthropologist.

Founded a prestigious literary
periodical, the *London Mercury*.
Works include: "Approaching
America"; "Winter Nightfall";
"The Poor Old Man."

Stanley, Arthur Penrhyn (1815-
1881) English churchman.

Dean of Westminster; leader in
the "Broad Church" party,
which emphasized free thought.
Works include: *Historical
Memoirs of Westminster Abbey;
The Athanasian Creed*.

Stanton, Frank Lebby (1837-
1927) American poet and journalist.

Compiled popular anthologies:
*Songs of the Soil; Up from
Georgia; Little Folks Down
South; Songs from Dixie*.

Stedman, Edmund Clarence
(1833-1908) American banker
and poet.

He achieved prominence and influence with his poetry compila-
tions, *An American Anthology*
and *A Victorian Anthology*.
Works include: *Lyrics and
Idylls*; "Dartmouth Ode";
"Gettysburg."

Stein, Evaleen (1863-1923)
American magazine and juvenile
writer.

Works include: "In Mexico";
"Wild Beasts"; "Budding-Time
Too Brief."

Stephen, James Kenneth (1859-1892) English barrister.

Works include: "Lapsus Calami"; "England and America"; "The Last Ride Together."

Stephen the Salbaite, St. (725-794) Palestinian monk of St. Sabas.

Works include: "Art Thou Weary?."

Stephens, James (1882-1950) Irish poet and novelist.

Works include: *The Crock of Gold*; "Follow! Follow! Follow!"; "Breakfast Time."

Sterling, George (1869-1926) American poet.

Works include: "A Deserted Farm"; "In Autumn"; "Three Sonnets on Oblivion."

Sterling, John (1806-1844) Scottish editor and essayist.

Born at Kames Castle, Isle of Bute. His biography was written by Thomas Carlyle. Works include: *Arthur Coningsby; Minor Poems*; "The Election."

Stevens, George Alexander (1720-1784) English poet.

Works include: "The Storm."

Stevens, Wallace (1879-1955) American poet and business executive.

Although not a full time poet for much of his life, his body of verse occupies an important place in American letters. Works include: "Peter Quince at the Clavier"; "The Worms at Heaven's Gate."

Stevenson, Robert Louis Balfour (1850-1894) Scottish novelist, poet, and essayist.

A popular storyteller whose books endure. Works include: *Treasure Island; A Child's Garden of Verses; Kidnapped; The Strange Case of Dr. Jekyll and Mr. Hyde.*

Still, John (1543-1607) English clergyman and writer of comedy.

Works include: *A Ryght Pithy; Pleasant; Merrie Comedy Intytuled Gammar Gurton's Needle.*

Stillman, Annie Raymond ["Grace Raymond"] (b. 1855) American novelist.

Works include: "Birth."

Stirling-Maxwell, Lady (see Norton, Caroline Elizabeth).

Stoddard, Richard Henry (1825-1903) American journalist, and lyric poet.

Edited the *New York Mail and Express* and the *New York World*. Works include: "Songs of Summer"; "The Lion's

Cub"; "Abraham Lincoln: A Horatian Ode."

Story, Robert (1790-1859) Scottish poet.

Works include: "The Whistle."

Story, William Wetmore (1819-1895) American sculptor and essayist.

Practiced law, then went to Rome to study art. His sculpture of Edward Everett is in the Boston Public Garden.

Stowe, Harriet Beecher (1811-1896) American novelist.

Began teaching school at the age of fourteen. Sold more books than any previous writer in English fiction, with *Uncle Tom's Cabin*.

Strangeford, Lord (1789-1855) English poet.

Works include: "Blighted Love" (Portuguese of Camoens).

Street, Alfred Billings (1811-1881) American librarian.

The state librarian of New York. Works include: *Fugitive Poems; Woods and Waters; Forest Pictures in the Adirondacks.*

Strode, William (1600-1644) English poet.

Works include: "Kisses."

Strong, William (d. 1654) English clergyman.

Works include: "Frithiof at the Court of Angentyr" (Swedish of Tegner).

Sturm, Julius (1816-1896) German lyric poet.

Works include: *Devout Songs and Poems*; "Israelite Songs"; "To the Lord My Song."

Suckling, Sir John (1609-1642) English poet.

Implicated in a plot to rescue the Earl of Strafford from London Tower, he fled to France where he is reputed to have committed suicide. Wrote the first plays produced with elaborate scenery. Writings consist of letters, poems, songs, a prose treatise, and four plays.

Surfaceman (see Anderson, Alexander).

Surrey, Henry Howard, Earl of (1516-1547) English poet.

First used blank verse in English; popularized the sonnet. Apprehended attempting escape from imprisonment for treason, he was beheaded. Works include: "In Windsor Castle"; "A Satire on London"; "Frail Beauty."

Swain, Charles (1803-1874) English engraver and songwriter.

Works include: *The Mind and Other Poems; Songs and Ballads.*

Swift, Jonathan (1667-1745) Anglo-Irish author.

The most gifted satirist in the English language. Works include: *Gulliver's Travels;* "A Modest Proposal"; *Tale of a Tub; The Battle of the Books.*

Swinburne, Algernon Charles (1837-1909) English lyric poet and critic.

His early poetry, sensuous and amatory, brought mostly unkind notices; his later work was political in theme. Works include: "Atlanta in Calydon"; "The Garden of Proserpine"; *A Song of Italy.*

Sylvia, Carmen (see Elizabeth, Queen of Roumania).

Sylvester, Joshua (1563-1618) English author.

A source of inspiration for Milton's *Paradise Lost.* Works include: "Contentment"; "Were I As Base As Is the Lowly Pain."

Symons, Arthur (1865-1945) Welsh poet and critic.

Prominent in the English Symbolism movement. Works include: "Days and Nights"; "Silhouettes"; "Confessions."

Symonds, John Addington (1840-1893) English critic and historian.

Works include: *The Renaissance in Italy; Study of Dante; Animi Figura; Essays Speculative and Suggestive.*

Tabb, John Banister (1845-1909) American clergyman and author.

Works include: *Poems, Lyrics and Child Verse.*

Taggard, Genevieve (1894-1948) American poet.

Awarded a Guggenheim Memorial Foundation Fellowship for creative work abroad. Works include: "The Enamel Girl"; "The Quiet Woman"; "The Still Search."

Talfourd, Sir Thomas Noon (1795-1854) English statesman and poet.

Works include: *Poems on Various Subjects; The Athenian Captive and Glencoe; Critical and Miscellaneous Essays.*

Taliessin (6th c.) Welsh poet-bard.

Famous for fifty-six poems contained in the *Book of Taliessin.*

Tannahill, Robert (1774-1810) Scottish weaver and poet.

Wrote primarily in Scottish dialect. Famous for *The Soldier's*

Return with Other Poems and Songs.

Tasso, Torquato (1544-1595) Italian epic poet.

A major Italian poet whose influence extended to Milton and Goethe. Works include: "Rinaldo."

Tate, [John Orley] Allen (1899-1979) American poet and critic.

Won Guggenheim Fellowship in 1928. Edited important literary journals and taught at several colleges. Works include: *The Pathers*; "The Buried Lake"; "John Brown"; "The Trout Map."

Taylor, Bayard (1825-1878) American novelist, printer, and journalist.

One of the most honored and gifted men of letters in his day. Works include: *A Book of Romances; Lyrics and Song.*

Taylor, Benjamin Franklin (1819-1887) American war correspondent and author.

Works include: *Pictures of Life in Camp and Field; The World on Wheels Summer Savory; Song of Yesterday.*

Taylor, Edgar (1793-1839) English poet.

Works include: "Song" (German of Walther von der Vogelweide).

Taylor, Sir Henry (1800-1886) English government service worker, author, and editor.

Works include: "The Virgin Widow"; The Eve of Conquest and Other Poems; "St. Clement's Eve"; "Isaac Comnenus."

Taylor, Jane (1783-1824) English poet.

Works include: "Pretty Cow."

Taylor, Jeffreys (1793-1853) English author.

Wrote stories for children, and books on geography, natural science, and religion. Works include: "The Milkmaid"; "Harry's Holiday"; "Aesop in Rhyme."

Taylor, Jeremy (1613-1667) English theological writer.

A champion of religious freedom. Works include: *A Discourse on the Liberty of Prophesying*; "Holy Living and Holy Dying."

Taylor, Tom (1817-1880) English dramatist and editor.

Editor of *Punch* and art critic of the *London Times*. Wrote more than one hundred plays including: *Still Waters Run Deep; The Unequal Match; The Overland Route.*

Taylor, W. (n.d.) English poet.

Works include: "My Recovery" (German of Klopstock).

Teasdale, Sara (1884-1933) American poet.

Descendant of the founder of Concord, Massachusetts. Contributed verse to leading magazines such as *Harper's, Scribner's, The Century.* Works include: "Water Lilies"; "August Night"; "The Crystal Gazer."

Tegner, Esaias (1782-1846) Swedish poet.

Elected to the Swedish Academy. Works include: "Svea;" "Mattvardsbarnen"; "Axel and Frithjof's Saga."

Tennant, William (1784-1848) Scottish poet and scholar.

Professor of Oriental languages. Works include: "Anster Fair"; *Life of Allan Ramsay; Syriac and Chaldes Grammar.*

Tennyson, Alfred Lord (1809-1892) English poet.

Became poet laureate upon the death of Wordsworth. The most eminent poet of the Victorian era and a giant among English poets. Works include: "Morte d'Arthur"; "Idylls of the King"; "Beckett"; *The Holy Grail and Other Poems.*

Tennyson Turner, Charles (1808-1879) English poet.

Brother of Alfred Lord Tennyson; collaborated together on *Poems by Two Brothers.* Works include: *Sonnets and Fugitive Pieces; Collected Sonnets: Old and New.*

Terret, William B. (n.d.) American poet.

Works include: "Platonic."

Tersteegan, Gerhard (1697-1769) German lyric poet.

Works include: "The Spiritual Garden"; "Crumbs"; "The Day Is Now Ended."

Thackeray, William Makepeace (1811-1863) English novelist, satirist, essayist, and critic.

Born in Calcutta, India. Under financial pressures, he wrote continually, contributing to magazines under various pseudonyms. Works include: *Henry Esmond*; "The Crystal Palace"; "The Pen and the Album."

Thaxter, Celia Laighton (1836-1894) American poet.

Works include: "Driftwood"; "Among the Isles of Shoals"; "An Island Garden."

Thayer, William Roscoe ["Paul Hermes"] (1859-1923) American historian.

Editor of *Harvard Graduates'
Magazine.* Works include: *The
Best Elizabethan Plays; The
Dawn of Italian Independence;
Poems, New and Old.*

Thom, William (1798-1848) Scottish poet.

Works include: "The Mitherless
Bairn."

Thomas, Dylan (1914-1953)
Welsh poet.

One of the most accomplished
and popular English language
poets of the twentieth century.
Works include: "Fern Hill";
"After the Funeral"; "Do not
go Gently into that Good
Night"; *Portrait of the Artist as
a Young Dog; Death and En-
trances.*

Thomas, Edith Matilda (1854-
1901) American poet.

Works include: *Lyrics and Sonnets; Children of the Seasons; A
New Year's Masque.*

Thompson, Ed. Porter (b. 1834)
American magazine writer.

Works include: "The C.S.
Army's Commissary."

Thompson, Francis Joseph
(1859-1907) English poet.

Struggling against poverty and
illness, his literary output was
limited. Works include: *The*

*Hound of Heaven; Poems;
Sister-Songs; New Poems.*

Thompson, Maurice ["James"]
(1844-1901) American essayist
and novelist.

Confederate soldier in Civil
War; state geologist of Indiana.
Works include: *Byways and
Bird Notes; Sylvan Secrets; The
Story of Louisiana.*

Thompson, John Randolph
(1823-1873) American journalist.

Works include: "Lee to the
Rear"; "Music in Camp."

Thompson, Will Henry (1848-
1918) American lawyer.

Works include: "The High Tide
at Gettysburg."

Thomson, James (1700-1748)
Scottish poet.

Surveyor general of the Lee-
ward Islands. Works include:
"The Seasons"; "The Castle of
Indolence."

Thoreau, Henry David (1817-
1863) American naturalist, philosopher, author, and carpenter.

Coedited the *Dial*, a transcendentalist magazine, with his
close friend, Ralph Waldo
Emerson. His experiences in a
cabin on Walden Pond for two
years were recorded in a journal

which resulted in a book, *Walden*. His philosophy of individualism and civil disobedience has been influential internationally.

Thornbury, George Walter (1828-1876) English man of letters.

Works include: *Shakespeare's England: or Sketches of Our Social History During the Reign of Elizabeth; Life in Spain; Haunted London; Two Centuries of Song.*

Thorpe, Rose Hartwick (1850-1939) American author.

Works include: "Curfew Must Not Ring To-Night"; "Drifted Out to Sea."

Thrale, Hester Lynch [Mme Piozzi] (1741-1821) English poet.

Works include: *Anecdotes of Dr. Johnson; Autobiography.*

Thurlow, Edward Hovel-Thurlow, 2d Baron (1781-1829) English poet.

Works include: "Beauty."

Tichborne, Chediok (1558?-1586) English poet.

Works include: "Lines Written in this Tower."

Timrod, Henry (1829-1867) American journalist and poet.

Works include: "Spring in Carolina"; "A Cry to Arms."

Torrence, Frederic Ridgeley (1875-1950) American poet, editor, and librarian.

Friends with William Vaughn Moody and Edward Arlington Robinson. Edited the *New Republic*. Works include: *The House of a Hundred Lights; Granny Maumee.*

Townsend, George Alfred (1841-1914) American journalist.

Special correspondent for the *New York Herald* and *World*. Works include: *Poems*; "The Entailed Hat."

Townsend, Mary Ashley van Voorhis ["Xariffa"] (1832-1901) American author.

Works include: "The Brother Clerks"; "The Captain's Story"; "Down the Bayou."

Trench, Richard Chenevix (1807-1886) Irish Archbishop of Dublin, philologist, and essayist.

Works include: *Notes of the Parables; English Past and Present; On Plutarch.*

Trowbridge, John (1827-1916) American novelist, poet, and editor.

Works include: *The Scarlet Tanager; Darius Green and His Flying Machine.*

Tuckerman, Henry Theodore (1813-1871) American author and critic.

Co-edited A Smaller History of English and American Literature. Works include: *The Italian Sketch Book; Isabel: or Sicily; Rambles and Reveries; Thoughts on Poets.*

Turner, Charles Tennyson (see Tennyson, Charles).

Tynan, Katherine (see Hinkson, Katharine Tynan).

Uhland, Ludwig (1787-1862) German dramatist, lyricist poet, politician, and professor of German literature.

Works include: "The Landlady's Daughter"; "The Passage."

Ulrich, Anton, Duke of Brunswick (1633-1714) German poet.

Works include: "God's Sure Help in Sorrow" (Winkworth's translation).

Untermeyer, Louis (1885-1977) American poet, editor, lecture, and critic.

Compiled many widely read and well regarded anthologies of English and American verse. Works include: "Swimmers"; "Steel Mill."

Van Doren, Mark (1894-1972) American poet and critic.

A popular and influential professor of literature at Columbia, he was awarded the Pulitzer Prize for *Collected Poems* (1939). Works include: "Civil War"; "The Orchard Ghost"; "Going Home."

Vandegrift, Margaret (see Janvier, Margaret Thompson).

Van Dyk, H.S. (1798-1828) English poet.

Works include: "On the Death of an Infant" (Dutch of Smits).

Van Dyke, Henry (1852-1933) American clergyman and professor of English Literature at Princeton University.

Works include: *The Reality of Religion; The Poetry of Tennyson; The Friendly Year; The Ruling Passion.*

Vaughan, Henry (1621-1695) Welsh poet.

Trained at law, he became a country doctor. Religion is the main theme of his poetry. Works include: "The Mount of Olives"; "Flores Solitudinis"; "The Retreat."

Vaux, Thomas, 2d Baron Vaux of Harrowden (circa 1510-1556) English poet.

Works include: "Of a Contented Spirit."

Vega, Lope de ["Felix Vega Carpio"] (1562-1635) Spanish dramatist.

Works include: "Country Life"; "Pantomime."

Venable, William Henry (1836-1920) American author, educator, and lecturer.

Works include: *June on the Miami and Other Poems; The School Stage; Melodies of the Heart and Other Poems.*

Vere, Edward de, 17th Earl of Oxford (1550-1604) English poet and actor.

Reputed by some to have written Shakespeare's plays. Works include: "A Renunciation" (from Byrd's "Songs and Sonnets"); "A Doubtful Choice"; "Fair Fools."

Verlaine, Paul (1844-1896) French poet.

A leading symbolist poet. Works include: "Sagesse"; "Amour," "Pantomime."

Very, Jones (1813-1880) American professor of Greek, essayist, and poet.

Contributed to the *Christian Register* and other journals. Works include: *Essays and Poems.*

Villon, Francois ["Montcorbier"] (1431-1500) French poet.

One of the great medieval poets. Works include: "Ballades";

"Petit Testament"; "Grand Testament."

Vinci, Leonarda da (see Leonardo da Vinci).

Virgil or Vergil [Publius Vergilius Maro] (70-19 B.C.) Roman epic poet.

Greatest Roman poet. Works include: "Ecologues"; "Georgics"; "Aeneid."

Vogelweide, Walther von der (1170-1230) German lyric poet, liberal politician, and reformer.

Works include: "Awake! Awake! The Day Is Coming Now"; "Under the Lime Tree."

Waddington, Samuel (1844-1923) English civil servant and poet.

Works include: "Mors et Vita."

Waller, Edmund (1605-1687) English poet and member of Parliament.

Works include: "The Dancer"; "'Go, Lovely Rose."

Waller, John Francis (1810-1894) Irish man of letters.

Wrote for the *Dublin University Magazine.* Works include: *Poems* (1854).

Walsh, William (1663-1707) English poet.

Works include: "Rivalry in Love."

Walton, Izaak ["John Chalk-hill"] (1593-1683) English land-scaper, angler, and author.

Fame is based on "The Compleat Angler, or the Contemplative Man's Companion."

Ware, Jr., Henry (1794-1843) American clergyman and writer.

Active in organizing the Unitarian movement. Works include: *On the Formation of the Christian Character; Life of the Saviour; Scenes and Characters Illustrating Christian Truth.*

Warren, Robert Penn (b. 1905) American author.

Wrote verse-sonnets, lullabies, lyrics, and tales. Won the Pulitzer Prize in 1946 for his novel *All the King's Men.*

Wastell, Simon (circa 1560-1627) English poet.

Works include: "Man's Mortality."

Watkins, Vernon (1907-1967) English poet.

Published over ten volumes of verse. Works include: "Discoveries"; "The Mother and Child."

Watson, John Whittaker (1824-1890) American journalist.

Wrote stories for periodicals. Works include: "The Beautiful Snow."

Watson, Rosamund Marriott (1863-1911) English poet.

Works include: "Ave Atque Vale."

Watson, William (1858-1935) English poet.

Works include: "The Prince's Quest"; *Wordsworth's Grave and Other Poems*; "The Purple East"; *For England: Selected Poems.*

Watts, Isaac (1674-1749) English poet, and clergyman.

Considered one of the finest English hymn writers. Works include: *Hymns and Spiritual Songs; Divine and Moral Songs; The Use of Children.*

Watts-Dunton, Theodore (1832-1914) English novelist, critic, and poet.

Works include: *The Coming of Love; The Christmas Dream; Old Familiar Faces.*

Waugh, Edwin (1818-1890) English poet.

Works include: *Poems and Lancashire Songs; The Chimney Corner; Posies from a Country Garden.*

Weatherly, Frederic Edward

(1848-1929) English barrister and songwriter.

Works include: "Darby and Joan"; "London Bridge."

Weaver, John V.A. (1893-1938) American writer.

Assistant book editor of the Chicago *Daily News* in 1916. Wrote for the motion pictures. Works include: "Drugstore"; "Ghost"; "To Youth."

Webb, Charles Henry (see Paul, John).

Webster, Daniel (1782-1852) American statesman and orator.

A senator and leader of the Whig Party, he was a presidential candidate in 1836. Two presidents appointed him secretary of state. Works include: "The Memory of the Heart."

Weir, William Harrison (b. 1834) English artist, author, and journalist.

Noted for his engravings of animals. An original member of the Society of Painters in Watercolors. Works include: "The English Robin."

Welby, Amelia B. Coppuck (1819-1852) American poet.

Works include: *Collected Poems* (2 volumes); "The Old Maid."

Wesley, Charles (1718-1788)

English clergyman and hymn writer.

Brother of John Wesley, he wrote over 6000 hymns. Works include: "Bid Me Sin No More"; "Claiming the Promise."

Wesley, John (1703-1791) English preacher.

A founder of Methodism. Works include: "Hope Springing Up"; "What to Do."

Westwood, Thomas (1814-1888) English poet and bibliographer.

Friend of Charles Lamb. Works include: "The Bee and the Lily"; "Night of Spring."

Wetherald, Ethelwyn (b. 1857) Canadian journalist.

Works include: "The Snow Storm."

Wheelwright, John (1897-1940) American poet.

Descendant of Boston's first multimillionaire. Became a Socialist and a Trotskyite. Works include: *Rock and Shell; Mirror of Venus; Political Self-Portrait.*

Whewell, William (1794-1866) English scientist and philosopher.

A Fellow of the Royal Society. Works include: *Astronomy and General Physics; Philosophy of the Inductive Sciences; Platonic*

Dialogues, Lectures on Political Economy.

Whibley, Charles (1859-1930) English poet.

Works include: "Eros Is Missing" (Greek of Meleager).

White, Henry Kirke (1785-1806) English clergyman and poet.

Protege of Robert Southey. Works include: "Star of Bethlehem."

White, Joseph Blanco (1775-1841) English clergyman and editor.

Edited (in English) "El Espanol"; "Las Variedades"; *London Review.* Works include: *Letters from Spain; Practical and Internal Evidence Against Catholicism.*

Whitman, Sarah Power (1803-1878) American poet.

Engaged to Edgar Allan Poe. Works include: *Hours of Life and Other Poems; Fairy Ballads; Edgar A. Poe and His Critics.*

Whitman, Walt (1819-1892) American printer and poet.

One of America's greatest poets, and an innovator in the use of free verse, his work celebrated the common man, brotherhood, and democracy. Works include: *Leaves of Grass.*

Whitney, Hattie (see Durbin, Harriet Whitney).

Whittier, John Greenleaf (1807-1892) American poet.

An ardent abolitionist and political activist, together with his friend William Lloyd Garrison, he devoted most of his energies after the Civil War to poetry. Works include: *Among the Hills; Legends of New England in Prose and Verse; Snowbound;* "The Tent of the Beach."

Wiffen, Benjamin B. (n.d.) English poet.

Works include: "To Rome" (Spanish of Luevedo).

Wilbur, Richard (b. 1921) American poet.

Won the Pulitzer Prize and the National Book Award for *Things of this World* (1957).

Wilcox, Ella Wheeler (1855-1919) American poet.

Contributed to periodicals. Works include: "Maurine"; *Poems of Passion and Poems of Pleasure;* "Drops of Water"; "Sweet Danger."

Wilde, Oscar [Finga, O'Flahertie Wills] (1856-1900) Irish writer.

A flamboyant figure who was imprisoned for homosexual offenses, he wrote many successful and witty comedies. Works include: *Lady Windermere's Fan; A Woman of No Importance; The Importance of Being Earnest; The Picture of Dorian Gray.*

Wilde, Richard Henry (1789-1847) Irish lawyer and lyricist.

Works include: "My Life Is Like a Summer Rose."

Wilkins, William (b. 1852) Greek poet.

Works include: "Educator"; "In the Engine Shed."

Wilkenson, William Cleaver (b. 1833) American clergyman, poet, and textbook writer.

Dean of the department of literature and art at Chantauqua University. Works include: *Dance of Modern Society.*

Willard, Emma Hart (1787-1870) American educator, author, and historian.

Founded the Emma Willard School to offer women a college education. Works include: "Rocked in the Cradle of the Deep."

Williams, Charles (1886-1945) English writer.

Appointed lecturer at Oxford University. Best known for his religious books. Works include: "Night Song for a Child!"; "After Ronsard."

Williams, Oscar (1900-1964) American poet.

Best known for his poetry anthologies. Works include: *The Golden Darkness.*

Williams, William Carlos (1883-1963) American physician and author.

One of the major twentieth century American poets. Works include: "Kora in Hell"; "Sour Grapes"; *The Great American Novel.*

Willis, Nathaniel Parker (1806-1867) American author.

Established and edited several magazines and was a frequent contributor of verse, prose, and travel pieces to periodicals. Works include: *Famous Persons and Places; Outdoors at Idlewild.*

Willson, Forceyth (1837-1867) American journalist.

Works include: "In State."

Wilson, Arabella M. (n.d.) American poet.

Works include: "To the Sextant."

Wilson, John ["Christopher North"] (1785-1854) Scottish author and scholar.

Works include: "Noctes Ambrosianae"; "The Isle of Palms"; "The Trials of Margaret Lindsay''; *Essay on the Genius and Character of Burns.*

Winkworth, Catherine (1825-1878) Scottish translator and poet.

Chief interest was the education of women. Works include: *Lyra Germanica; The Christian Singers of Germany.*

Wither, George (1588-1667) English soldier and poet.

Imprisoned for his satire *Abuses Script and Whipt.* Works include: *The Shepheard's Hunting; A Collection of Emblemes.*

Wolcott, John ["Peter Pindar"] (1738-1819) English poet and satirist.

Works include: *Lyric Odes; An Epistle to the Reviewers; Peeps at St. James.*

Wolfe, Charles (1791-1923) Irish clergyman.

Gained fame with "Ode on the Burial of Sir John Moore."

Wolfe, Humbert (1885-1940) English poet.

Works include: "The Blackbird"; "For Omar"; "A.E. Housman and a Few Friends."

Woodberry, George Edward (1855-1930) American critic and educator.

Works include: *A History of Wood Engraving; Life of Edgar Allan Poe; The North Shore Watch and Other Poems.*

Woods, Margaret L. (b. 1856) English novelist.

Works include: *A Village Tragedy; Vagabonds; Lyrics and Ballads.*

Woodworth, Samuel (1785-1842) American poet and journalist.

Founder of the *New York Mirror.* Famous for "The Old Oaken Bucket."

Woolner, Thomas (1825-1892) English sculptor and poet.

Sculpted statues of Carlyle, Tennyson, and Darwin. Works include: "My Beautiful Lady"; "Pygmalion"; "Silenus and Tiresias."

Woolsey, Sarah Chauncey ["Susan Coolidge"] (1835-1905) American poet.

Gained popularity as a children's writer. Works include: "The New Year's Bargain"; "What Katy Did"; *Verses*; "A Little Country Girl."

Wordsworth, William (1770-1850) English poet.

Poet laureate. His great love of nature and his exceptional poetic skills resulted in some of the best nature verse in the English language. Works include: "To the Cuckoo"; "Daffodils"; "To the Skylark"; "Tinturn Abbey"; *The Prelude.*

Wotton, Sir Henry (1568-1639) English diplomat.

A member of Parliament and ambassador to Venice. Works are compiled in *Peliquial Wottonianae* (Wotton's Literary Remains).

Wyeth, John Allen (1845-1922) American surgeon and missionary.

Fought in the Civil War. Works include: *A Textbook on Surgery; Life of General Nathan Bedford Forrest; With Sabre and Scalpel.*

Wright, Elizur (1804-1855) American reformer, journalist, and author.

Published works on life insurance and a translation in verse of La Fontain's "Fables." Edited *The Emancipator* and *Human Rights.*

Wright, Richard (1908-1960) American author.

One of the first popular black novelists; his works portrayed the dire circumstances of blacks in America. Works include: *Native Son; Black Boy; The Outsider; White Man, Listen.*

Wylie, Elinor (1885-1928) American poet and novelist.

Works include: "Bells in the Rain"; "Demon Lovers"; "The Pebble."

Xariffa (see Townsend, Mary Ashley).

Xavier, Saint Francis (see Francis Xavier, Saint).

Yeats, William Butler (1865-1939) Irish poet and playwright.

Recipient of the Nobel Prize for literature in 1923. Founded and wrote for Abbey Theater of Dublin. A chief organizer of the Irish Literary Theater. Works include: "The Land of Heart's Desire"; *Plays for an Irish Theater; Responsibilities and Later Poems; The Hour Glass.*

Yendys, Sidney (see Dobell, Sidney Thompson).

Young, Andrew (1885-1971) Scottish clergyman, poet, and botanist.

Won the Queen's Medal for Poetry in 1952. Works include: "The Dead Crab"; "The Ruined Chapel"; "Late Autumn."

Young, Edward (1683-1765) English clergyman.

Famous for "Night Thoughts." Works include: "The Revenge"; "The Love of Fame."

Zangwill, Israel (1864-1926) English novelist and poet.

Famous for *Children of the Ghetto.* Works include: *Ghetto Tragedies; Dreamers of the Ghetto.*